Transition
in African Beliefs

TRANSITION IN AFRICAN BELIEFS

Traditional Religion and Christian Change:
A Study in Sukumaland, Tanzania, East Africa

Ralph E. S. Tanner

MARYKNOLL PUBLICATIONS

Maryknoll, New York

1967

To Penelope

Preface

CHRISTIANITY'S IMPACT on Africa has been studied more often as a religious invasion than as social change within a religious context. The study of organized Christian activity has been largely ignored by sociologists, particularly in Eastern Africa, and such work as has been undertaken has concentrated on religious problems and has been written by religious.

Since Christianity, sociologically speaking, has been introduced into Africa like topsoil over the base of traditional religions, anthropologists coming from the West have seen little to interest them in Christianity and have concentrated on traditional religion; they search for the primitive as an earlier form of organized religion.

Much of the anthropological material in its modern context has been found somewhat inadequate because these studies have been of diminishing segments of the societies examined—dying cults in a rapidly changing world. They are inadequate also because the writers have made an essentially agnostic approach to religious activity, which has been analyzed in terms of social function and psychological experience. Faith as such was to be explained away rather than appreciated. Missioners' studies may also have failed because their approach, just as much as their conclusions, has been predetermined by their own devotion and often by failure to understand social function in its local context.

Sukumaland in northwestern Tanzania is an interesting area not only because of its enormous size and large population but because it has been relatively free from the appalling consequences of divided Christianity. Much change has occurred there but much has passed by, leaving the majority of the Sukuma untouched, particularly by the calls of Christianity and Islam.

Field work at any time offers the fascinating experience of failure to understand the society in which work is being undertaken. My work in Usukuma between 1951 and 1954 resulted in a superficially detailed understanding of the traditional religion in a neohistorical sense, while leaving unanswered many of the questions which ought to have been asked and answered. However, my Sukuma material rested undeveloped.

In 1959, as a result of the influence of the Rev. E. Welbourn, who was then working on his study of the separatist churches in East Africa, I became interested in the probems of conversion, particularly as it became obvious that the overwhelming predominance of rational pragmatic reasons for becoming Christian did not prevent the growth of religious faith when these reasons no longer applied.

In 1962 the Maryknoll Fathers (The Catholic Foreign Missionary Society of America), who had taken over the Shinyanga diocese in Sukumaland from the White Fathers and were new to East African missionary work, suggested that a book on Sukuma traditional beliefs would be both useful and necessary for their members.

After this project was accepted, a preliminary tour of Usukuma showed that the traditional religion, in the face of modern pressures, was becoming increasingly fragmentary, and that to produce a study of this nature for the use of priests could give them an entirely wrong emphasis in their relationships with the Sukuma when they were perhaps already too much inclined to see in the past unrealizable benefits for the future.

The problems facing them were not related specifically to these traditional fragments. In conversations with priests it became evident to me that the essential problems were the social and economic changes affecting the Sukuma, without their being able to exert more than minimal influence over their own destiny, and the difficulties relating to adapting the ideals of Christianity to their contemporary social, economic, and religious practices. It was accordingly decided to base the study on these contemporary issues and to draw attention to traditional beliefs when they were found to be of importance to these problems.

This study is not an attempt to assess Christian progress, in which the Catholic Church has made notable achievements, particularly in the fields of medicine and education. These standards are essentially Western and exterior to the traditional values of the Sukuma, and I did not think that any study on this basis would serve my expressed purpose of providing a theoretical and factual background to the missioners' Christian activity.

If the study appears to be essentially critical of Christian and particularly Catholic activity, it is because I have looked at this activity through Sukuma and thereby specifically restricted eyes. It is therefore not a balanced assessment, for the Sukuma themselves do not and cannot see Christianity in such a balanced, dispassionate, and depersonalized manner. It is nevertheless a study made in faith and should be read as the comments of one who sees in East African Christianity much selfless devotion and yet also the long crooked path to an impossible social ideal.

The object of a religious study must be religious activity as concerned with the general needs and expectations of the *people* who are the subjects and objects of it. The social activities of a religious body must be peripheral to this assessment; for a man's appreciation and understanding of God to be dependent on a parallel provision of a whole complex of social services would be entirely wrong in this context.

Apart from my long association with and liking for the Sukuma, with whom I have been in contact on and off for more than fifteen years, which has made me acutely aware of their problems and interests, my experience of priestly activity and the personal and religious difficulties of priests has made this Sukuma bias rather unfortunate.

I also feel that the impressionistic nature of this study of religious activity should be recognized despite the broad nature of the title. Impressionism all the more recognizable since I have been very much in the hands of friends—rather than informants—whom I have now known for years.

My grateful thanks are due to Joseph P. Baggot, M.M., Bishop Joseph Blomjous, James W. Bradley, M.M., David Clement, W.F., Hans Cory, the late Jan Hendriks, W.F., Nfumo Kabadi of Nyegezi, Ntemi Kapongo of Nassa, Raymond Kelly, Ntemi Daudi Kidaha of Shinyanga, Matthias Koenen, George M. Mikolajczyk, M.M., Juma Ndamulo, Alden L. Pierce, M.M., George L. Weber,

M.M., Ntemi Lupembe of Massanza, A. C. A. Wright, and Maurice J. Zerr, M.M., and to the editors of *Africa, Tankanyika Notes and Records, African Studies, Anthropological Quarterly, Ampleforth Journal,* and the *South-Western Journal of Anthropology* for permission to quote from my articles in their journals.

Table of Contents

Part IV   The Adoption of Christianity

Transition
in African Beliefs

PART ONE

THE TRADITIONAL CREED
AND
CULT OF THE SUKUMA

THE SUKUMA are pastoral agriculturists, numbering well over a million, living on the semiarid steppe of northwestern Tanzania, to the south of Lake Victoria. They speak the same language and have an overall similar culture but, just as each chiefdom has a different history and origin outside of Sukumaland, so there are variations from area to area both in accent and in social practice, as well as wide variations in ecology between the well-watered north and the dry rolling plains of the south.

These differences in origin of the inhabitants of each chiefdom and of the clans and lineages living therein, and the absence of written traditions, have given their beliefs wide variations. These beliefs are not formed or diffused by a deliberate system of propagation, but are absorbed into the consciousness of the child as he grows up in his homestead, and the degree of his appreciation of such values will depend on the amount of influence his elders have on him and his neighbors as he grows up, by a combination of intelligence and practicability.

Similarly, when their traditional religious practice depended on a combination of misfortune and ill-health and successful divination by professional diviners, who were able to prescribe the necessity of carrying out any number of variations of social

1

activities, which were not purely religious in form, the Sukuma varied widely in what they felt they ought to do.

So their religious practice comprises a large number of inter-locking systems, depending on the success of a particular diviner in one area and the failure of another next door; the development of a particular society with ancestor support near one hill and the complete absence of the same ten miles away; steady and regular rain, good cotton prices, and veterinary success against stock dis-eases. All this will have had some influence.

Thus traditional practice depended on a number of varying factors, but as so much of this semisecret religious information can be obtained only from informants who are both few in number and dedicated to the propagation of their own successes, it is too easy to generalize and to assume generalities. Documents describ-ing a particular religious incident usually show these same ten-dencies, ending with the statement that, from that day to this, no one did that act again and everyone followed the new procedure, because it had been so successful.

In addition, almost nothing done by the Sukuma in their tra-ditional religious practice can be ascribed to religion alone. The observer may see an act which can be religious or purely social, according to the unspoken intentions of the persons concerned and, accordingly, the assessment which is then taken depends upon how much the informant is willing to say and explain about what has occurred.

So far, they have been little influenced by Christianity or Islam and continue to practice their own forms of ancestor worship, and it is essential, before we consider their religious practices, to un-derstand what they appear to regard as the principles of life and to proceed from that to their worship and some of the reasons for their beliefs.

Few Sukuma have given thought to eschatological problems, so that it is only from the everyday idiomatic phrases exemplify-ing certain words that a loosely coherent system can be con-structed. Although these words and phrases form the substratum of their religious knowledge, the possibility of understanding de-pends very much on individual explanations from men who have both imagination and the ability to verbalize their own understandings.

It is impossible to say that the Sukuma do this or believe that; only the broadest principles may be common to them as a whole. Thus the explanations of a lake-shore elder will almost certainly be totally different from those of equally knowledgeable elders from an inland parish; even the explanation of elders from the same parish may differ. One elder may practice his religion in one way as it has proved to be successful in that form, while another may have had a totally different experience. There is an area of consensus but not of conformity. Also, these elders will be able to answer only the questions which they have asked themselves and answered within the context of their own culture.

Questions related to the concepts of other religious systems, particularly the Christian one, such as the soul, resurrection, heaven and hell, do not serve any purpose. We can only pick up trends and incidents, remembering all the time that, while Sukuma religion is the object of our study, we are more likely to be sifting the explanations and knowledge of a small number of elders who will have made contact with the enquirer.

CHAPTER I

The Supreme Being

THE RELIGION of the Sukuma, in its practical aspects, is composed almost entirely of a direct ritual relationship with the spirits of their ancestors. Behind and above these ancestor spirits, they recognize the existence of a Supreme Being, to whom they attribute a wide variety of power, under various names, depending on the locality concerned. It is difficult to analyze their ideas about the Supreme Being since their conceptions have not become the subject of a cult or of speculative discussion.

In their ideas of the Supreme Being, they have two basic concepts. Firstly, that the Supreme Being is a solitary spirit and that the various names under which he is known are nothing more than different aspects or intentions, more in the nature of facets of his character. The other and more widespread concept considers the Supreme Being to be preeminent over a series of lesser spirits, who deal with the different aspects of life concerning human beings and the world in general.

In no sense are they polytheistic; it is rather that each function is either localized, as with Ngassa with its association with water holes, rivers, and Lake Victoria, or the names are alternated within the concept of a Supreme Being in accordance with local usage. They do not group these different aspects or usages into a system of parallel functions; there is always a hierarchy in which the Supreme Being is preeminent. These beliefs parallel their social system; sub- or supra-ordination puts everyone and everything in its prescribed place.

That they are essentially monotheistic is shown by the ease with which the would-be Christian convert accepts the Christian explanation of God; in a sense, he is already at home with it and

5

need make no great concessions of traditional belief in order to accept Christian faith.

This Supreme Being is not so much the major power in a hierarchy of spirit beings as a force upon which everything else is contingent. He is deemed to be responsible for maintaining the world, more or less as a passive guarantor of the status quo. Success and skill may be due to the orderliness of the world guaranteed by the Supreme Being, but are more directly caused or enabled by other agencies rather than by the direct action of the Supreme Being.

He is regarded as being male in essence and has no particular living place. When questioned, the Sukuma cannot say positively whether he lives in the sky or on the earth, but invocations, which usually start with his name, are addressed to the sky.

In general, it seems that the idea of a Supreme Being has a normal everyday utility in the sense that all their cosmological ideas depend on this, insofar as they have given any thought to the matter as a coherent whole, but there is no expletive use of his name such as is common in English.

The word used for God in the Christian context (*Mungu* or *Mulungu*) has a mixed Bantu origin; it may not be specifically Sukuma and may have been imported through the medium of Kiswahili, the present-day national language of the country.

Missionaries chose this Kiswahili word for God in their religious teaching and Bible translations when they first arrived in Sukumaland, because their ideas had been worked out first in that language; they were naturally unwilling to use Sukuma words for their concepts before they had learnt the meaning of new words by prolonged association with their use and users. Present-day Sukuma prayers used by the Catholics contain phrases with *Seba* and *Liwelelo* as translations for the Christian "God"; a return to traditional usage after possibly half a century of using the Kiswahili word, which had by then become synonymous with their own words. The existence of a Christian phraseology involving specific words has not affected their use in traditional phrases, so that there is a conflict between the meanings which can be attributed to these words in two parallel usages, fundamental to this being the loving God of the Christian and the seemingly indifferent Supreme Being of the Sukuma.

There is no one and nothing superior to the Supreme Being and such ideas as they have of creation go no further back than to say that the Supreme Being brought about certain conditions under which man was able to develop into his present social form. They have no idea that the Supreme Being created anything of his own deliberate volition, and indeed they seem to regard him as a totally independent spirit, very largely indifferent to man's activities. The Supreme Being is so great that he has very little to do with them in their petty human problems, which can better be solved through the intercession of their ancestors, who, at least by definition, are involved in the solution of these.

They do not regard it as essential that everything must have, or indeed should have, a cause. Their speculation is confined to the causes of their present-day troubles and, in the absence of any need to consider creation in order to understand these immediate causes, they do not speculate about it. It is possible to gather creation stories, but they are not spontaneous, and when analyzed, they appear to be more relevant to the psychology of the individuals who recount them than to the functional understanding of the community's beliefs.

The character of the Supreme Being is constant and does not change from good to bad and vice versa according to the situation. The fact that he is above the petty influences of man and does only what he himself wants is thought to make his character primarily good.

Their concept of good in religious and social matters seems to be negative rather than positive. The Supreme Being refrains from doing both evil and good, and this withdrawal from the affairs of man is conceived of as good in a sense unknown to Christian thought; good action is a desirable state of neutrality. He refrains from causing sickness in cattle, who are thus able to increase on their own without interference, and he is therefore good. It is not necessary for him to actively promote the good health of these cattle.

This lack of involvement in human affairs seems to have meant that he is interested in the moral aspects of conduct rather in the abstract than in the concrete. Possibly the explanation is that the Supreme Being does not control nature and society, but is nature as a whole. There is, then, some vague idea that he is interested in actions which are not controlled by the normal rules of society, but since their morality is almost always the social control of the community, there are few references to the Supreme Being as a sanction for any particular conduct. They do not say, "God help you if you do not behave." The Supreme Being is interested in maintaining the unity of nature, rather than in particular offenses, except where they are disruptive of this unity.

The Sukuma consider that death is necessary for the survival of the social world—the Supreme Being's unconcern for and lack of action to prevent death is an example of his inherent goodness —and that the pain, sorrow, and fear in the world in no way detract from this goodness. He is not an agency to whom one could appeal with any hope of success to prevent or delay death.

The Supreme Being has no regular connection with the earth and there are no direct isolated invocations to him or shrines in his honor. He is referred to directly in ancestor-propitiation ceremonies and in the initiation rites of special societies, when his name precedes the invocations. He is not invoked in tribal or clan situations as the support of a particular section of the community, so that he does not appear in any way to be the personal guardian of the social order. There are no stories showing how he protected or guided any part of the tribe during their migrations to their present localities, nor is he used in attempts at explaining present social situations.

No particular representation is called for in their lives to make their ideas socially meaningful. For a people who are not very imaginative in their religious ideas, their explanations of place-names are both long and imaginative folktales, but few are connected with ancestor worship and none were found to be connected with the Supreme Being under any name.

No one, even those unusually perceptive in regard to spiritual activity in present-day life or folklore, has seen the Supreme Being. He is recognizable only in his actions. There are some who have dreamed of him and who have been able to talk to him through that medium. A traditional Sukuma, with Moslem rather than Christian connections, described such a dream.

> When I was sleeping, the Supreme Being came and called me by name with a harsh voice. I answered at once and asked who was calling, and he replied, "It is I, the Supreme Being," and that if I came out of my hut, I should be astonished, as many had heard his name and that he was on the earth, but did not know where he lived. I got up and went outside my house and saw there a light brighter than anything that I had ever seen in my life. I asked who was turning the night into day contrary to nature. The Supreme Being told me to sit down on the ground and he would tell me news of my brothers who were dead and no longer on the earth.
>
> I could see nothing at first but eventually I could distinguish a white mass within the light and I began to be afraid, but he reassured me and I listened to his words. He told me that I should have money and cattle and that I should marry and that my firstborn would be a daughter; she would be married later to the chief of that area. When he said this he went up and disappeared and I saw him no more.

It seems that the point in the story of such a dream is not that it shows analogies to Christian myth, but that the story is completely isolated from religious practice. It neither validates nor does away with anything which the teller might have practiced or believed in his social life. For all the importance given to the Supreme Being, he is still apart from their everyday religious life.

Below the Supreme Being and his inferior spirits or character aspects come the ancestor spirits, who are subject both to the propitiation of their descendants and to the overall control of the Supreme Being. A bad event can occur because it is willed by the Supreme Being or by the ancestor spirits. If the sufferer goes to a diviner for the divination of the cause of his troubles and a cure involving the propitiation of the ancestors has no effect, then it is assumed that the trouble has been caused by the Supreme Being. If that is the case, there are no means of working for a recovery; the sufferer can beg but little can be expected from this begging, as the Supreme Being has already made known his intentions. If a sick person should ultimately recover, it is a sign that the Supreme Being has changed his mind, not necessarily in response to prayer.

The Supreme Being is concerned with the activities of the ancestor spirits because they are, relatively speaking, nearer to him than to living man, in the natural association of supernatural agencies. Similarly, the instinctive interest of the living man is in his ancestors, to whom he is related, rather than in the Supreme Being and nonancestral spirits, on whom he has no automatic influence, nor is there any community of interests between them and him. The sick or troubled person deals with the spirits of his ancestors because they are essentially human and can be thought of as humans and act in a human way with their jealousies and conceits. Also, since they are related, there is always the hope that they will automatically act in their descendant's favor. As this is the fundamental tenet of their spiritual life, the idea and possibility that the Supreme Being will be of personal assistance to them is beyond the existing needs of their religious life.

The more astute diviner (*nfumo;* pl. *bafumo*) would consider himself able, through his divining, to recognize cases of misfortune involving the Supreme Being. He would probably avoid further consultations on the grounds of futility of intercession for diseases which to him, and probably to the majority of ordinary people as well, would appear to be already incurable. However, it is generally recognized that misfortune cannot occur without the connivance of the Supreme Being, irrespective of the attitude of the ancestor spirits.

There is never any direct thanksgiving to the Supreme Being for recovery from illness or for material benefits which have been received. The good result is nearly always regarded as being due to the intercession of the ancestor spirits, to whom such thanks are due; but the ancestor spirits are not dominant, for, if that were so, the Sukuma would admit that there would be no death.

The control of the Supreme Being over a Sukuma is completed at his death, and a man who has been much troubled by him during his lifetime, with poverty and sickness, will not have the same attentions carried over into his existence as an ancestor spirit.

The diviner, whose powers are inherited from ancestors in the same profession, requires the benevolence or at least the indifference of the Supreme Being for the proper practice of his skill. The invocation of one diviner to the Supreme Being when he first started this work was, "Supreme Being, I beg you to give me the power of divination which has been offered by my ancestors. I implore you to listen to my supplications, O Spirit of good luck, so that I may have strong powers and be greater than other diviners. My urge to divine is genuine and handed down by my ancestors, so that I may give accurate divinations and thoughts of herbal medicines to both treat and cure."

Although the Supreme Being functions beyond the normal boundaries of men's influence through invocations, it is possible to anger him. A wealthy man sneering at a beggar would make him angry, not because it was an uncharitable thing to do, but because it was sneering at the Supreme Being's method of dividing up property. It would be unwise to speak unkindly about a sick person, for the same reason. So a Sukuma would say that if you have the good fortune to get many cows you must not laugh at a poor man, for you are laughing at the Supreme Being, who gave the poor man his poverty.

The Supreme Being would also be angry if relatives wailed excessively at a death, because everyone is made by him to live for a certain period, neither longer nor shorter than that. If the dead man was old, it would not matter so much, as he has lived out his allotted time. If the relatives should lament at the death of a young person, he will be angry with them for refusing to accept his wishes. There is, of course, considerable difference between this theoretical explanation and actual practice. In a wider sense, the murderer will incur the anger of the Supreme Being, because he has taken over the latter's work of disposing of human life.

In conclusion, although belief in the Supreme Being and his subordinate spirits or character aspects is widespread among the Sukuma, it has not taken upon itself more than the faintest tinges of ritual. The main spiritual force is their conception of the influence of their ancestors for good and bad, and belief in the Supreme Being is in practice subordinate to this. Although, in theory, he is the controlling force behind these ancestors, the average man is content to leave it at that and deal spiritually with his ancestors. With this more pragmatic approach to troubles, it is difficult to see in what way the Supreme Being could be more present in the practice of their religion. Perhaps a parallel would be, in England, that a practical understanding and appreciation of the love of God is experienced by a very limited number, while an acceptance of God as a background to material existence would probably be admitted by the majority without their feeling any need to conceptualize the matter any further.

There is no doubt that a belief in the Supreme Being is not a practical force in their spiritual life, but it is a necessary background to their ritual activities. Possibly their very lack of positive beliefs about the Supreme Being and his practical separation from their system of ancestor belief and propitiation have combined to give them an easier understanding of the Christian need for positive theism. In addition, the separation of their belief from practical ancestor worship has kept it apart from missionary attack.

It is hard to state where spirit-empowered activity stops and the ordinary processes of nature begin. To the ordinary Sukuma, there is no hard and fast line; some restrict the Supreme Being and the subordinate spirits' activities to the invisible power behind their day-to-day activities, while others bring them further into the open by referring to the dawn as a spirit by saying that someone has suffered great trouble because of the dawn, but this could also mean "such is the way of the world."

Father Bösch, in his study of the beliefs of the Banyamwezi,[1] a tribe closely allied to the Basukuma both in language and culture, gives no less than thirty-six names for their Supreme Being, of which more than three-quarters are known to the Sukuma, who have added several new ones, all of which have their extremely variable characteristics, which cannot be deciphered into exact components.

---

[1] F. Bösch, *Les Banyamwezi, peuple de l'Afrique orientale.* Münster i W.: Aschendorff, 1930.

CHAPTER II

The Ancestors' Behavior

A POTENTIAL ancestor spirit (*isamva;* pl. *masamva*) is in the blood of every man and becomes active after death. It is all that remains after death, when the human being dies; there is nothing left when an animal dies, even a cow specially consecrated to the ancestors of a family. All the spirits of his ancestors (*nkurugenji;* pl. *bakurugenji*) are in his blood and the blood of his relatives. If a man dies without child, the spirit of the dead man goes to his brothers, by reason of the blood relationship through father and grandfather; it is not necessary for him to die in order that his spirit be present in the body of his son, and they allege that a living man, by this means, is able to affect another living relative.

The dead, the living, and the unborn are a continuum and represent not so much a personal immortality but a survival in an ancestor group, just as he or she has lived in a group in life. The unity of the living and the dead is expressed in their ceremonies, when ancestors are referred to by kinship terms more appropriate to the living, whereas the word for ancestor spirit, *isamva,* is rarely used in propitiation, although it is quite common in everyday conversation.

The Sukuma concept of a spiritual hierarchy is clear enough, with the ancestors, nearer to them, more approachable than the distant Supreme Being. The names of more recent ancestors are remembered and recited in order at propitiation ceremonies, but their number is indicative of social status—the ordinary cultivator remembering no more than four, whereas an important chief might recite as many as twenty.

In these recitations, the ancestors are usually referred to collectively as brothers (*badugu*) in the usual sense of being members of the same agnatic line, and, even in the ceremonies which are usually specifically directed to one ancestor, the relationship is not made more definite, possibly because the one dissident spirit must be propitiated without antagonizing the rest of the lineage. This avoidance of singularizing any particular ancestor, although only one is considered to need propitiation, occurs in all aspects of their religious life.

The ancestors are also referred to as the great ones of the family, as in remarks after a good harvest that they are laughing—*Batale biswe ba kale basekire*—or, when there is some misfortune, that they got angry—*Batale biswe basayaga*. When nothing is wrong, human terms are used for the ancestors, "the great ones," "those who preceded us," "our brothers," and so on, but once misfortune becomes apparent, the word *isamva* comes into use; it is the spirit of the ancestor, almost, rather than the ancestor, who is discontented. If someone becomes ill, *wadimilwe nzimu*—"he is held by a spirit"—is used, while if the person becomes personally possessed by an ancestor in a divination ceremony, they say that he is held by the spirit of an ancestor—*wadimilwe masamva*.

There is an element of spiritual unity among the dead, so that the recently dead and the ancestors of long ago are one. The progenitor of a lineage is rarely mentioned, and then only in a chief's ancestry. There are no good and bad ancestors whose characteristics are constant—only ancestors who are angry in relation to particular circumstances. The ancestor who has been killed because he was a sorcerer (*nogi*) is included in the general invocations at a sacrifice; he might turn nasty, but he has no predisposition to continue his acts of sorcery from the spiritual world. The greatest disaster that can overtake a Sukuma and the family which surrounds him is that the family should be extinguished. It is descendants who keep the individual spiritually alive. Similarly, expulsion from the family would have the same end of depriving the individual of survival as ancestor, both for himself and his children, and this is the strongest sanction for conformity.

The traditional concept of the ancestor spirit has been confused by the Christian concept of the devil and the angel, for which Christians used the Swahili *shetani* and *malaika*. In addition, the Moslems have used *shetani* in a much more general sense for evil spirit, demon, and devil, particularly in connection with possession and hysteria. Also *nzimu* is used for ancestor spirit, which has general Bantu derivations, rather than specifically Sukuma ones, and may be an addition to their traditional usages. It seems now that the terms *isamva* and *ishitani* are used indiscriminately for ancestor spirits and that, accompanying an overall change in their traditional religious practices, the ancestor spirits have taken on a more punitive nature than was the case in the past, so that they are more interested in aggression toward their descendants than in their welfare.

The whole cult has thus taken on many aspects of the Swahili cult of nonancestral spirit possession, divination, and release by the performance of certain acts. This suggests that the Christian concepts have not gained a separate identity and that the ancestors have not been easily added to the category of All Souls, for and to whom prayers can be addressed. There seems to be no connection between the heart of the man (*moyo* or *ng'holo*), in life and when he dies, and the spirit (*isamva*) of the same person when dead—one does not elide into the other so that his heart becomes his spirit. In life there are a body and spirit which become extinguished at death and are replaced by the ancestor spirit.

As descent is patrilineal, there could be no continuance of life through daughters who, upon marriage, become attached to other lineages. Some chiefly families who traced descent matrilineally are not considered here. Nevertheless, the married women still remain members of their own lineages and are not only able to take part in the ritual activities of their own families, but would be called home to do so. It should be clear that the Sukuma do not see this continuum of the living and the dead as being a single line of descent from father to son which alone can ensure survival as a spirit.

Just as the individual has innumerable ascendants, to whom he has a lineal relationship, so the ancestor looks to the broad extent of family development for his descendants. Their use of classificatory kinship, by which a father's brother is also a father to whom the relationship is as close as to the father himself, means that after death relatives other than one's own children may continue to give due honor and remembrance. This extended relationship is not entirely confined to classificatory kin, as the headmen of villages (*banangwa*) and hereditary councillors (*banang'oma*) also paid attention to the ancestors of the chief. Similarly, the followers (*bahemba*) of diviner-magicians and rainmakers may give honor to the deceased members of their craft and to the particular specialist who started the society to which they belong.

Cases are encountered in which the true lineage has been falsified in order that the inheritance of a chieftainship should be passed down in direct line. Such circumstances could be when a chief in the past has had only one child, a girl; he prevents her from marrying; in the course of time, she bears an illegitimate son, which then belongs to her father and not to the genitor; the chieftainship has thereby been kept in the family of the old chief. This could happen as well with ordinary men who have neither male children nor brothers, but these are exceptions and, although the arrangements would be elided into an assumption of orthodox patriliny for ancestor worship in succeeding generations, their validity at the time is sniggered at in conversation.

A man's ancestor spirits are within him and look after him. They made themselves felt in the traditional family by the generalized feeling of support and comfort which came from the performance of regular rites of propitiation and remembrance and the possession of paraphernalia inherited or assumed in response to divination, or from the maintenance of cows, sheep, goats, dogs, snakes, porcupines, and so on, in response to an ancestor's needs. This aspect is on the decline.

In their other form, these spirits are felt to cause sickness and misfortune in the individual, regardless of the physical cause, by which method they draw attention to themselves, so that their descendant has to resort to divination to find out their needs. This has resulted in a great increase in the numbers of practicing diviner-magicians. The spirits are not located in any particular part of a man. They can maintain the man in good health, but they do not help him to think or feel, abilities reserved to the activity of the heart. A good harvest or intelligent cultivation is a result of the direct help of the ancestors.

Living people have no direct communication with their ancestors and it is the ancestor who makes himself known to his descendants through the mediumship of a diviner-magician or by possession, in which the person behaves uncontrollably.

The ancestors can and possibly do perform various acts which have a bad effect on their descendants; the Sukuma do not consider it possible to say that any particular misfortune has the one cause. When a man is sick, it may be caused by the Supreme Being, his ancestors, witchcraft, or poison, or indeed a combination of all four allowing a certain situation to arise. The Supreme Being is indifferent, the ancestors annoyed, which enables the wizard to be consulted, who uses magic to poison him. Direct causation is alien to their ideas of misfortune and, of course, the inexactness of their metaphysical ideas allows explanations for both success and failure.

Thus the ancestors may be the cause of death, the thunderstorm that destroys the harvest, the drought that shrivels the growing crops, the sickness of the man and his wife—particularly her inability to conceive, her tendency to abort, and the still-births of her babies—the failure of the young to grow well, and of the cattle and small stock to increase. They might also account for the forgetfulness which loses money and the thief who steals their property, the failure to pass an examination or defeat in a political election, losing one's way at night, loss of profits on a commercial deal, the upsetting of a boat on a river crossing, being bitten by a dog or knocked over on a bicycle. The whole gamut of human success and misfortune may be subject to their influence.

Although name-giving is usually done soon after birth, names may be changed later in life because of illness which has been attributed by divination to a dereliction of filial duty. The fulfillment of the obligation is in the formal taking of the name and there is no equivalent obligation to use it, so that an individual with a troubled life may run through a series of names in order to get relief. At the time of such name-changing, the person will be asperged by the head of the family, who will make an invocation to the ancestors: "I am summoning my ancestors, I am calling them because of the name of your child here. You are wanting him to be called Masanja and from today this will be his name. This was as you wanted, and from now on leave him alone that his family may increase and gather property and that he may regain health with plenty of food." The formal ceremony and the mention of the name therein is deemed sufficient to alleviate the troubles from which he has been suffering.

After a child has been born, the ancestors come and look at the child to see its intelligence, before the coming-out-of-the-house ceremony, at which it is given a name, which they themselves may have decided upon before the birth and planted in the hearts of the parents. If the birth is difficult, the child is thought to be refusing to acknowledge the power and position of his ancestors, and they in their turn despair that he will be one of them. Accordingly the ancestors pin their hopes on another subsequent child to take the wanted name.

When a child is called by a name willed by a particular ancestor, all the ancestors are informed so that none of them will be angry. A man will take names only from the male side of his family and a woman from the female line. There is no limit to the number of names which any individual can take on, and some men have been through the ceremony as often as four times.

The importance of names cannot be overstressed, since the name, rather than the individual, is the operative element on which most of his ritual life, before and after death, will depend. This fact is emphasized in witchcraft, where it is essential to obtain not only something of the individual who is to be bewitched or something which he has used, but also to know his full name. Otherwise the magic will be ineffective.

The study of texts seems to suggest that, although a person's father may have an operative ancestor spirit, in actual practice the taking of names is always referred to as from grandparents to grandchild. There is a telescoping of generations beyond this, so that all ancestors may be referred to collectively as grandparents.

There is a continuity of the parent relationship carried on from life into death, but it is no longer centered on individuals, and the loves and hates of the family life of this world are projected onto the ancestors more as a corporate body than as a collection of individuals. The concentration of propitiation on unknown ancestors by the descendants who have been suffering from their activities supports this conclusion. The recently dead parents are actively used as links with the mass of ancestors preceding them, in the sense of mentioning the line of descent, but there are very few cases of propitiating an ancestor who has been known personally to the person involved.

Another feature is the neglect of the dead as individuals in contrast to the remembrance of them as ancestors. For instance, there is the lack of attention to graves. These are often in the cattle pen for the man and his first wife if they are wealthy, and are unattended almost from the time of the funeral. Sometimes the grave is marked with a small upright stone (*ishigo*) but as the earth on the grave is levelled off, there is often little to distinguish it from its surroundings and it soon disappears as a physical reminder of a particular person. A basket is often left upside down on the grave, but this soon rots away.

The term *ishigo* for gravestone has a much wider use in reference to groves of trees and thick bush, which they reverence and do not cut for firewood. Such groves contain the reputed graves of chiefs or are the sites of historical events such as at Burru near Mwanza, where a grove hid the chief from his enemies, and his family worshiped there from then onwards. It has also been used in some places for houses in which parents and grandparents are still alive, where such reverence has to be shown.

No visits or periodic sweepings of burial places are required of the descendants unless they should be particularly prescribed by diviner-magicians. Except for the graves of chiefs and notable magicians, or occasionally as a result of divination, graves in general are not the scene of ceremonies.

This lack of interest in graves should not lead to the supposition that they are not important. They are the evidence of ownership in a Western sense, while to the Sukuma they are sacred in general rather than in the particular. The ancestors are present in the dust of their graves and diviner-magicians, in their divinations, sometimes allege that they can see this dust rising, as an indication of ancestor displeasure. Catholic Sukuma have said that the possession of the Tomb of St. Peter must validate the Church, and that, for this reason alone, the Protestants cannot have the true religion. The graves of their dead are the justification for their present existence. The graves of famous people and some places of long-forgotten importance, which they assume to be graves, are recognized by those passing, who throw twigs, grass, and leaves onto them, while the passing Christian would make the sign of the cross.

The Sukuma do not say that the spirits live in their graves or in the spirit houses erected to them in propitiation. Just as invocations starting with the name of the Supreme Being are directed toward the sky, so they continue with the names of their ancestors, turning toward the different directions from which parts of the family are thought to have migrated. There is a connection with the Supreme Being, as "he has been come for"—*wizilwe na Liwelelo*—and "he has gone together with the Supreme Being"—*waja na Welelo*.

It does seem that they consider these spirits to have a life comparable to their life on earth, for they are offered, in propitiation, the earthly compensations which they would have enjoyed there. In any case, graves as such have no interest for the Sukuma in general, only those of their own family. Digging into a grave while laying down foundations does not disturb the workers because the bones are not those of their ancestors, who are the only ones who can harm him.

The living and the dead have an essential and continuous unity, in which the two are interdependent. Each depends for its existence on the other, so that the higher the social standing of the descendant, the greater the number of ancestors with whom he has to keep in touch.

In their attentions to ancestors, the Sukuma do not seem to take particular care with the agnatic line; all or any of a man's ancestors may be called into prominence and propitiated. As inheritance is normally from father to son, it seems strange that this line is not stressed to the exclusion of others. Marriage is exogamous for those who have great-grandparents in common. Consequently, there may be a considerable number of common ancestors beyond that degree, which would tend to make ancestor worship cognatic rather than agnatic. A great many propitiation ceremonies are, in fact, for female ancestors and it is probable that, as the women lose their kinship in their children, there may be a degree of counterbalancing through their predominance in such ceremonies.

This could also be looked upon as a belated recompense for such injustices as they, the female ancestors, may have suffered in their lives.

In their ideas on causality, benevolent and evil forces are not equally divided among the various spiritual agencies. In their investigation of illness and misfortune, there is no known direct line of causality which they and their diviners can follow for all matters. Rather, there is a process of elimination, which removes possible causes one by one and allows them eventually to hit on the remedy which is the true cure for ill health or misfortune in that particular context.

It does not seem that the ancestors are considered specifically as the protectors of the family and this may possibly be a consequence of the nonlocalization of lineages. Localization would have necessitated individual rather than lineage welfare. There is no question of loving the ancestors, and they are feared rather than venerated. There is a marked degree of informality in addressing them, with no display of honorifics; in fact there is often no means of telling by the language whether the Sukuma are addressing the living or the dead.

The ancestors, through the medium of divination ceremonies, do not offer guidance and advice to their descendants and, as often as not, they are asked to agree to lines of action or states of affairs that have already been decided on or carried out. The head of the family asks for their intercession with powers greater than their own rather than for their help, and in general they are asked to abstain from evil rather than to bring about unexpected good.

These propitiation ceremonies are not directed to relatives who can be remembered even by the oldest of the family. The relative causing the trouble comes from the distant past, so that the production of his name in a divination ceremony usually occasions considerable surprise, as the name and the incidents complained of are unknown, even in tales of the lineage. The survival of an individual ancestor in name form depends on remembrance as an individual, and considerable stress is laid on the unfortunate circumstances of losing one's name. Nevertheless, the individual soon fades into the group ancestry and no longer has any individuality in the social sense.

As an influence for good and evil, the position of the ancestors is much more complex. It is doubtful whether the people have any conception of good and evil abstract forces that are equally valid at all times and places. The average Sukuma would seem to grade his ideas of right and wrong according to the degree of relationship which he has to the person in the context. Since his primary obligations are to his own family and diminish with increasing kinship distance, it follows that the presence of ancestors must be a sanction on the behavior of the individual which can, in this context, be described as moral.

Their concepts of justice are thus closely aligned with their kinship structure and the ancestors backing it. They see nothing wrong with Christian concepts such as, "Thou shalt not steal"; it fits in exactly with their family idea that it is unthinkable to steal from a close relative; they have qualified the precept without actually stating the qualification—it is so obvious that they see no linguistic need to express it. The restrictions on stealing cattle from the Masai are related to political power and not to any moral restraints, which may, in fact, be rather more permissive than restrictive. There are thus no absolute values in their morals and these issues become qualified by relationship, locality, and the circumstances surrounding the incident, and the ancestors add a religious sanction to the family's need to maintain itself in opposition to the other lineages, clans, and tribes surrounding it.

If they understand that the living and the dead have an essential unity, and that sins are acts against the interests of an obligation to one's relatives and neighbors, then failure by an ancestor to carry out his duties to another ancestor when they were both alive can be seen to have an effect on their mutual descendants. Thus they consider much of their misfortune to be the result of such a sin, of and for which they could have no possible cognizance or direct responsibility, which turns back on the family of their descendants.

The chief, who was the leading descendant of the dominant clan in each chiefdom and whose relationship with his ancestors in the past concerned the welfare of the whole chiefdom, was responsible for performing ceremonies of propitiation involving large numbers of people. Now little or no interest is taken in these activities relating to chiefs' ancestors, since chiefs no longer have political power, in comparison with the past, when they were the very center of the life cycle of the chiefdom and the religious symbol of its identity. Under the colonial government, the chief was under the eye of an alien administration and usually considered, rightly or wrongly, that it would be inadvisable for him to take part in such ceremonies, apart from his probable conversion to Christianity. The chief had a deputy under customary law, whose role has changed to that of a substitute for the chief when these ceremonies are carried out in semisecrecy, in response to emergencies such as widespread drought or cattle sickness.

Although the ancestors are dominant in the ritual life of these people, they are relatively weak in their powers and they are never considered to have any direct control over the forces of nature; in fact they have no overall control over any particular facet of life, and are themselves considered to be ultimately dependent on the Supreme Being. The invocations in propitiation ceremonies start with the name of the Supreme Being and then mention the ancestors. The latter can cause trouble and misfortune, but they are never considered to have power over life and death. There is no idea that the ancestors will automatically look after their descendants or that illness and death result from their inattention.

There is the necessity of intercession, since the goodwill of the ancestors is essential. Magic medicines, however well divined, may be ineffective by themselves. In the course of a disease, if the sick man is holding his own, this may be because the majority of the ancestors are battling with the ancestor who caused the trouble, and that is the reason why he has not died. The effect of a ceremony, in such a situation, would be to ignore the help which some ancestors were giving, and to antagonize them rather than to get the man well again.

Regular everyday ritual directed to the ancestors is no longer considered a necessity in order to obtain a pleasant and satisfactory life and, even in the more out of the way parts, it is no longer carried out. The invocation for such a ritual was recorded as saying, "See, all you who are our brothers, this is your goat of sacrifice. You like to eat in your own home, so let the owner be well; let him get everything in life and do not complain of his

success, but leave him alone. This is your sacrifice to bring peace
to the household, so eat it, all of you." Perhaps there never has
been regular ritual as such and the informants may have attributed to the past all the ideal aspects of life which they find to
be absent from their present existence.

Now both the educated and uneducated persons neglect their
ancestors for years and consider propitiating them only when they
are in trouble, so that the cult of the ancestors has changed from
maintaining their goodwill by regular rites as was done in the past
to the present intermittent recognition of their powers to harm
and the ceremonies, individual rather than collective, necessary
to recover their goodwill. It is their interference rather than their
benevolence that occasions the ritual.

The ancestors themselves are very capricious and do not appear ever to complain of neglect in general but only of some particular desire that has not been followed—a desire which, in the
majority of cases, could not have been anticipated; people say
that their ancestors are difficult to please, *batale biswe bali
balambu no*. Possibly, neglect is not quite the correct word; it
may be rather that they wish to be remembered in some particular way because of something that was done to them during their
lives; for example, a man's dying away from home while on a
journey. The fact that so many of the divined reasons for ancestor
anger concern their death and burial in the correct way at their
homes stresses the importance of burial, as a family link, rather
than of graves alone.

In a Sukuma's life, which may be pleasant and successful, with
plenty of cattle and a large family, there is never the suggestion
that this well-being is in any way related to the number of propitiation ceremonies that the householder has performed. Only in
the case of the diviner-magician, whose art depends on the active
co-operation of his ancestors, can it be said that he has been in
active satisfactory communication with his ancestors. Such well-
being may be related to the fact that, on the one hand, his ancestors have not noticed it or rather have refrained from doing evil,
and, on the other, that its existence is due more to the actions of
the Supreme Being.

They have no firm idea of when the spirit of a dead man becomes active after his death and there are no ceremonies in which his spirit is activated into the community of the ancestors, nor any formal bringing home of the spirit of a dead relative. They acknowledge that his powers are latent and some say that he can begin to influence the living as early as six months after his death. In other tales, they do suggest that the spirit of the dead man does remain in the area of his home for a time and that, under certain circumstances, he can be both seen and felt.

However, we must examine these folktales against the background of their social life. A man is never on terms of great intimacy with his father and it is thought that such attitudes would vitiate some of the other practical aspects of their relationship. A deceased father is also too near to the living to be considered as a spirit in a group of spirits. The grandparent is a more distant relative in years, while at the same time his role is one of personal intimacy with the grandchild. Thus it seems likely that the spirit does not become active until there is a gap of one generation between the deceased and the living.

Although it may be supposed that the processes of ancestor worship act as a sanction for their form of morality, there is no indication that the connection is close and that infringements of their code are immediately followed by supernatural action. If this were the case and people relied on this connection, it would suggest that their processes of customary law were weak. This, however, is not the case, as it seems that the ancestors do not act on matters which are more readily dealt with by legal processes. They are certainly not the upholders of custom in general, nor do they appear to take any action in cases where particular individuals are thought to have caused general misfortune, such as the alleged starting of a drought. No cases have been found in which they took action in cases of adultery, theft, and other private delicts.

The ancestors are not a separate series of beings but they are, if not one with their living descendants, at least a part of the same family in the relationship of father to son and mother to daughter. Between these categories, there always exists a very wide measure of tolerance and it would hardly be likely that the father would take action against his son for theft, etc., nor the mother against her daughter should she disgrace the family by being caught in adultery. Just as in real life a father would take action against his son with extreme reluctance, so in the life of the ancestor spirit, he would be similarly reluctant to be angry, except under what he considers to be extreme provocation.

Very few cases can be found in which fathers or mothers have disowned their children, and even then it has been caused by the children's flagrant neglect or disobedience, rather than because of some more public or private delict of no immediate concern to the family. The ancestors are therefore interested in the continuation of the lineage and its maintenance, and are only likely to take action when they feel that this unity is being disrupted. The majority of cases of ancestors' possession result from their descendants' neglecting them within the framework of the parental relationship.

There is a sense of dependence on their ancestors as being one with them in the same family, rather than an aggressive control over their descendants by dominating ancestors. It is not a fact that, if the man behaves well and remembers his ancestors, they will bless him, but rather that the man will be upset by his ancestors for reasons of their own choosing, which the man will not be able to find out in advance. The function of the ancestor worship is not to dispose of individual troubles, but to unify the family in response to a challenge to its continuity.

The land is not considered as belonging to the ancestors, since none of the lineages, except the dominant lineage of the chiefdom headed by the chief, was in any way localized. The ancestors of the earth and any ritual association with it are absent from their religious life. Ownership of land is only by active occupation and any conception of ritual ownership would be alien to this, apart from the fact that every lineage has a mythological charter, which, even in historical sections, contains many migrations.

Although in the past the worship of ancestors had a very wide field of activity both geographically and socially, it is doubtful nowadays if it has any influence outside the extended family. It is not to be viewed as a field of ritual collaboration, overlapping kinship ties and extending into the necessity of neighborhood unity.

Sometimes the informants say that the murderer cannot commit such a crime without having first committed many sins against

his ancestors, and it is the latter who drive him to kill. Although
he does not usually take a knife out with him, he will take it on
that day. The man who is to be murdered cannot be called to the
place of the killing by the ancestors of his murderer, so it is considered that he is called by witchcraft, with which his own ancestors have concurred. In fact, the whole thing is regarded as rather
a foregone conclusion, and even more so because sometimes the
murder would take place in the presence of many people, when,
by all the odds, it should have been prevented. The overt reason
for the murder is not the real cause, which will have been provided
by the ancestors.

The wizard, if he has failed to kill someone through sickness,
might find out the man's ancestors and attack him before the latter are aware of what is going on. The ancestors are not propitiated during the night or at midday, so such attacks would be
made at these times, when the ancestor spirits are not in attendance at the homes of their descendants. The idea may be that
such serious public delicts must involve a prior rejection by ancestors who have no further interest in that individual as a member of the lineage.

There is little attention to the purely personal side of remembrance and it is doubtful whether any individual would carry out
a ceremony for a particular ancestor purely out of affection for
him as a remembered individual. This may indeed seem strange,
but there do not appear to be any customs, other than those connected with the funeral, which would testify to a prolongation of
personal grief. It is considered that the elements of personal grief
may well be acted out in the responsibilities of inheritance, especially when there are cattle to look after in the compound.

In conclusion, we find that the Sukuma have no consistent cos-
mology, but a rough theory of causation, which is not specifically
dependent on the results or failures of ancestor propitiation. In
their worship, there is little to distinguish the living from the
dead and the parent relationship becomes submerged in the ancestors as a corporate body, to which it is directed. The relationship with the ancestors is founded on expediency within the
framework of continuing remembrance as the only means of ensuring survival. The ancestors act as a sanction for the mainte-

nance of moral standards, which appear to be definable only in kinship terms. Their ancestor worship has no part in their knowledge of the spirits and phantoms that make them frightened of the night and of lonely places. It is the key to the functioning of their culture and not a ghost story.

CHAPTER III

The Cult of the Ancestors
in Everyday Life

THE ACQUISITION and retention of a specified article (*kitongelejo;* pl. *shitongelejo*), which itself becomes part of the family's ritual paraphernalia as a permanent act of propitiation, is the most obvious sign of the practice of this cult. People believe that these objects, by their existence in the household and their use at times of sacrifice and propitiation, have the power of giving peace to the family—not positive benefits, but leaving the living alone to prosper, with more children and cattle and better crops. While the general term comes from *kwitongeleja*, "to exorcise," which suggests the removal of something unpleasant, they are also called *maholelo*, objects which bring the even successes of everyday life.

Many Sukuma wear amulets (*lupigi;* pl. *mnigi*), which may be but are not necessarily connected with ancestor worship; only the individual himself can say for what particular reason he is wearing a strip of hide around his wrist, why she has a piece of wood on her thigh girdle or, indeed, why they hang holy medals around their necks. It is not possible to assume exact categories, and the early missionaries' wholesale categorizing of these objects as contrary to Christian morals has undoubtedly made the Sukuma use their wrists less and their thighs more for wearing traditional religious, magical, and medicinal objects, where they will no longer be seen.

These relics or keepsakes of the ancestors do not appear to be necessarily articles which the ancestors actually possessed in their lifetimes. The baskets, bows, stools, and the hide clothing of a previous generation will have perished very quickly, and the

fact that there is a practical gap between the death of an individual and his existence as an active ancestor spirit means that there is
no particular merit in keeping your father's bow or sleeping
hide when it no longer has a practical use in the household. Such
objects do not go up into the attic for children of later generations
to discover, but are kept in use with less and less utility until they
disintegrate. The bow splits, becomes a stick, and ends up in the
fence or on the fire; the sleeping hide becomes holed, gravitates
to the floor, is used for winnowing grain, and is finally eaten by
the dog and white ants.

Other artifacts, such as spears, arrowheads, bracelets (*itendele*)
of iron and copper, ostrich eggshell beads (*isanga*), and seashells
(*kilungu*), will not decay and, hung on the walls or pushed or
plunged into a crack, can survive as long as the hut stands. They
stay there unnoticed until family necessity makes the members
resort to divination, where they are told to wear or use, for example, a bracelet of copper (*itendele lyaza*). The one on the wall
is remembered, thankfully, and brought back into their lives, as
otherwise they would have to buy one, and indeed some of the articles required are virtually unobtainable and require years of
searching before they can be used in propitiation.

Nothing is thrown away in a Sukuma house because it no longer
has an immediate utility, and often the weirdest articles are accepted with evident pleasure because they fulfill a still uncompleted obligation, or might possibly fulfill one in the future. The
head of a vulture is cut off and dried with delight, because the
son of the father's sister wanted one for propitiation several years
before. Similarly, such articles about the house can be sold or
given to neighbors in the same sort of difficulty.

The seashells and ostrich-shell beads came into use as fashionable everyday articles and, as they went out of everyday use, became of ritual value to later people. The same process is continuing with plastic badges, coins, holy medals, and safety pins,
which are beginning to be seen in the equipment and costumes of
diviner-magicians. Almost everything which the Sukuma use or
have used has come into ritual use in some part of Usukuma; pot-
ters' and ironsmiths' equipment, household utensils, the bones,
claws, and skins of wild animals and the bark, leaves, and roots of

plants. A list would become no more than a vocabulary of their material culture.

If the owner is asked, he will, of course, state that these are the actual objects which belonged to his ancestors, and the fact that they are obviously not, as in the case of diminutive shields, stools, and baskets of recent make, in no way affects their practical utility. The pragmatic questioner sees but does not believe, while the Sukuma believes but does not see in the same way. Not only did these objects belong to the ancestors but they still belong. Just as the ancestors are a continuation of the living household, so these objects are still used and wanted by them. Although they look like a worthless collection, often of moth-eaten rubbish, they are in use—the division between spiritual and practical utility is not at all clear.

When these objects are not worn in everyday life, they are carried or worn by the family head when particular ceremonies of propitiation and remembrance are carried out. The diviner-magician also does this when he carries out a divination. Thus skins are worn over one shoulder, while another lies on the ground in front, covered with other ritual apparatus. He may wear a fur hat and have numbers of necklaces of skins, beads, wire, and small gourds covering his chest and a ceremonial decorated fly whisk (*singwanda*) in his hand. Beside him there is a thin iron spear or an iron rod with bells at one end (*nanga gwa kisinza gulina ng'hinda*), or a pole decorated with strips of hide from propitiatory sacrifices which have been carried out at his direction or in his family. On the mat in front there will be baskets and trays containing more objects. The quantity and variety of these objects depend upon the person's involvement in ancestor propitiation; some families have very few and others a sackful.

Similarly, the house compounds, or property nearby outside, may have cleared areas, plants, and small houses dedicated to and used in propitiation. These small houses (*numba ya msamva* or *kigabiro;* pl. *mhigabiro*), are possibly more common in the north than elsewhere, varying from five-foot traditional beehive-shaped thatched houses to small, roughly tied lines of sticks symbolic of houses, or three flat upright stones covered by a fourth, often smeared with cow dung.

Those houses with such spirit hutches usually have one or two small structures, while diviner-magicians themselves might have a number of grandiose structures, or a dozen or more hutches lining the outside of the compound fence or surrounding the divining space. While these are only models of actual houses, there are cases in which a traditional house has been constructed and lived in, as an act of propitiation. Sometimes these small houses are clustered at the gates of the compound to right or left, according to the relationship of the ancestor propitiated, or around the cleared area of beaten earth (*lubuga*), in which the diviner-magician carries out his divinations, to which perhaps some euphorbia or aloe plants have been transplanted.

An additional gate may be made in the compound fence in response to ancestor spirit requests, and there are cases in which ten or more additional gates have been constructed as a result of repeated divinations. The small houses are constructed from specific trees which have symbolic meanings, just as the main house has the wood of certain trees in certain places, which cannot be explained in terms of their natural properties.

These houses are not treated with any reverence and are not shrines maintained and used for the continuing welfare of the family. Their construction fulfills the obligation and they are not repaired or reconstructed should new troubles beset the family; they fall down, sheep sleep in them, and dogs urinate on the poles. In fact, they are treated just as the Sukuma would use them if they were real houses. The area where these houses are clustered would be the place for a family sacrifice and special invocations, at which times they are asperged (*kufuka lwanga*), and small portions of a meat or beer sacrifice would be left in them by the celebrant during the ceremony for the household animals and ants to eat, but for the remainder of the time they have no attention paid to them. They represent a localization of cult activity, rather than the homes of specified spirits.

A further everyday link between the ancestors and their descendants is the keeping of particular animals, for which a variety of names—*ya kwitongeleja, ya maholelo, ya kifumo, ya masamva* —testify to their importance, not only as a symbol of the ancestors' peaceful interest in the household, but as a living part of the ceremonies necessary to the welfare of the family. In the same way as in other difficulties, the magician divines the source of the ancestors' displeasure, suggesting that it was the tradition of the family to consecrate a particular animal to their ancestors, and that they should do so.

The animals required are usually cows and goats with specific coloring; totally black cows and goats for chiefly families, white male goats for the Bubinza and Bukwaya clans, black male goats with white spots on the foreheads, white male goats with black patches on the sides for Bushi, Bugunda, and other clans, white she-goats for the Bunega and Butimba clans, red sheep for the Busabi and Bukundihave; and so on, but these are not exact and there are many variations. Sheep tend to be used for women. Chickens are also used and the Bukwimba clan have dogs with eyebrows of contrasting colors (*mva ya miso anne*; lit. "a dog with four eyes") dedicated to their ancestors, in remembrance of a tradition of hunting successes.

Chiefs usually had black cows dedicated to their ancestors, possibly as a symbol of their rainmaking importance. Members of the Buyeye society of snake charmers would keep a snake and those from the Bungunguli society of porcupine hunters would keep a porcupine as essential links between their present powers and those of their ancestors, who practiced these arts and upon whose benevolence they are still dependent. The reasons for venerating such animals are always given as historical events, which were so successful that other successes followed.

It is possible for a family to have several animals in one compound dedicated to their ancestors, and the sound of their clanking bells, indicating their ancestor-propitiation role, makes their identification easy. They are never slaughtered and are kept until they die, at which time their meat will be eaten only by members of the family as a whole and not merely by those in the agnatic line. The animal would probably be skinned near the spirit houses and the hide kept, on its death, and it would probably not be replaced, unless the family again suffered misfortune and was similarly advised to dedicate another beast. In the past it would

have been replaced by a young animal as soon as possible after
the death. The milk from such a dedicated cow can be drunk
only by those who have spent the previous night in that family's
compound or by the family itself.

CHAPTER IV

Propitiation Ceremonies

IT HAS BEEN seen that the Sukuma, in his traditional everyday life, surrounds himself with objects and animals in response to the demands of his ancestors. These are material facts which can be observed in a visit to his home, but the anger of his ancestors requires a formal ceremony in propitiation, of which the objects and animals are only leftovers of diminished importance.

Propitiation ceremonies cover a wide range of activities from the almost automatic asperging of the ancestor shrines at a family feast to the prearranged full-scale ceremony of the sacrifice of a bull for a serious family trouble. Apart from the simpler and more casual everyday ceremonies which are gradually dying out, these propitiations are performed only as a result of a divination to discover the cause of the trouble which is worrying the individual or family concerned. It does not appear that there is any obligation on descendants to initiate these ceremonies; they are, in fact, considered to be suggested by the aggrieved spirit at the time of the divination.

Honorific ceremonies, such as those performed for a chief by his courtiers, the sacrifice of the grave stones (*kitambo sha mashigo*), a sacrifice by a husband in honor of his wife's grandfather (*kitambo sha kukwisha*), by hunting societies for success in the chase (*kitambo sha bawimi*), and by a man on obtaining the status of elder (*kitambo sha kugwila*), are markedly on the decline. Ceremonies connected with the agricultural cycle and the life of the compound, as when the householder builds a new compound (*kitambo sha kuhoja kaya*), or for the first-fruits of the harvest (*kitambo sha kunga shiliwa shipya*), or when the chief desires to ensure rain in his area (*kitambo sha kulomba mbula*), have all virtually disappeared.

There seem to be two stages in the decline and extinction of a ritual; firstly, when it is possible to get information only from the old, who may or may not have witnessed such a ceremony in their youth, and, secondly, when these rites are known to middle-aged men who list numerous alternative and varied sacrifices which are latent in the community rather than extinct. They can be reactivated if the tension is sufficiently strong; nothing has to be invented to deal with such a situation.

Only ceremonies related to the death of ancestors in unusual circumstances or those aimed at eliminating known evils—usually in the form of sickness—are still carried out as frequently as in the past. In the first group, there are ceremonies (1) connected with ancestors who died away from home; for example, men who died on overseas service in the Second World War (*kitambo sha kucha lwichimu mbulugu*), or who died alone in the bush (*kitambo sha kucha lwa kuliwa noni*) ; and (2) for those who died at home under unusual circumstances; for example, the ancestor whose corpse was mishandled at burial (*kitambo sha kucha kuponya shiti*); or for the man who died outside his compound in order to curse his relatives (*kitambo sha kucha kwa kudukwa*) .

The absence of the corpse is a breach of lineage unity and the lineage is thus more exposed to sickness, since a wandering spirit is an unpredictable factor, and this will always be a potential danger to it. The diviner, in his investigations, will give priority to any such possibilities, and a large proportion of all ceremonies carried out to reduce sickness are attributable to happenings of this sort.

Although the sacrifice is the most involved ceremony of propitiation, all the simpler ceremonies, such as blessing ancestor-cult objects (*kulibirija maholelo*) or the ancestor's grave (*kulibirija ishigo*), have the same procedure. The unit for ancestor worship depends upon the severity of the problems confronting them and the social status of the individuals concerned. As the importance of the family rises, the cost of the ceremonies of propitiation must increase and the number of persons involved rises. For the simpler ceremonies, the nuclear, or immediate, family alone attends, just the man with his wife and children. In a situation involving the infertility of a sibling, the extended family attends, and so on, until classificatory kin become important enough to be present.

These ceremonies are, in effect, a ritual of reunification in which no constant attention is paid to a particular line of descent —sometimes patrilateral and sometimes matrilateral, as in the ceremony for a wife's kin already quoted, and typical invocations are as follows: "Now, grandfather, I have come to take you from the forest; let us go home where you will spare me from these ills and let me live in peace"; this was followed later in the ceremony by, "Now we have built your house so you may not let us suffer and may never complain against us, as we have removed you from the forest and have brought you back into your house, so please let us live in peace." The central ritual of the ceremony, which starts outside the compound, is the bringing back into it of the symbolic body of the aggrieved ancestor, just as it began with the acting out of the event which originally caused the ancestor's anger.

The remaining ceremonies are held to propitiate ancestors who have been found, by divination, to cherish specific grievances that have caused the sickness of the sufferer or his family; these ceremonies take the name of the central act or article of the ritual, as in the ceremony for building a second gateway for the compound (*kitambo sha mibita ibili*), or for using a lion's skin in the ancestors' honor (*kitambo sha ngobo ya shimba*), and so on through a list which might well contain as many as two hundred different articles. These ceremonies can become so symbolic that they lose most of their physical relevance, as in a two-gateway ceremony for a household which had no compound fence, which necessitated the construction of imitation gateways on the open ground in front of the house.

Through these ceremonies, health and wealth can be regained; but they also serve as periodic reminders of family unity, which is not always confined to the agnatic line, as well as providing a practical manifestation of communal unity. As so many families have moved out beyond walking distance of the majority of their relatives, it is often no longer possible to demonstrate this family unity, so that, in some invocations, the names of relatives

too far away to attend are mentioned to the ancestors. The ceremony is often conducted by a diviner-magician in association with
the grandfather, as head of the extended family. Gatherings of
large numbers of lineage members may have occurred in the past,
but they probably served as expressions of political power associated with the chief; clans are widely dispersed and the largest
localized group is often the chief's lineage extending over the
geographical limits of a single chiefdom, which it dominated in
the recent past.

Agnates carry out the central ritual; a woman participates in
ceremonies, together with her own agnatic kin; thus, in a certain
ceremony carried out by a diviner-magician for the purpose of
keeping his own ancestors in a favorable mood, the cow of the
ancestors was anointed by the agnates only, just as the sacrificial
goat was connected with them only. The affines stood around this
group and were not directly connected. The sacrifice is, however,
eaten by everyone attending, which would include some of the
parish elders as well as neighbors. The latter would not have
come just out of curiosity or because of the meat, which is one of
their overriding passions, but because of the sense of unity of the
community, which functions through reciprocal obligations expressed in such gatherings and is felt as an urge to share in the
tribulations of its members. It is a social occasion, in which there
is no distinction between those involved in the ceremonies because of their troubles and their relatives and friends and neighbors, who have the time and inclination to attend. There is nothing secret in the ceremony.

Apart from any other consideration, the Sukuma have a passion
for meat, and the holder of a sacrifice is, at least for that day, the
center of the social life of his community and he must benefit indirectly from the ceremony. The diviner-magician, who carries
out numbers of ceremonies in the name of his own ancestors, is
not only establishing himself as a person with whom the ancestors
are in strong communion, but becomes a dominant personality
in his community, and this must also contribute to his material
success as a satisfactory diviner. This factor becomes all the more
important when it is realized that the old system of prescribed
status promotion through feasting is gradually breaking down.

The gap thus left, as well as the function of these feasts, may now have been taken up by propitiation ceremonies.

Another factor inherent in the propitiation ceremony and allied usages is the possibility of overdoing something through fear, so that repeated ceremonies do something to control a form of neurosis and may be of psychological as well as social utility. Mwanza, the principal town of Sukumaland, on the lake shore, has a far larger number of diviner-magicians in its immediate neighborhood than are to be found in the most distant parts of the area. Possibly the function of the propitiation ceremony has changed from relief of purely personal ills to the relief of some forms of underlying social insecurity.

Because of their fundamental idea that the dead and the living are one uninterrupted line, it is natural that they have affection for the dead of the family, both in the general and in the particular. Although so many of their troubles are thought to be due to angry ancestors, there does not appear to be any fear of them even when the descendants are suffering from their activities, and these ceremonies can only be described as loosely formal.

The ceremonies follow a traditional pattern, but the details of the ritual are not prescribed with any degree of certainty; they are protracted functions in which the leader proceeds with many hesitations—something is forgotten or missing, someone is not ready. But, though there are many variations, a pattern may be discerned from a study of a number of such ceremonies. An important part might be omitted, as indeed was the case in one of the ceremonies witnessed, and this was pointed out by the observer, but the omission was not considered to have vitiated the ceremony, so that right intention seems to be more important than correct ritual. Of course, in the absence of recorded ceremonies, there can be no right rituals, only ones which satisfy the performer and which are subsequently proved to be correct by the relief which they bring to the sufferers.

This absence of a correct ritual accounts for the variations which appear in the ceremonies and the bizarre nature of some of the acts, such as the walking on fire that was witnessed in a certain ceremony, and this is certainly not a continuation of any previously known Sukuma traditional rite. No parallels have been found to it elsewhere and no explanations of its origins were forthcoming. Possibly its explanation lies in the Indian community of the nearby town of Mwanza and some now forgotten demonstration of fire-walking, which this person had watched.

Many of these rituals seem to be performed on the basis of trying anything in the hope of success. There is certainly no need for all the participants to understand the meaning, but there is the practical necessity of participation for all the members of the family which has sinned; it is necessary also for them to be in a state of right-mindedness, resulting from a confession of their sin. Both of these are more important than functional correctitude amounting to dogma.

The ceremonies appear to be loosely divided into five parts. At the beginning there is the presentation of the sacrifice to the ancestor to be propitiated, through the medium of the spirit cow or goat belonging to the family; the simpler propitiation, in which the sufferer puts on an amulet, may terminate there. This may occur before the ceremony proper; next there is the consecration of the sacrifice to the ancestor by connecting it with the members of the family which has sinned and is suffering, carrying with it the suggestion that the sin is transferred to the animal which is, as a rule, ritually used in reconstruction of the historical event which caused the ancestor to be aggrieved. The characteristics of the sacrifice are decided in divination and a ceremony in which a fine animal is used has no better chance of success than one with a handful of porridge, provided that there has been a correct diagnosis.

The invocation, which is repeated throughout the ceremony, is a straightforward confession of sin, usually starting with, "We beg you, grandfather, to forgive us for our offences," or some similar phrase, followed by a request for his benevolence; here the sacrifice is spoken of as a gift but it is, in reality, an exchange in terms of goodwill and ill health. This is followed by the killing, which is not of great importance, since it is not carried out by the leader. It is followed by an examination of the entrails to divine whether the ceremony will be successful, which appears to be purely confirmatory, before the meat is cooked and eaten.

While the central meaning of the ceremony is expiation for

the wrongs which have been done, the sin is got rid of by means of sacrifice. There is no bargaining and the ancestor is entirely free to accept or refuse the propitiation, but the Sukuma, in their own explanations, suggest that the dead wish to be equal, not only among themselves, but with the living, and that their jealousy can be averted only by regular propitiation, which usually requires the divination of sin and its expiation through confession and sacrifice.

CHAPTER V

The Diviner-Magician

THE DIVINER or magician (*nfumo;* pl. *bafumo,* which may be derived from *kufumbula,* "to discover") uses magic powers legitimately to enable the person in misfortune to find the ancestor or other cause of his misfortune, and to provide the means by which it can be propitiated or in other ways put right, a dual role, with separate but connected functions. This is a very broad field and he appears in many social forms.

There are the diviners who diagnose misfortune by examination of the entrails of chickens (*nfumo wa kuchemba ngoko* or *njanda*), and those who, after a propitiatory sacrifice, discover whether it has been successful or not from an examination of the entrails of the sacrificial victim. There are those diviners who manipulate material objects in order to be able to tell the future, throwing shells, watching a floating stick, and so on. Others are specialists in particular matters, such as the magician who is able to keep seed-eating birds away from the harvest fields (*nfumo wa noni*), the rainmaker (*nfumo wa kugema mbula*), those who prevent and cure snakebite (*nfumo wa nyokanyoka, ngoyangi* and *nswilili*), and the female specialists who deal with infertility (*nfumo wa nengo*).

Next there is the class who, after a material link with a sick or suffering person, enter a state of autohysteria, by means of which they are able to diagnose the cause of the patient's misfortune (*nfumo wa ntwe*). Also those who are able to induce hysteria in others as a means of finding out and releasing ancestor anger and curing the person (*nfumo wa kuchunja*). These and others are loosely organized in the Bufumu and Bumanga professional societies of diviners and magicians, which form small local groupings in which there are graded ranks and special rituals of entrance and promotion. None of these categories are exclusive, methods and means vary, and most give herbal advice as well as providing the magic ingredients thought to be necessary for a particular case.

The leaders of dance and other societies who are able to promote their own and their society's welfare by the use of magic medicines and the support of their ancestors and, in their songs and feats of physical skill and sleight of hand, are also classed as a type of diviners. Even the physician, who deals entirely with herbal and physical remedies (*nfumo naguji* or *ngota*), comes into the same class, as he is dependent on ancestor support for his ability to diagnose trouble and supply the corrective.

These are not exact categories and perhaps it is more correct to suggest that every Sukuma, in the traditional life, had some connections with the divination of ancestor anger and the encouragement of their support in his attempts to manipulate his environment by other magical means.

There was no priestly caste, socially isolated and marrying within itself. Everyone attempted his own magic, which may have developed into a skill useful beyond his family. Others deliberately seek such a skill and succeed or fail, in their opinion, because of the support or neglect of their own ancestors. There is no passing on of mystical disposition to a person when he starts to practice, and such supernatural power as he needs for his work, he must obtain from his ancestors on his own application. The power to practice is not considered to be automatically inherited from father to son or from mother to daughter, but there is a tendency for it to be passed down within a particular lineage, either because the ancestors themselves have made known their desire to this effect or because of the natural association between parents and children, which would lead to the growing interest of the latter in the profession.

Anyone wishing to become a diviner-magician attaches himself as an apprentice (*nhemba*) to a practicing diviner after giving him a present. He lives with the magician, more or less as his servant, and learns by participation, as an assistant, in the rituals which his master performs, as well as doing the tiring work of pounding up and drying his medicines. It may be years before he considers himself ready to go off on his own. It is certain that no secret information is passed on without additional payments being made to the master magician, because so much of the professional's success is thought to be due to the possession of magic and herbal medicines personal to their creator and his ancestors. This secrecy is stressed, because so much of their method may be common knowledge.

Although the desire to practice may well be occasioned by the possibility of economic gain, the fact that he has to practice whenever patients appear and, further, has to spend considerable time looking for herbal and magic medicines, probably means that his earnings will be about the same as his losses and that he will be unlikely to become richer, unless he is unusually successful. The outward expression of wanting to be a diviner-magician seems to be a form of mental disturbance, which is resistant to the everyday cures and propitiation rituals. Beyond these two incentives of money and mental disturbance, it is necessary to consider why so many Sukuma stay on the fringe of, or take up, this work. Before and during the early days of the colonial administration, the career of diviner magicians was the only position to which the nonchiefly Sukuma could aspire; it may have provided the channel for the person with greater ambition to improve himself.

Similarly, the practice of diviner-magician, in any of its forms, allows behavior which, in everyday Sukuma life, would be quite abnormal. The average Sukuma's behavior is noticeably quiet and restrained and this work provides an approved opportunity for the exhibitionist and extrovert to do what he likes—to behave in an un-Sukuma way.

Also, in his search for new herbal and magic medicines and his working contacts with people in misfortune, the success of a diviner-magician seems to imply an unusual and higher degree of intellectual curiosity than the average Sukuma has. He is an intelligent person who lives by his wits. Perhaps this is also shown in the much wider range of general knowledge which he soon amasses, not only in this search for medicines, but in the variety of contacts which he gets, as pupil and master, with people outside his own immediate neighborhood. He meets those who come in and he goes out to look for information.

After the man has been troubled for a time, divination establishes that there has been a magician in the family at some time,
who wishes the art to be practiced again by his descendants. The
man takes up training and the mental disturbance recedes.

After he has been under training for some time, he will gradually take on patients as his confidence grows, until he becomes
independent of his master. There is no formal graduation, nor
is the ability or right to practice connected with the loose association of magicians, of which he may become a member when he
feels the need for more social eminence rather than for magical
background to his work. However, this association has only a very
intermittent corporate life and may, in fact, become active in a
particular area as a part of the propitiatory needs of a particular
diviner-magician. Such an association has grades within it, but
they have no universal application and will be of value only to
the incumbent and his associates and neighbors.

Meetings involving diviner-magicians from a wide area have
now probably ceased. They have no group cohesion and more
important than this is the permanent social relationship which
exists between the diviner-magician and his teacher, after he has
started practicing. For the former, it is a valuable business connection and for the latter, a ready means of extending his influence and possibly of forming a local branch of the professional
association, in which he would be preeminent. Each practitioner
is responsible to himself alone for his use of medical knowledge,
his scale of fees, and the secrecy of his consultations.

Although the cures diagnosed by the diviner are alleged to be
supernaturally provided, each is much concerned with the individuality of his own pharmacopoeia, and there is a constant
search, through the medium of dreams and bought confidences,
for new herbal and mineral medicaments.

The compulsion under which a man considers that he must
practice as a magician is regarded as the fulfillment of an obligation and is referred to as *igasa lya bufumu*, the debt of the practice of magic. The same word in the plural, *magasa*, is used for
the unpaid cattle in bride-wealth payments and both uses have
the same literal meaning of an uncompleted part of a bargain. A
number of other activities which are caused by ancestor activity

are also referred to as *igasa,* so there is, in all their spiritual life, this intermittent compulsion to fulfill obligations made known to them by their ancestors. There is no obligation until the person himself becomes aware of it, through illness and divination, and there is no way of getting out of such an obligation once the person is aware of it, except by its fulfillment; he cannot practice for a commercial motive.

There are no interior states which create subconscious compulsion. A written description of an initiate under training states that he goes first to be cut and rubbed with magic medicine, is given a name and a date to return, and until that date he is still under an uncomplete obligation to his ancestors. He cannot go to the aid of anyone else in misfortune. On the day of removing this debt, he goes into the forest with his master, to complete his initiation. He is shown plants with which he can help himself in his smaller troubles and he is told to pay up, so that he can be shown the really strong medicines. Thus it is that he fulfills his debt and can practice successfully. This appears to be an open commercial transaction, but it has been initiated and completed in terms of traditional religious values.

The whole role of the diviner-magician is a form of propitiation and is separate only in degree and ritual from all other forms of ancestor ritual. He must show that he is living his propitiatory role by carrying out rites and following ritual prohibitions and obligations which have religious and very little social utility. They discipline him in his moral obligations. He becomes the center and main exponent of his own cult and likewise he is dependent on it for the continuation of his role as magician.

This is the case whether he becomes a magician for religious reasons or whether he started to train originally for commercial or prestige reasons; when he becomes wealthy from successful divination he becomes the victim of his own success and must now court the support of his ancestors for the wealth which he accumulated initially without too clean or clear a sense of obligation to them. Some diviner-magicians drop their professional activities when they become wealthy, possibly because, in the eyes of their ancestors, they have fulfilled the debt obligation (*igasa*) to them, which was the initial impetus to their spiritual practice.

When someone comes to a diviner-magician for the diagnosis of his misfortune, the latter, no matter what particular method he uses, has a large number of socially recognized answers which he can provide and which can be tried in turn or in combination for the patient's relief. He can diagnose that the patient has an angry ancestor who must be propitiated, that the Supreme Being has decided that he must suffer, that he has been bewitched, or that someone is trying to bewitch him and that he needs protective magic medicine, or, possibly, that he has a minor ailment which can be put right with herbal medicine.

Although private comments are made about the frauds committed by some magicians, the core of people's belief is that the man has been caught and forcibly detained by his ancestors; he is doing what he has to do. There is never any idea of free and willing service. The man must carry out certain actions in order that he can return to the optimum state of being left alone to profit from life in ritual neutrality. Yet it must not be thought that the diviner-magician is an unwilling victim of circumstances; he may well profit from having to fulfill this obligation and, in the meantime, he has a position of some social prominence, which will compensate him for his constant preoccupation with ritual necessities.

After discussions with a number of magicians, it seems to me that their attitude to their powers could be compared to that of some Christians of former times who thought that sacraments administered by those without freedom from sin were not real or effective. Magicians seemed to realize that they were not doing the things which they purported to be doing, but they nevertheless felt that, should they be able to get into greater communion with their ancestors as they were endeavoring to do in their ritual, then they would be able to have the exact powers which they were now pretending to administer. This is not to say that they are sceptical of their powers and the forces behind them, but the reverse—they are very humble and realize their dependence on powers outside of themselves. Their insistence on the minutiae of their own personal rituals goes far beyond anything that would be necessary for the mere maintenance of their position as administrators of village rituals largely for personal gain.

Although, in its crudest sense, the whole of their ritual activity is directed toward the restoration of each patient to a state of ritual neutrality, from which the hostility of his ancestors has moved him, the magician's activities as a ritual specialist seem to be directed more toward maintaining or regaining the unity of the lineage in which the living and the dead are not differentiated. He provides a social service to the persons who consult him, which is incidental to his own need to propitiate his own ancestors. In a sense he has to go on working as a diviner, so that he and his family will remain in good health. As he propitiates his own ancestors by practicing, he enables others to propitiate their ancestors.

A sense of inadequacy seems identifiable in their attitude to their work; this is shown sometimes in the almost frenetic activity to seek for greater knowledge. There is always the hope of being able to do better to spur them on, while at the same time there is the realization that they would indeed be able to practice correctly if they were really what they were pretending to be. Sukuma scepticism about their powers might well come from the diviner-magicians themselves and their apprentices, if they are not successful, rather than from any other source.

The magician may create a reality through his expression of possessing a form of interior grace, the communion of the living and the dead which exemplifies the theoretical foundations of the whole of Sukuma social life. The people see, in the successful diviner-magician, the continuing value of interest in ancestors and the constant propitiation of them.

The ability of the magician to receive the knowledge necessary for a cure through dreams and self-induced hysteria is dependent on the goodwill of his ancestors as a whole. He appears to have no power relationship with a particular spirit, but is supported by the family's ancestors, of whom he is a lineal descendant; when there is one ancestor who had practiced as a diviner he then invokes both him and the other ancestors for continuing help. Although he is a practitioner of ritual, he makes no claim to having thought out his actions unaided.

None of the magicians considers himself to have ever acted on his own, and an increase in his power is always attributed to increased spiritual assistance; he searches continually for new medicines, herbs, and ritual, but it is not his intelligence which selects the successful ones, it is the ancestors acting on him. It follows from this system of ancestor support that a practicing diviner-magician is always a successful one, and failure is never attributed to the lack of knowledge or personal ability of the magician himself; he must either find the cause of his failure or attach himself to someone who has proved himself successful.

A written account of such an event stated that Lyabubi went to his fields and saw there the largest snake he had ever seen, so he ran back home at once and told what he had seen. That night he developed a strong fever and by morning he was even incapable of speaking. By good fortune, Gharabilo, a herbalist, was passing and the relatives called him in. He had a look at the sick man and gave as his opinion that he had been struck by the sticks of sorcerers. He was asked to try and cure him and went through no less than twenty medicines without bringing any improvement, and finally he stated quite openly that he was beaten.

Just then, another herbalist, Masaga, happened to be present and he asked whether he could try his medicines. He got permission, as possibly the Supreme Being would give him success. So he tried, and almost at once the sick man started to improve, even beginning to eat again so that he soon recovered completely. From that day Gharabilo went as an apprentice to Masaga, who both taught and respected him so that the success of his medicines would be better known.

The diviner-magician is a member of the community, and in his day-to-day activities it would be impossible to distinguish him from his fellows. He is not exempted from communal duties, but leads the same life as his fellows except when patients call upon him for help. He is not the religious leader of the community, nor could he be, when so many persons practice to some degree, and if one had attempted to be, the results would have been so factional as to have defeated the community's ends. He is only a diviner-magician when he is actually practicing and, at other times, he is not treated in a special way; people are not afraid of him. His prestige depends on the success of his practice, not on the practice itself.

This practice, moreover, is kept largely within the magico-religious sphere of their community life, and the results of his divinations are not used as additional evidence for a particular solution in any judicial process.

Although he is resident in a particular locality, his work is not confined to his neighbors, and indeed it would be rare for a sick man to consult a magician from his own parish. It seems that diviner-magicians are links between the various segments of the chiefdom and beyond and that, speaking in terms of the whole area, they are unifying agents. Few people mention the diviner-magicians in their own parish and there is a constant stress on the notably successful ones who live in different areas; the barren wife in Shinyanga goes to Nassa for diagnosis, while the sick man there travels to Kwimba. Possibly the usual move is not so far as this and the person goes only to a nearby village.

Sukuma life is very dull for months on end, with its widely spaced houses and uncertain livelihood, so that the ceremonies of divination and propitiation provide some excitement for those who are onlookers and a welcome topic of gossip for the community, about those currently going on and the reasons for them.

In the past, as the chief and his family were the dominant and also the only localized lineage in the chiefdom, controlling all the important political positions, it follows that, without a controlling counterforce, there would have been considerable instability in the chiefdom. It is suggested that, in the past, the diviner-magicians, who were then few in number, formed one of the counterbalances, without which the chief might have become absolute in power within his own area. Perhaps also there was an element of patronage on the one side and, on the other, the diviner-magician may have functioned as an informer who could warn from a privileged position. At that period, the number of diviner-magicians was controlled by political expediency and their own proven efficiency, but now, with the removal of these controls, their numbers have increased greatly until there is almost a plethora of magicians among whom the sufferer can make his choice.

The exact number of practicing diviner-magicians cannot be determined, even by careful enquiry, because their activities are known only when they are in demand; and further they function intermittently, except for the few who are widely known and have a sufficient number of clients to be at work every day. Checks which have been made seem to suggest that about one per cent of the adult population seem to have some claim to be called diviner-magicians. There is no clear dividing line between the old man curing a few neighbors of their minor problems and the popular practitioner with a widespread clientele—both are known by the same terms.

There is a very heavy concentration of them around Mwanza town, which is the only big population center in the area. These function mainly over the weekends, when the town-dwellers have time for such consultations. There is a suggestion from the details which have been collected that the most inaccessible areas have the lowest numbers of diviner-magicians and that the number increases in proportion to the amount of interference there has been with the old way of life by the advent of Christianity, Islam, and industry.

During work in the Mwanza area, it was possible for me to go from practitioner to practitioner on Sunday morning, and to find almost all of them busy with consultations, while other patients were waiting for attention nearby. Although all the diviner-magicians were Sukumas, it seemed that their patients were mostly migrant laborers, which again illustrated their role as unifying agents.

There is no doubt that the diviner-magician looks to his profession to bring him power and respect as well as economic security, but this does not detract from his practical ability to help people through his consultations. His power over his neighbors is related only to his economic position, as he has little professional contact with them. He is not the focus of parish activity, but probably his prominence accords more with his age than with his practice as a magician. Indeed, the vagaries of ancestor support, which may permit the man to practice only for intermittent periods, make it almost impossible for any permanent social position to be dependent upon his professional activities alone.

Observations of diviner-magicians in their own villages show very clearly that they are not feared, nor indeed are they treated with any marked degree of respect. This may be because the magician has no powers peculiar to himself, apart from the support of his ancestors, by whom he is completely controlled, and also because his social position locally, since it does not rest upon any religious function, must depend upon the amount of sacrificial beer and meat he makes available to the neighbors and the parish elders. Nevertheless, because of his specialist knowledge and the success which it has brought, he is exposed to jealousy, not so much because of his medicines but because he tends to cure those who have been marked for death by sorcerers; accordingly he has to pay particular attention to protective magic medicines (*lukago*) against sorcery.

His professional activities vary from being a very small sideline to his life as an agriculturist to being a full-time specialization, and it is in this variation that he perhaps has the greatest influence on his community. His success rather than his failure is a guide to the ritual tendencies of his neighborhood, and a certain amount of imitation in rivalry results from his practical work, which is usually carried on out in the open.

The female diviner-magician may continue to function after she is married, and her parents are entitled to an extra head of cattle in respect to her powers, or else her husband will not be entitled to share in the proceeds of her practice. Her patients are both men and women.

Although large numbers of people consult these diviner-magicians every year, considerable scepticism is evident in almost all discussions on the subject. This is directed against individual magicians and is never against the basic principles of ancestor influence and control or witchcraft. This scepticism is expressed in the fluctuations of the popularity of individual diviner-magicians as well as in the tricks designed to show that they are faking their answers.

There are the additional factors that the diviner-magician will grasp at any opportunity to make money and will accept any number of apprentices. Also, belief in their powers has lessened with the increase in their numbers and the fact that it is no longer a dangerous profession in which he could suffer the consequences of an inappropriate diagnosis by death or property loss, in the absence of any supratribal legal system. Nevertheless, these tricks and their disclosures are not made public or communicated to the diviner-magician and remain the secrets of small groups. A pagan chief gave the following description of such a test.

I hid one of my shoes outside my house in the fields and tied a small packet of wood powder in maize leaves to the leg of my bed. I then called a diviner to diagnose the problem. I spat into the bill of the chicken which was going to be used for the haruspication and it was left for the night under that bed while I was advised to sleep elsewhere. In the morning I was made to stand in the doorway holding a spear in my hand with my wife beside me, while the chicken was cut open and examined. I was then taken to one side and the diviner explained that the magic medicine tied to the bed leg had been put there by girls whom I had seduced and not given cattle compensation to and that the shoe had been taken by my own relatives for the insertion of magic medicine which would have given me a serious leg disease. I did not tell anyone that I had set a trap because he would have been angry.

In this and in every other situation in which patient and magician are linked together, they are never cut off from their communities and remain subject to most of their controls. The patient is a sceptic but will not do anything about it because he is never quite certain whether the diviner is reliable or not in his professed powers, while the latter will deal with his client largely in terms of information which he has been able to glean from the patient's own answers to his questions and from his apprentices, who either have some knowledge of the problem from their own places of origin or have been sent to find out between one diagnostic session posing the trouble and a subsequent one to complete it. The scepticism is greatest among those who have failed to get relief from their troubles after repeated consultations with diviner-magicians, and among those who have never had cause to consult them.

It must be remembered that overt scepticism carried to its conclusion would be suspicion of the foundation of their whole spiritual life, on which so many of their material benefits have been founded and, for that reason rather than any other, there is little attempt to act on these suspicions, even when money is involved.

Diviner-magicians have always been a prominent part of Sukuma culture and, in the stories of the past and reverence for their graves, the diviner-magician becomes a great chief and the chief becomes also a diviner-magician—the two roles perhaps were so interrelated that they elide in myth. If the Sukuma is brought up in such a system, there is no incentive to carry this scepticism into agnosticism; one can make a few sly remarks but go no further, as it would be cutting at the foundations of his own social-religious experience.

Education, perhaps not so much as Christianity, encourages outright disbelief as an article of faith, whether as moderns or in religion, but this itself allows for considerable credulity and does not appear to inculcate scepticism. It is usual to find that sceptical tales are often qualified at once by stories of miraculous activities of ancient as well as recent magicians. These stories have considerable circulation and include how the living tree turned into firewood at a blow, milk that would not curdle, the sick man who got up and danced, and so on; a part of the golden age of the past, when the Sukuma, living in a wonderful land, were great in all they undertook to do. Credulity is greatest among those who have benefited from the help of their ancestors and diviner-magicians. These would include numbers of the dominant lineage in each chiefdom, the rich fertile fathers of many progeny, as well as the leaders of dance groups (which are both popular and highly competitive).

It would be hard to say that there has been any diminution in the faith of the whole community following the increase in the numbers of diviner-magicians practicing. The whole mass of magical activity has hardly been touched. Ideas and recent political changes, both at national and local level, may have made the average man feel more unprotected than previously and, with this, he has a greater tendency to use magicians and magical activity. Certainly, some magicians seem to be more prosperous than in the past. At worst, it gives comfort to the sufferer by canalizing his hates onto those whom he has already learnt to dislike in their social setting and, at the least, it is an inoffensive herbalism which would compare favorably with our own extensive use of patent medicines.

This whole system of divination and legitimate magic is to be distinguished from sorcery. Sorcery is immoral and involves the practice of bad magic, malevolence, and hate; the sorcerer (*nogi*) is by definition an enemy of society. Minimal ideas about sorcery are universally known and believed, although active sorcerers are rare and officially it is considered out-of-date superstition.

That it survives at all may be explained by the fact that the whole religious system is concerned with the mechanics of the control of unknown forces. A person in misfortune or illness may have, through divination and legitimate magic, eliminated as causes malevolent ancestors, an indifferent High God, and direct causation, yet he as much as ourselves feels the need for certainty. In his anxiety he may hold witchcraft responsible for what remains unknown and inexplicable. Thus in spite of modern developments, sorcery retains its hold on imagination.

PART TWO

THE CHRISTIAN
AND
TRADITIONAL SOCIETY

CHAPTER I

The Background to Conversion

THE SUKUMA are a conservative people, slow to see the need for or the inevitability of change and even slower to act. An unfavorable environment and a very narrow margin between success and failure have made them wary of innovation, which springs from more secure economic backgrounds than they possess now or have done in the past. Further, they are not a unified people in the sense that they have had one culture for a very long time, and each chiefdom and its people has its origins elsewhere. Their ecology varies from the lake shore to the hinterland, their language and customs as well.

This diversity of backgrounds has been further complicated by the larger conflict between the Kiswahili national language used by government, business, and education, and the Kisukuma of the people. It seems that the absence of a single culture has been a factor in delaying change, certainly in ecclesiastical matters. Government has always assumed a uniformity and it may be that the people have used the idea themselves in favor of opposition to government's plans. It is difficult to divide Unyamwezi from Usukuma except politically, and the reasons given for dividing these two tribal groups might just as cogently have been used to divide Usukuma. The assumption of uniformity lulls the onlooker into making totally unwarranted conclusions.

Similarly, political federation attempted by the British failed to achieve even administrative success because of this diversity, which prevented or hindered overall legislation drafted on the assumption of Sukuma uniformity. Equally, political activity in the name of the Sukuma as a tribe, with a party dedicated to that particular end, was soon swamped by, if not allied from the beginning to, the Tanganyika African National Union, the only

national and effective political party to have functioned in Tanganyika, which has now developed into a one-party state. Similarly, attempts to run newspapers and newssheets in Kisukuma
did not succeed because education and politics were conducted
in Kiswahili, the official African language of the country, and the
only practical use for Kisukuma was in the social and political
field for the purpose of hindering relationships with the central
government during the struggle for independence, when the Sukuma often refused to use Kiswahili and forced government officials to use an interpreter, which bolstered up this conservatism.

The huge size of Usukuma not only hindered communications
for trade, but also prevented the population from being influenced by many of the changes inherent in a situation of rapid
national political evolution. It prevented the population from
being communicated with and even from communicating among
themselves as a stimulus to change. The whole of Usukuma has
had a relatively slow rate of exposure to external and internal
influences toward change.

This provincialism or tribalism has to be considered in assessing the possibility of a universal Church; furthermore it is a question of the political and social aspects of religious practice in a
new country dedicated to the creation of a national identity. The
wider aspects of universality are not really cogent at this level.
In Kisukuma a man can follow the services of the Church only
visually, he cannot participate. Kiswahili must be his only link,
and then a partial and stunted one, with the non-Sukuma world—
and the Church must plan toward this national universality. If
the Church aims at an understanding laity there can be little case
for Latin, and a continued use of Kisukuma could be taken as going against the expressed wish of the government to end tribalism.

An equally powerful factor almost inevitably leading to the extinction of Kisukuma as a language to be used in the Catholic
Church is the cost in time and effort of providing the necessary
religious books, which would have to be passed as correct by the
Church itself. The Church would proceed with caution so that
there would be no difficulties over meanings; this would take decades and the effort would be worthwhile only for a national language. An important factor in the change to Kiswahili have been

the Sukuma priests, the first of whom was ordained more than twenty-five years ago; they were expected to stand for their own language, but they opted for Kiswahili. It was significant that among themselves they were using Kiswahili in conversation.

The people's interest in Christianity has varied from more or less indifference in Shinyanga and Maswa to the growing movement toward conversion along the shores of Lake Victoria and in the Geita district, to which large numbers of Sukuma have moved from overcrowded and infertile areas, principally in order to grow more cotton. Perhaps their subservience to cattle values in Usukuma proper has made for conservatism, and the peripheral area, with its economic opportunities with cotton and better ecology, has stimulated change in many fields.

In the immigrant areas, the newcomers are from the younger age groups and from different families, clans, and chiefdoms, and have not had time to congeal into conservatism, particularly as the magicians, members of the established order and the specialists on whom the ordinary people depend for their contacts with the remnants of traditional religion, rarely moved into these new areas. There is a greater readiness to accept change away from their elders and traditional surroundings. A further differential which may account for these variations in convention is that economic change brought on by bigger and better cotton crops benefited the older and more conservative Sukuma element, which controlled land usage and livestock, more than the younger generation, which benefited from educational change—two divergent value systems.

In their traditional chiefdoms, the innovator, the man who goes ahead, becomes the proud one (*ndoshi*), for whom the majority feel envy and resentment, while in the immigrant areas the external ecological pressures of animals, forest, and isolation have gone far to dispel their apathy and to make them not only ready to change but also more ready to help each other and to initiate Christian activity as well. Although the priest tends to see the Sukuma failure or success to follow Christianity as an isolated series of events peculiar to religion, the Sukuma must see Christianity as just one facet of an almost overwhelming process of social change in which he finds himself entangled, without being aware either of its inevitability or of its causes, and conversion itself as the result of a multiplicity of causes.

The priest may feel with some justification that the analysis of these socioreligious processes is an encroachment on his pastoral field and that he is concerned with unobservable factors—the intangible processes of salvation and the spiritual values within the temporal. He is confined in his observations, while the Sukuma and the social scientist are not so constricted. From the dedication of his calling, his conviction of ends results in a human tendency to distort his assessment of means. The latter can study means and evaluate their degree of coincidence with ecclesiastical ends without any constriction.

In considering conversion, there have to be reasons for leaving one set of beliefs and for accepting an alternative set, or indeed, trying to practice both sets at once. The Sukuma do not react to Christianity as a blank sheet of paper waits for writing; they are more willing to justify their own beliefs and to see values and disadvantages not acceptable to a Christian or appreciated by a Christian foreigner. An average Sukuma might say, "There is no Sukuma who does not believe in God. I believe in God, so why should I come to your instructors?"

It is not inertia when a Sukuma says that every tribe has its own religion and every religion is good and that for this reason he could not change. Others are more explicit, explaining that all religions have the same purpose of appearing to appease the dead, slyly adding that Christian missionaries had obviously been unsuccessful in appeasing Jesus in Europe, so they had therefore gone abroad to get African assistance in their efforts. There is nothing abnormally ethnocentric in seeing Christianity as another form of propitiation.

Others speak from tradition, and indeed for their growing materialism, when they say that their cows are their God, and that these are so sufficient for them that they do not want other things. The elderly polygynist may accept the need for baptism but will say that he will become a Christian as soon as his wives have died. He cannot face the social upheaval in his family life which would follow conversion, or, in plain terms, reject the women with whom he has shared his life for years and return them to their parents, unwelcomed and unlikely to marry as well again.

Whatever the spiritual consequences of conversion, there will be social consequences, of which the adult convert is certainly aware and which he is prepared to consider when he weighs the advantages and disadvantages of Church membership, particularly since an emotional conversion is prevented by the long training required before baptism. The priest, particularly one from overseas, does not realize the social consequences of conversion. He may have experienced at home differences between man and wife over the issue of religious conversion, but he will know nothing at all of the difficulties involved in leaving the social practices of one group and joining another.

It will be necessary to refer repeatedly to the fundamentals of Sukuma life which relate to the fertility of their wives, their cows, and their fields. This trilogy has formed, forms now, and will form for the foreseeable future the background to their culture and, as has already been seen, the substance of their traditional religious practices. If the irrational belief in the ability of politics to alter the basic disabilities of their habitat is disregarded, then their concern for these problems overlaps into every part of their emotional life. So it is not unexpected that those involved directly in these three facets of fertility are those who find it hardest to break away into Christianity, where there has been no proven success in the control and manipulation of these essentials.

It follows, therefore, that those least involved are the most likely to convert, the young who are not yet involved in the fertility of their wives, the old who have biologically or socially failed to produce and sustain a family, and the unsuccessful farmer and cowless small-holder who have little chance of regaining or retaining a position without these assets, and lastly the person in employment who may be so involved in urban economic values as to be at least partially free from the dominance of cow and field fertility while retaining the same obsession for marital fertility. The religion of a community is expressed through its dominant values and through the socially important person's control over these values. The disparity of the Church views and local

values is a constant feature of the Sukuma's attitude toward Christianity, and for want of another phrase, the partial failure of
Christianity in the religious rather than the social sphere.

Christianity has been present in Usukuma for such a short time,
since World War II, in its present form of numerous churches,
hospitals, schools, and social organizations, that only a small number of today's adult Christians are the children of Christians.
Christianity has a depth of one generation at the most, and the
problems of a Christian are those of a man practicing a new religious system in the surroundings of a traditional order which has
not yet disappeared. It is certainly not the situation of the Western
Christian, who practices his religion in the surroundings of de-
caying Christianity and a growing materialism.

The missionary priest similarly is faced with a practice of Christianity basically different from that in which he was brought up.
This trite statement may seem unnecessary after the missionary
priest's training, but nevertheless it comes as an exciting shock to
many, when faced with its reality, that they will be working with
people who have no, or very little, knowledge of Christianity. The
convert from one variety of Christianity to another is an interesting but not significant object of priestly activity in Western countries, which on the whole is concerned with the maintenance of
Christian values in the community. The attraction of the mission field lies in the existing Christian nullity, and activity is hu-
manly directed at those most receptive to the new doctrine; numbers become an indication of success because the situation is being judged according to the priest's home-country values.

In Western countries so many converts means almost that number of enduring Christians, while this is very far from the reality
of Usukuma conversions. This reality is even more obscured by
the Western preference for success in numerical terms and the
relationship between this and the provision of money by overseas
donors for further work.

The peasant sees the changes of the present in the small ways
in which they affect him and has little conception of the whole,
and he sees religious change and the possibility of conversion in
terms of advantage and disadvantage to himself, as a person, in
the circumstances in which he is living. He can have no conception

of a universal Church, since the Sukuma have none; he has no knowledge of disinterested or status-motivated public service, sacrifices which may not be motivated by Sukuma values, or all the multiplicity of factors and ideas that surround missionary activities. He must see the Christian activity with clouded eyes, only some points coming into his vision which will certainly not be the salient features in the eyes of the Church itself. Odd impressions, just as much as obvious attractions, will sway his judgment, and many of these impressions will be associated with building— "The priests are coming to build here"—rather than the permeation of new religious values.

There is no doubt that Christianity is thought to give more status to the individual Sukuma at the moment than the surviving traditional beliefs do, for the latter have never received any political support. This compulsion has been described time and time again in the phrase, "It is civilized to have a religion." There is accordingly status to be obtained from using a Christian name and, up to the present, few persons with any ambition would care to use full traditional names now out of a sense of identity with and pride in the past rather than as a sign of approval of the traditional religious system.

Although this name-changing may be an incentive to conversion, few seem to take the obvious way out and just change their names without baptism, because baptism, as a *rite de passage,* has value for them possibly partially independent of its Christian meaning. Name-changing in propitiation of disturbed ancestors causing misfortune has always been a prominent feature of ancestor worship, so that a person might take on a series of names during his lifetime.

A high percentage of the chiefs in the past were Christians, of whom the majority were Catholics, and the consequence of getting a convert in a key position should have been considerable influence on subordinates with whom he was connected in both family and political affairs; however, it does not appear that such key converts had any general influence comparable to Tusi over Hutu conversions in Rwanda-Burundi. If anything, there have been converts who have become key men after conversion, which they were certainly not before, and who have become quite apostolic.

Few conversions result today through the influence of those in positions of power, most of whom are new to their positions, and it would appear to be impossible for them to be leaders in the Christian community and at the same time maintain their positions politically. The key convert in a closely integrated lineage may have been of value in the past, but influence in the present is confined to the immediate family, as when the lapsed family head affects the practice of his family.

Many acknowledge themselves to be Christian although they live as pagans and may not have completed their courses of instruction before baptism. In areas in which there have been mission stations for some years, a high proportion of the nearby people will have had this fringe contact with at least some parts of Christian doctrine and practice; it becomes a part of their lives, an awareness of alternatives within their own conservatism. Their appreciation of Islam, localized in towns, does not clash with this conservatism until a man has moved away from home.

While the association of missionary churches with the colonial power has often been stressed, and the difficulties which are inherent in this situation are much mentioned in the postindependence era, Christianity has been connected from its initial appearance with mechanical, social, and economic progress in general. It supplied an atmosphere of "getting on" and, in almost all spheres, seemed to the people to be ahead of the government, though past progress is unlikely to be remembered in considering its present position.

Even if the Christian church concerned is sure of its doctrine, the Sukuma will certainly not be clear about their beliefs. As Father Horan explains, "We are attached to a dogmatic formula because we love the Church because we love Christ in her. We do not usually become converts because the Preface of the Trinity or the Athanasian Creed suddenly hits us as the way things have to be."[1] The Apostles' Creed, as a statement of beliefs regarding historical events, will not impinge on their credulity, and they will pick on externals rather than the finer metaphysical points

---

[1] H. Horan, W. F., "Why Is a Sect a Sect," *The Homiletic and Pastoral Review*, Vol. 65, No. 5 (Feb. 1965), p. 420.

on which to base their interests. Change can occur only in terms of what has gone before and, similarly, it would be almost impossible to feel the emotions appropriate to a Western religious practice unless they fitted in with a predisposing Sukuma cultural heritage.

These statements of fundamental belief may be the sure foundations of church cohesion, but they have no attraction in themselves to nonbelievers. It may well be that what the Church considers essential are not the elements attracting the layman and vice versa. He is more likely to see a church as offering him a new devotional life that will fit in as well as possible with his traditional life. The sacrifice of many of the more socially valuable practices of their otherwise dull lives cannot appeal to more than a few.

CHAPTER II

Conversion as the First
Available Alternative

IN THE INITIAL STAGES of Christian mission activity, the Sukuma were shown an alternative system of religion where no alternative of any kind had existed before. This very fact led to a questioning and an uncertainty about their traditional practices. Faced with the insistence of Christian dogma, a Sukuma will say that he did not think there could be another world after death, and this future life may even be seen as a material rather than a spiritual reason for conversion. Doctrinal teaching such as this, expressed with certainty in the same unchanging form by succeeding priests and in printed matter, has a special attraction for the undecided and uncertain.

Colonialism further disrupted the common interlocking social-political-religious system. Under the Germans the subordinate government posts were held by Indians, Arabs, and Swahili from the coast, under the British by colonial civil servants who were usually nominally Christian but often not interested in Christianity or bound by its beliefs. Chiefs and their subordinates became more secure in their positions. There were thus even fewer opportunities for advancement than in precolonial times.

The peaceful or violent political revolutions of the postcolonial period have once again enabled the clever person to better himself by his own efforts without being dependent on fixed establishment lines. In the initial years of contact it was Christianity that provided some opportunities of advancement, alternative ways up the ladder. Persons associated with the missions as catechists and lay helpers, for example, gained protection from too much interference from government servants and chiefs and an increase in status from being in association with Europeans, albeit missionaries, who were automatically associated with the new power, and from being the lay purveyors of a new cult, the intermediaries of the priests in their dealings with the laity.

This situation has been confirmed by both administrative and missionary experience. The colonial government may well have been indifferent to the Protestant churches, except when a particular issue brought them into conflict, but it retained the usual European suspicions of the Catholic Church. The Church benefited from this in its relationship with the Sukuma, for they could see that the English Protestant Church had much closer social links with the colonial administration. This slight but significant antipathy was described by one priest as his having had "some nice fights with officials." Nevertheless the Sukuma seldom saw a clear difference between the Catholic missionaries and the government officials, although there was never the close social connection between the two groups that there was in the Congo, where the officials went to the refectory on Sundays after high Mass for coffee with the priests, although this is usually the priests' main time for dealing with their African parishioners' personal problems.

The priest, when he saw something that he considered wrong and against the interest of the Church, tackled the government official or department concerned. Whatever the result, he was seen not as an intermediary, which he undoubtedly considered himself to be, but as one of two persons of a similar tribe and identity quarreling or agreeing about a third party of lower status who could not bring to the dispute any recognizable or equivalent power. Disputes with governments, then, underlined the sameness of priests and officials, not their divergence. In the postcolonial period the positions are reversed and the dangers similarly alternated should the priest endeavor to act as an intermediary.

Although the missionary churches would have denied that they were able to act as intermediaries, some Sukuma saw that they were potentially able to assist them in gaining influence and may have approached conversion with this in mind, particularly in the early days of Christian penetration.

Since the missionary priest had easily observable high status, a further inducement to conversion for some was the fact that all the denominations offered the possibility of ordination to the laity, whose advancement in other spheres had been severely restricted by the racial stratification of government service and business.

Conversion was also a means of revolting against traditionalism for those who, by their very nature, wanted to be different. There are a few men in any society who are evolutionaries rather than revolutionaries; here they saw the new Christianity as a method of manipulating traditional forces to their own advantage and that of their families. The intermittent palace revolutions of the past in almost every chiefdom, when the chief had failed to ensure the welfare of his people by magico-religious means, were no longer possible under the colonial rule. Some must have seen Christianity in political terms, just as their traditional religion had political aspects, and approached conversion as a means to support their own positions or to attack the political structure, which had become solidified by the existence of the colonial power supporting permanent chiefs.

CHAPTER III

The Choice Between
Faiths and Churches

IN THE CHOICE of religious change, the Sukuma can turn to Islam, which at the moment is concentrated in the towns and trading centers, or to Christian churches based on overseas administrative foundations. The only independent African separatist church so far seems to be practicing only in the Nassa division of the Mwanza area, and to be on the decline from a peak of activities in the thirties corresponding to the aging of their bishop! The choice is thus between the Catholic Church and three Protestant churches, the Church of Central Tanganyika based on the Church Missionary Society in communion with the Church of England, the African Inland Church based on the African Inland Mission, which is an American missionary organization of very low-church tenets, and the Seventh Day Adventists.

The first and third of these are small with few churches and have made little progress, while the African Inland Church, with a wider spread of churches and hospitals but without any system of out-stations, has been established since the earliest years of colonial rule, without any great upsurge of conversions. The Catholic Church is ubiquitous and has expanded greatly in the last decade, with the Maryknoll Mission coming in to found an additional diocese based on Shinyanga, to build on the work begun by the White Fathers, who remain within the Mwanza diocese.

In their choice of church the Sukuma must choose between Protestant groups offering a hard devotional life from which drinking, dancing, and smoking have been banned as directly evil, and the Catholic Church which is seen as being more permissive toward these essential elements of customary life, allow-

71

ing that the intention to sin of the individual is of more importance than the circumstances alone, requiring both deliberation
and the full consent of the will for a serious act. This striking difference between the obligations of church membership sometimes
gives rise to naive questions from Catholic catechumens—for example, whether they are obliged to drink and smoke after baptism. Possibly some catechists overemphasize these differences
and say, "This hard Protestant life is not for us, and we drink,
smoke, dance, and use nail polish."

The demands of much of Protestant practice seem to make it
difficult to attract converts unless their personalities are possibly
so divergent that there is a sense of group identity and satisfaction from belonging which they have not been able to get elsewhere. The Seventh Day Adventists, who not only have these
prohibitions, but who also have Saturday as their day of devotion and many dietetical restrictions, seem to have been successful in gathering a core of converts who have been noticeable for
their success in gaining office both in the Tanganyika African National Union and in the important and all-embracing Sukuma co-
operative movement.

The non-Catholic missionaries in their moral opposition to
Catholicism, by reason of which they have had to differentiate
themselves clearly from Catholic practices, have of course established for themselves an obvious social distinctness. What they
see as doctrinal differences may in fact be making ritual out of
antiritual. The Sukuma see the lack of vestments in their worship
not as a non-Catholic gesture, but possibly as making the celebrant indistinguishable from an ordinary European or a Sukuma
of rising status.

The ordinary Sukuma cannot see the historic or religious reasons for schism in the context in which this arose, but sees these
Christian groupings as variations to attract converts in the same
way as their own magical practitioners vary their activities to add
weight to their status. They may well see this Protestant nonritual
as an unsuccessful gimmick, just simply because the unorna-
mented church, for example, is not ritually satisfying. It is also
likely that they see the different Christian sects as European equiv-
alents of their own societies, which have magico-religious as well

as the social-basis forms of Bugika and Bugaru dance societies, in which comparison the Catholic Church obviously wins over the Protestant churches.

The more realistic approach to custom is the most prominent reason for the attraction to Catholicism, allied to a dislike of what is taken to be Protestant harshness and the realization, whatever the human reasons real or implied, that the Protestant African and overseas clergy have widely divergent standards of living.

CHAPTER IV

The Availability of Christianity

THE NEARNESS of missions to the home and the availability of priests is important. If a sacramental religion is offered, opportunity to receive the sacraments must be provided regularly. Catholic Church records show a marked decline in practice and financial support in proportion to the distance from a resident priest. The Church's network of out-station (*kigango*) churches is now reasonably well established and covers most of Usukuma, but in the earlier years the mission stations were widely spaced and there was a correspondingly lower availability of priests.

There are, of course, other aspects to this extension of the priest's activities, such as the fact that his regular but widely spaced appearances at out-station churches get better regular attendance from the local Christians than is the case at his parish church; either way there is little continuity and the priest is not personally committed to any particular group of Christians. Now, with the Church's social commitments in schools and other training establishments, it is doubtful whether this availability is any higher per Christian than it was in those early days, particularly since this expansion in activities has not been balanced by a similar expansion in the numbers of priests available.

Perhaps the Church in Usukuma could be described as an institution to provide baptism, and certainly the amount of priestly time and energy going into catechetics is extremely high and related to a relatively minor part of the total Christian life. This concentration of effort on catechumens detracts from the priest's ability to assist those endeavoring to lead a Christian life. In a city parish two thousand families to a priest would be regarded as an almost impossible burden and in Usukuma even more so, where there can be no such geographical concentration of Catholic families, whose parish may be spread over two hundred or more square miles. The devotion to catechumens means that less and less time is available for the pastoral problems of the faithful. Concentrating on getting baptisms may not establish a Church; it initiates a problem and there seems to be an error in emphasis here.

The Catholic Church in Usukuma certainly has an acute staffing problem which cannot be eased by the short-term recruitment of lay workers who have no long-term commitment to the Church's work and whose goodwill and enthusiasm have to be balanced against their ignorance of the language and the additional financial burdens for the Church itself for leaves, housing, and family problems.

The convert alone in a traditional environment has little enough to support his faith. The majority will probably be illiterate or so marginally literate as to be unable to get any practical help from simple religious manuals printed in Kisukuma. He needs the physical presence of the priest and the opportunity to receive the sacraments and may also try to influence a relative to be converted so that he will not be the only Christian in the family. He has to participate in traditional rituals and he may not be sufficiently prominent socially to stand alone, so he attends with a rosary in his pocket. Although in the past there was some movement of Christian converts to be near a mission, it is now more often the case that a church with a resident priest becomes surrounded by a predominantly Catholic population.

The mere creation of a parish in a new locality results in the conversion of a large number of local people, everyone going to instruction since there are no social advantages in staying away. Perhaps the majority of churches have been placed as far away as possible from other outside influences in order to get converts and this circle of converts has been the result of their isolation, or were established in an empty area which would soon be filled with immigrants.

Also, in the initial stages of any mission church there is a very personal connection between the priest and his neighbors and the few Christians available. Today the commitment to the individual is no longer possible, for the priest's work expands, and must be replaced by an individual's commitment to the Church instead, which will not be as satisfying to the Christian unless it is adequately supported by an all-embracing religious and social organization. The Church has tried to deal with this increasing load of work by providing better transport by using motorcycles and cars, but this has resulted in the expansion of the priest's radius of activity without really increasing the depth of his contacts; the tempo of his life accelerates and much of his work is done under the pressure of the very human desire to get home for the night.

In the early days it was possible for the Sukuma to approach the catechetical class as an undifferentiated mass, but as their social life changed with political and economic evolution there has been a move from a Sukuma problem to individual problems, and the parish can no longer be regarded ideally as containing very similar people. Possibly the Church is confused, as the colonial government was, in thinking that increased mobility means increased contact and efficiency, whereas in fact the individual parishioner may well see less and less of his parish priests as the number of Christians increases and the geographical and social area of Christianity expands.

CHAPTER V

Christianity and Education

IN AN ENVIRONMENT in which houses are widely spaced and schools few and far between, except in the towns and trading centers, catechetical courses for the instruction of would-be converts provide, in many cases, the only possibility of acquiring literacy. Even with the expansion of primary schools, the need for literacy cannot yet be satisfied entirely, although it is no longer such an inducement to attend catechetical classes as it once was. It is not that literacy is taught as such, but there is at least contact with the possibility of learning to read and write. Converts have even given as the reason for their conversion that the Church provided them with "the book." They do not take it that the Bible is the most important of all books and that this is their recognition, but that it is the only substantial book available to them in a language which they can understand, a very potent attraction.

To most Sukuma the only works available in their own language are newssheets and Kiswahili pamphlets. There are also, of course, books usually of small size, comparatively high-priced, and dealing with matters of purely functional interest such as improving agriculture and rural health, account keeping, or documentaries, or fiction of a rather serious nature. These types of books, together with political manifestoes, have limited attractiveness to the slow reader. The Bible, in contrast, is low-priced and of large size, although available only in a Protestant edition. The Catholics have a comparable amount of religious literature available, but not the complete Old and New Testaments. In the Bible they can read of marvelous happenings and great events, stories that are exciting by any standard and analogous to their own myths and stories. The attraction of the low price under these semiliterate conditions does not make the reading of the Bible a specifically religious exercise.

There is no doubt that conversion to Christianity and Western education were very closely linked in their minds initially, and the same words "to read" are often used for attendance both at catechetical centers and schools, rather than the more ambiguous "to learn"; the catechumen is called "a reader." It seems that the Protestants press literacy and education as a factor in the conversion of further church members much more than the Catholics; possibly they aim at the creation of a religious elite upon which a growing Christian community can be built in the future.

All the churches have been active in education, and Christian schools have provided the large majority of all places available in primary, intermediate, and secondary schools in Usukuma, particularly in the last decade, when education has increasingly come to be regarded as the only reliable method of personal advancement. As these schools, except for those of the Seventh Day Adventists, are now supported mainly by government funds, the churches are not allowed to confine pupils to those of their own faith; indeed the churches themselves would deny that their schools are specifically designed as a method of forcing conversions rather than a means of attracting converts by example and explanation. Before government grant-aided schools came into being, the incentive to conversion was very strong, since the missions ran their schools entirely without government assistance and naturally gave places to their own church members.

Although there has been some expansion in primary education, there is a continuing shortage of places for secondary education. This has made the junior seminary attractive to youths not fully committed to their vocations, who may have seen it as their only opportunity for further learning; they study for their School Certificate examinations and then leave the junior seminary. The Catholic Church does not regard schools, especially primary ones, as a particularly good method of extending church influence, although it has always appeared ready to put up primary schools whenever the government allowed, as a means of tying down a particular area to a potential Catholic commitment.

Teachers in these schools appear in many ways to be poorly

trained, as indeed the shortage of teachers in an expanding educational system has made many secondary-school rejects take up teaching. In addition, many are poor Catholics, whose moral failings in a church school in a small community may seem to have church support, because some acts are known to parishioners but not to the parish priest. Some priests state that it is easier to have contact with government teachers and their schools, for which they have no administrative responsibilities and where the pastoral and administrative functions do not clash. It does not appear that the Church regards its schools as an essential commitment; and it would probably prefer to leave the ownership of these schools in government hands, while the Church continued to provide at least a nucleus of staff.

The shortage of places in postprimary schools has meant that there will be a tendency to become a Christian, not because a boy or girl would be specifically chosen as a member of the Church, but because in competition for a limited number of places, the Church administrator would be bound to tend to choose those of the same faith, all other points being equal. Even if this were not the case in fact, the people, from possibly their more supple awareness of the functioning of human nature, would assume that this policy existed and take action accordingly.

CHAPTER VI

The Converted Child
as a Christian

EVEN IF THE CHILD is not a Christian before entering a church school, there is a strong tendency for him to become one during his schooling. Catechetical classes are provided there in the school and he need make no effort to go and learn. If the majority of the pupils are Christian and church services and activities are provided for the school pupils, few children will like to be the odd man out and remain isolated from these group events. In one school a girl was even produced as "our pagan" and the embarrassment of the occasion in a Christian context was far stronger than any leanings toward the Christian faith as a desirable thing in itself.

The Church has long been aware that school conversions have been one of the most undesirable features in church practice, conspicuous by the very high proportion of converts who cease to practice almost as soon as they leave school. Most can rattle off the catechism, but in fact some further signs of persistence must be required in order to justify these unrewarding conversions.

Just as the child becomes subject to Christian organizational pressure in school, his process of conversion is divorced from his outside life. He is converted without the real cognizance of his parents or indeed without his being aware of the social consequences of following his faith. Removed from school he no longer has any incentive to live up to it and, on the contrary, there is considerable pressure against his doing so. The beginnings of these pressures are shown when the child is told to attend church

on Sundays outside of school hours and immediately becomes the
center of tension and oppression in his home. The child has no
real social existence as an individual and cannot make a stand.

There are now, of course, a growing number of Christians who
were baptized in infancy, not only the children of Christian parents but those of pagan parents who have had the children baptized *in articulo mortis,* either possibly as a magical rite when all
else had apparently failed or, certainly in the case of twins, in order to avoid the cost of traditional rites for the birth of twins.[2]
The priest has the difficult choice of deciding whether to baptize
or to require the parents to undergo instruction in the faith which
they allege they want for their children, to ensure that, if they
do not die, they will be brought up in a Christian atmosphere.
Although priests stress that anyone can baptize a child in danger
of death, it is rarely considered as effective as priestly baptism
and many will go to great lengths to get a priest to the dying, often
requiring him to make long journeys if there is any possibility of
getting there in time.

Children born to Christian parents, particularly the Catholics,
have received little or no instruction in their faith and they have
little incentive to practice it. They see little value in something
which they have not chosen themselves if they are not members
of practicing Christian families; seeing Christianity from within
a circle of indifference, they can have no appreciation of the fundamental alternatives accepted by the adult convert. The main
problem of infant or child baptism to the Sukuma is that it does
not impose an obligation other than the using of the baptismal
name; it is conceived as a parallel to a Sukuma naming rite and
as conferring Sukuma benefits.

Emulation rather than specific teaching is the manner in which
the Sukuma learns; insofar as the family are practicing Christians the children will be practicing Christians. It is doubtful
whether many Christian children are specifically taught Christian
doctrine in the home. Just as baptism is a necessary social rather

---

[2] *Cf.* Hans Cory, "Sukuma Twin Ceremonies," *Tanganyika Notes and Records,*
No. 17.

than religious rite to many nonbelieving nominal Christians in England, so baptism to the equivalent Sukuma Christian becomes a matter of form. It is thus not surprising that many Christians do not know who Jesus was or how to make the sign of the cross.

CHAPTER VII

Adult Conversion

PROPORTIONATELY, women are more attracted to conversion than men, and young women attract and bring in the young men, who come to catechetical classes to look the girls over. Men may become Christians in order to marry Christian girls, but in married life, unless the husband practices, the wife is unlikely to be able to do so, or to be able to influence her husband over his religious practice, or to ensure the bringing up of the children as Christians.

Although the women in general are more inclined to practice Christianity than the men, it is likely that the move toward conversion is the first move toward female emancipation. By attending classes a woman has an identity independent of her family, in which she can speak for herself at a much earlier age than would be the case if she stayed in the traditional environment. She comes in touch with outside influences. She also knows that the Church requires her to say openly in a private meeting with the priest whether she agrees to marry the man chosen for her by her family.

The old often tend to ask for baptism, possibly more women, largely widows, than men. Perhaps they see in conversion a mental security which is no longer provided by their traditional environment, especially if the family is dying out; they also see the charity of the Church as assisting them. There was also the benefit of physical security after the phase of murdering witches in 1963, which must have been terrifying for any surviving lonely women.

They may also feel that it is necessary at the end of their lives to belong to one religious system and that the cheaper and apparently more successful Christian system is the best for them. This desire for conversion is certainly not entirely material, since they come for instruction over long periods without any real hope or possibility of ever learning their catechism, until at the very end they are probably baptized in recognition of their very apparent devotion to the Church as an institution and their knowledge and acceptance in the simplest terms of the basic tenets of the faith.

Much of the opposition to the baptism of sons comes from their fathers, who are worried that there will be no one to carry out propitiatory sacrifices for them in after life even though the fathers themselves are no longer practicing their traditional religion. The possibility of being extinguished by the conversion of a son to a religion brought in by aliens must be a severe shock to many older persons. The obligation to support parents is both spiritual and physical. The strictness of early missionaries about ancestor worship has meant that it is difficult to convince such people that in Christianity the living pray just as devoutly for the eternal rest of those who have died.

Conversion may also be seen as a way out of a serious family quarrel or an unpleasant social situation. A girl may wish to become a Christian as a means of rejecting the husband chosen for her by her family. Someone compelled to take part in a deliberate deception organized by a magician and the magician who caused the death of a man through an overdose of herbal medicine might see conversion as a moral release. Although preparation for baptism is a lengthy process, signing up for a catechetical course can be seen and used as relief; attendance alone gives such a person room to maneuver.

Also conversion permits the Christian to get out of many social obligations which he could have had no convincing reasons for avoiding otherwise. If twins are baptized soon after birth, the father can avoid carrying out much of the expensive traditional ritual, which he claims as un-Christian, although the Church has made no specific rulings on these traditional acts except to prohibit the obscenity in them as a part of general moral counsel. Although traditional rituals still provide many religious and social benefits, they are nevertheless expensive, and the Christian, by thus cutting down the size and extent of his obligations, is able to save money.

Similarly the man in regular employment prefers to be a Christian because the feast days of Christmas, Easter, Ascension, and Assumption in East Africa are known in advance, starting and stopping to a schedule, whereas traditional rites have no predetermined dates and involve much waiting about without pay. Just as a progressively economically centered way of life requires a schedule, so does the religious system catering for it require a parallel schedule.

The Christian bridegroom may stay only a few days in the compound of his father-in-law, rather than be obliged to stay much longer if the family is following traditional custom. In his desire to set up his own household he has the support of the Church, which considers it necessary that the married man should have the fullest opportunity to bear his own responsibilities. The married man may see this encouragement on its obverse side, that by leaving he can avoid many of the inconvenient aspects of subordination. This individualism of moral obligations, which is stressed by Christianity, in many ways cuts across the collective obligations of the average Sukuma. Whether this can be seen as a necessary concomitant to a growing materialism is doubtful, considering that the Sukuma still feels family obligations to be stronger than individual ones.

Further groups of converts, usually women, are those who have become possessed by an ancestor spirit, and conversion is seen as a means of relief and of getting away from further infestations in the future. This does not involve a ceremony of exorcism, and often a blessing of the individual, and possibly of the house as well, and the possession of a holy medal together with the burning of traditional religious equipment have some quieting effect. Others seek baptism because the normal processes of ancestor propitiation have failed to get rid of their troubles. They have gone repeatedly to magicians and carried out their instructions; there seems to be no end to their requirements for the elimination of a multitude of possible causes, so that it is possible to become impoverished by the demands for repeated propitiatory sacrifices. Just as little action is taken without divination, so it seems that people may prefer to have a reason recognizable to themselves before they seek baptism.

Conversion provides a way out, not only by providing an alternative religious explanation of their troubles, but economically, by the use of Church facilities for sick calls, the last anointing, and penance, possibly without making any contribution toward the maintenance of the parish and certainly without being required to make part payment in advance, as is the case with traditional methods. In comparison to this, such persons are indeed getting a far cheaper religious system, and relatively few Sukuma, so far, have attempted to bear the slight costs of the new religious rituals which they patronize.

It may even be that one of the reasons for Church membership is that it is so cheap, but with the coming of independence and the strong trend toward the nationalization of the Church in its priesthood and financial support, and the use of some pressure to contribute more to church and priest maintenance in terms of cash paid out, Christianity may be becoming as expensive as traditional systems of relief. It would be a mistake to think that traditional herbalists and magicians are very expensive; they are cheap to consult and get higher payments only when the patient is cured.

The pressure on women to seek new religious ways if traditional methods fail seems to be caused by the fact that their position in the household depends on their fertility and the survival of their children. A barren woman, or one who is dazed by the persistent sickness and death of her children, is defenseless against divorce and a low position in her own family afterwards. The husband is not nearly so involved, for if the one wife is unsatisfactory in these terms it is comparatively easy for him to marry again.

In a changing society in which there is much tension between the old and the young, conversion to Christianity and the following of its rules, at least externally, improves the social power of the younger generation. Although there may not be a direct challenge, the control of the elders is weakened by reference to another power system external to traditional practices. However, it is unlikely that any prospective convert sees the practice of Christianity in such broad terms, and upon conversion he will do all that he can to avoid a complete commitment on any particular issue, much less accept in its entirety his new way of life.

Although these reasons for conversion have stressed the material and social advantages of becoming a Christian, this does not in any way presuppose that converts may not develop, and afterwards maintain, a faith which is devoid of such considerations and a devotion which the observer cannot fail to be aware of and to admire.

CHAPTER VIII

Teaching for Baptism

AFTER THE INDIVIDUAL decides to seek to be baptized, problems of teaching him have to be considered, and linguistic difficulties related to the transfer of essentially philosophic terms from one language to another are the first complications. The first religious translation into an East African language were made into Kiswahili and, because of the absence in Kisukuma of the appropriate words, Kiswahili has continued to be used. *Mungo* (God), *nakatifu* (blessed), *bikira* (virgin), and *sala* (prayer) are some of the key words which have had to be used. This is not to suggest that linguistic adaptation has not been going on all the time, but these key words in a new cult have little in them to link with Sukuma experience.

More important than this transfer of key words is the absence in Kisukuma itself of important verb forms, which must give the Sukuma fundamental difficulty in understanding the Christian ethic. "To want" and "to love" are the same word, *kutogwa*, and it is a verb in which the "w" suggests a passive form in Bantu dialect, but it does not have a passive meaning. It is impossible to say, "I am loved," but only "he loves me," and "I like work" becomes "work wants me," *milimo yanitoga*. "We want work," *tutogilwe milimo,* and "we love God," *tutogilwe Mungu,* have the same verb form, so that the phrase can be understood only in its context. They have apparently no word for will, so that the Sukuma might be semantically incapable of accepting the Christian idea that he could determine his moral actions independent of outside causation. The dead bodies of a man and a cow have the same word, *mimba,* so that explaining the significance of a burial without a social situation to differentiate it again raises problems.

The Scriptures are full of allegory, which in translation may

well create innumerable problems. In the absence of a monogamous ideal of marriage, the spiritual marriage of Christ and His
Church involves the use of words which may conceivably have a
suitable meaning but are more likely to have an entirely secular
meaning. Doubtless allegory teaches an appreciation of spiritual
issues, but then transfer into another language may make nonsense. These semantic difficulties are enough to show that greater
knowledge of and more exposition through the medium of Kisukuma is not sufficient when certain concepts are absent from their
understanding.

In these matters there can be no assistance from the past and
nothing can be more tortuous than the nurturing of new ideas
which cannot be absorbed into traditional culture. The Sukuma is
mystified because example and practice cannot readily be provided within his own social orbit to support a new verb form.
Purely school teaching does not have this basic difficulty, because
children are being taught non-Sukuma facts and not moral issues.
The teaching of the catechism appears to give few problems and
the facts are accepted because the priest is an authority, not only
because of his social position, but for his religious knowledge as
well. If the priest says that something is true, it is true, and similarly when the priest says that he himself cannot understand the
Trinity or the Eucharist, they accept his belief in the ununder-
standable because he says it is true.

The process of preparation for baptism in any case is lengthy
and differs from parish to parish in practice, although there are
official systems on the books in each diocese. While there is a tendency to think of catechetical training as an organization problem
for processing numbers of individual converts, the difficulties are
many and varied. Some of these are the difficulties inherent in
mixing men and women, the old and the young, the literate
schoolboy and the completely illiterate adult, and in catering to
individuals and the place where they live.

The great length of these instructional periods is very striking;
the White Fathers talked of a four-year catechetical period. The
Maryknoll Fathers have now reduced it to three years in the Shinyanga diocese and do not seem to consider anything shorter than
two years reliable, but even adjacent parishes show considerable

variations both of time and of content. Criticism of this lengthy period seems to assume that attendance is regular in much the same way as an officer worker in a town might put aside Friday evenings for instruction in order to cover the six months' course starting on a specific date.

It is more likely that these long periods have resulted from the Sukuma's preoccupation with seasonal agricultural work and the demands of his family commitments. It is just not possible for him to attend as regularly as an industrial or office worker. He is dependent on the agricultural year, his own health and that of his relatives, and the social and political demands of his neighborhood. He is not independent in the sense that his time is his own, and the off-and-on nature of taking instruction is very noticeable, so that it may be years before he has mastered an adequate knowledge of the new faith. Also, in accepting instruction, he is being subjected to far stronger and more regular discipline than anything he will have experienced in his traditional life.

In addition, the Church does not view conversion merely as the memorizing of essential prayers and the answers in the catechism. All priests view this lengthy period of instruction as a test of constancy and devotion. The obligation is there as well to see that the convert does understand, and too much reliance cannot be put on the catechists to do it thoroughly. Converts live at the mission for periods of up to six months during the dry seasons, going home only over weekends, in order to be given more thorough instruction as well as a grounding and object lesson in the need for charity and self-help as a Christian, the practical side of a Christian community in action.

In the past the missions were able to conduct these classes with little interference from outside agencies, but it is now becoming more difficult to get would-be converts to spend such periods away from home, with all the attendant problems of eating and sleeping in the neighborhood of the church. This must cause hardship, since a husband and wife have to take turns looking after the house. The demands of the national political party and the cotton-monopoly co-operative societies for their attendance at meetings are not easy to resist.

Some priests do not realize the difficulties which any catechu-

men may experience in attending the classes regularly and may
cut the person out of the course for as little as three late arrivals
or nonappearances during a six-month course. This is quite unrealistic in Sukuma circumstances, since few have watches and an
overcast day may make their timing completely wrong. Furthermore there are any number of agricultural or personal emergencies which do not require that he should actually do anything except wait about in case he should be needed—he has to be seen to
be there.

Many priests stress that the proper role for catechetics in Usukuma is to impart knowledge from which comes love and the practice of Christianity. They suggest by implication that the intellectual development of the Sukuma is such that Christianity's
fundamentals can be absorbed only by rote, knowledge possibly,
but acquired by repetition. In this they distinguish between the
African and those from developed countries in the matter of learning. It is suggested that the intellectual or the understanding per-
ceiver of Christianity is a comparative rarity in any culture and
that to base any plans for the future on any other method of learning is bound to be illusory.

But if the Christian truths are to be got home to any person in
any culture, it can be done only in terms of that culture; the everyday terms of most cultures are extraordinarily alike: the affairs
of the immediate surroundings, family problems, social survival,
and aggrandizement. The greater world outside encroaches hardly
at all on this everyday pattern of egocentric involvement.

The majority of religious literature, though of the highest
quality and the most fervent intent, is distinguished by its virtual
unreadability and this applies as much to religious works in English as in Kiswahili or Kisukuma. There are, of course, many notable exceptions, but almost all of this literature is couched in very
general terms. The average catechism as printed is usually so un-
stimulating that the only conceivable way of learning it may well
be to regard it as a discipline and test of faith in order to get
through it satisfactorily. Certainly the would-be Sukuma convert
regards it as a hurdle to be cleared and not as a key to living.

Perhaps the Church has realized this. The African Way of Life
series is the beginning of a system of catechetics which is not plain

dull—there is an attempt to make it alive—but it is still alive very much in general rather than in local terms. Is it not possible that an intellectual perception of Christian truths is possible through the localizing of the catechism, not so much in language but in fact, and that when these facts are not localized then no one can muster the interest to learn by rote? Naturally the catechist or the priest in his classes illustrates his points with biblical references and stories, but how many people can get a sense of reality from things abstracted from another culture?

The catechism would be in the national language, but examples fitted into the explanations should come from the tribe or community in which the class is being held. The starting point for an understanding of Christian values must be the Sukuma culture, on which can be built whole sets of premises and intentions. The Sukuma probably have no conception of abstract ideas and their ideas are related only to specific instances of what has been or should be done concerning a known series of facts.

That they have this difficulty is borne out by their questions in catechetical classes; it is not the main tenets that are argued, if indeed there is any argument as such. They accept the existence of God without question; they question points of practical detail and they probably see Christianity in terms of just these particular points. Just as when questioned on the nature of love, they can only conceive it in terms of "What are you asking me to love? Is it my wife, my mother, my father-in-law, my ancestral tribal antagonist, or the European without the gate? Define the questions and we will give you the answers of this particular Sukuma and possibly that of the Sukuma in general."

Many priests have talked of the desirability of having a diocesan policy for baptism so that catechumens could not go to the parish that provided the quickest course, and accordingly there would be fewer administrative difficulties. This judgment seems to assume that all the Sukuma are the same and can be processed into Christianity in the same manner. Surely it is quite unrealistic to lay down lengths of time before baptism or between the stages of learning the catechism except for the reason that the priest is so shorthanded that he cannot make a personal evaluation of the catechumen.

Again, to argue that the long period before baptism is necessary to show devotion to the Church would seem to be unrealistic religiously, if not sociologically in conditions of political independence when such methods appear to be applied only to missionary work. It is not possible to have roll calls all the time without losing something of the truly religious element in the testing of devotion by attendance. Furthermore, who is to state that regular attendance has no opposition at home; the irregular attender may have a difficult social battle in coming even once a month. The system seems to be forced on the diocese by the large numbers of Christians per priest in any parish. Again, when we close our eyes to what is considered the purely Sukuma element in these problems and realize the parallels to Church practice in America and Europe rather than the differences, is it morally defensible to require of the Sukuma tests of devotion which are not applied elsewhere?

Although there does not seem to be any group feeling among those who are confirmed together, those of the same baptismal class do seem to feel a strong sense of identity, even though they may be of widely divergent ages. An adult woman will break down and cry when she cannot be baptized with the rest of the class because of some marriage difficulty.

CHAPTER IX

Christian Marriage

CHRISTIAN MARRIAGE is at the center of Church activity in Usukuma just as it is essential to Christianity, but the fact that it has become a central issue arises from the three problems of divorce, polygamy, and women's rights, and the inflation of the social importance of the marrying couple. From a place of relative unimportance in the traditional ritual, bride and groom are put into the position, in the Church's ceremonies, of being assumed to be socially adult individuals, capable of making mature decisions without the support and authority of their seniors.

It is fundamentally important to realize that the Sukuma have no conception of a stable and enduring marriage as an ideal supported and enforced by custom. The very exactness in time of the marriage in church—one moment more and they are exactly married—is against their whole idea of marriage as a developing institution. Christian marriage is described in terms of *kulagana*, "to take an oath," which is of course correct in Christian faith, but this word is never used in any way for Sukuma customary marriage, which uses *kulunja*. Oath-taking among the Sukuma is a very serious matter and accordingly very rare, and its association with the initial union of a young man and woman, which may or may not develop into a mutually satisfying marriage, seems to them totally inappropriate.

Since it is over Christian marriage that the most severe conflicts develop between the Church and traditionalism, the attitude to sin in this respect should be examined. The Church uses the word *zambi* for a religious sin, whereas the Sukuma would use the word *shibi* for a bad or evil thing, but without any religious connotation. Divorce is to break the house, *kubulaga khaya*, and not *shibi*, which they would use for fornication with an unmarried girl and for all unnatural sexual acts. Adultery, *bushiya,* would be regarded more as an injustice to the rights of the woman's husband than as a sin. The Church will talk about God's laws in the abstract, but the Sukuma will consider God's laws in the concrete in relation to his own personal position and the potential longevity of his family. They are in accord if they happen to coincide, but neither can by definition accept the other's basic terms; the split is shown quite clearly linguistically.

It is almost inevitable that an infertile marriage will end in divorce or polygamy, with the husband either taking a second and younger wife or the infertile wife going as a second or third wife to another man. The stress on children is so strong that virtually no Sukuma can maintain an infertile monogamous union.

Perhaps it is wise to consider the parallels with European practices before too ready a condemnation of Sukuma marriage is made. Once a marriage is established, the Sukuma are not particularly prone to divorce which, at the best of times, involves complicated negotiations and the disorganization of at least three families. The Sukuma man and wife are not as isolated as they would be in Europe, and compromise and reconciliation are the themes which govern marital quarrels, backed by a sound awareness of the economic consequences of a broken marriage.

Sukuma society is organized on the assumption that marriages will last and it is therefore extremely difficult for a Sukuma to break a polygamous marriage and to return to the first wife taken under customary law. Religious difficulties are not regarded as sufficient grounds for separation or remarriage unless both the parties consent, even if the claimant is prepared to forego any bridewealth claims. An examination of the problem discloses that an increasing amount of marriage trouble is economic rather than concupiscent in origin. Polygamy is not a serious problem, principally because the Sukuma men have never gone away in large numbers to work as migrant laborers, and there are not, therefore, an equivalent number of unattached women. Any tendencies to take several wives are unlikely to increase, with greater demands being made on their available income.

The baptism of polygamists is a difficulty because the husband has to send away all his extra wives, but he cannot divorce them under customary law, so he has to maintain them. Therefore he will have one household in which he will cohabit and one or more households which he has to maintain socially and economically without any cohabiting. He is still married to these other women, so they can still claim support in court or informally through their families, who would certainly press hard to have their relative adequately maintained. They do not want the messy problem of divorce to come up as it might well involve them in the return of the bride-wealth, a difficult problem if the marriage has lasted for some years.

He has to visit these households, at least to see that they are cultivating well and to contribute his share of the necessary labor, so that propinquity alone might lead to sin. He is still socially the father of the children born in the marriage before his conversion, although religiously they are illegitimate. The wife may need the physical contacts of marriage to which she has become accustomed and further children may be born after the husband's conversion. Again socially he is their father, and it would seem that he has to accuse his wife of adultery to clear himself in the eyes of the Church, or use the event as an excuse to divorce the wife while retaining the children.

These are complicated social problems, in which the Church may become too easily involved in what may really amount to detective work in regard to sexual practices. A further complication is that while the polygamous marriage exists neither the husband nor the wives can be baptized or receive the sacraments.

Another difficult problem is that the Church considers husband and wife as a unit, whereas the Sukuma rarely draw attention to this and, of course, it is not possible to observe them together; they do not eat together, walk together, or play with the children together, much less greet a visitor together. The priest may know the husband well and the wife just as well, but since he never sees them together he may never associate the two faces in his mind.

Many priests comment on the irresponsible way in which young men and women enter into Christian marriage, often on the flimsiest of pretexts and on very short notice, with partners chosen for them by their parents. It is difficult for a young man to resist the demands of his parents and he probably sees in an early marriage at least the beginnings of personal independence and a rise in status. It may even be that he sees the girl as a means to this end, and the fact that he has not personally selected her does not mean that he has in any equivalent way rejected her. Arranged marriages probably have a good or even better chance of success than an entirely free choice does. Perhaps, also, the Christian Sukuma takes an exaggerated view of the commandment to honor his father and mother, feeling that this builds upon traditional Sukuma values and that his father can command him to sin; to work on Sundays, marry a pagan, or do other things that are unacceptable to a Christian.

Marriage initiates a social relationship which may or may not develop into a stable union, depending, as the Sukuma realize, upon countless factors which cannot be anticipated or allowed for at the beginning: the fertility of the woman, her docility toward her parents-in-law's instructions, and her ability to work; the ability of the husband to generate children, beyond the simple question of impotence, his success as a provider of clothes, food, and a reasonable house.

All the denominations have been involved in the problems centering on bride-wealth. Although initially there were objections to bride-wealth as such with its implications of wife purchase, the tendency has always been to try to limit the number of cattle required. It has been assumed that Christian marriage as a sacrament cuts off the couple marrying from the wider obligations of family membership, and that the payment of cattle prevented the young persons from marrying as early in life as was deemed necessary if they were not to be in proximate danger of mortal sin. It is perhaps too easy to stress the traditional values concerning bride-wealth when straightforward commercialism has entered more and more into their calculations.

The more commercial attitude to bride-wealth is partially the result of a decline in the sacramental value of cattle. They no longer represent the principal means of carrying out essential sacrifices to propitiate the ancestors and to ensure the continuation of the family by legitimate marriage. The giving and receiving of cattle is now largely thought of in terms of money and, of course, the larger the number received the higher the status of that family in its own eyes and in those of the community. Bride-wealth does indeed validate the marriage, but the Sukuma father these days would want his daughter married to the man making the highest offer and would do what he could to see that his daughter agreed.

Similarly the attitudes of potential Christians may be conditioned by consideration for the Church's past rulings on bride-wealth limitations. Young men, and the parents of more sons than daughters, tend to find in conversion a justification and a way around bride-wealth demands, while the parents of more daughters than sons may oppose their conversion because it would reduce the bride-wealth cattle which they anticipate receiving. Since marriage negotiations are in the hands of the older men of both sides, who are everywhere the most resistant to social change and religious conversion, the Church puts itself in the middle of a ready-made dispute whenever it tries, from the highest motives, to counsel young men and women that they themselves must reach their own decisions about marrying.

Bride-wealth was originally seen as a group obligation of the man's family to provide and of the girl's family to receive and distribute, and this is still strongly felt; certainly the whole process of marriage as a group activity tended to result in stability. The passage of cattle from one family to another and the symbolism of the rituals connected with them all went to legitimize the marriage. Few Sukuma see any direct advantage in either receiving or paying the full bride-wealth agreed, and prefer to leave some unpaid (*magasa*) so that each family has an obligation and a hold over the other, which may be to the advantage of the married couple themselves in time of trouble. The Church has tended to forget the social value of this debt and has tried to insist that bride-wealth be paid in full at the time of the marriage.

The Church endeavored to restrict bride-wealth from the best possible motives, but the attempts were almost always thwarted by traditional forces. Couples would give details of the permitted bride-wealth to the priest, while the traditional negotiations had determined a higher figure; the priest was never in a position to get the truth or to insist on the restricted number without the use of religious or legal sanctions. That Christian parents would or could forego such economic advantages, which were anyway peripheral to the function of the sacrament of marriage itself, was too much to expect, and such a requirement would create a penalty for conversion and the practice of Christianity. In addition, many African local authorities attempted to control the use of bride-wealth with an equal lack of success, and it was undoubtedly very difficult for the average Sukuma to distinguish between the rules of government and those of the Church on this issue.

The Church views the proportion of unpaid cattle as an interference in the marriage of two Christians, in that it represents the debtor's and the debt-holder's continuing influence on the marriage, as is shown in the saying, "Unpaid bride-wealth cattle make the household" (*magasa gakalenyaga kaya*). The opposite view is that unpaid cattle represent proportionately less security for the continuity of the marriage, since the lower the number of cattle paid, the easier it would be for the couple to separate and the cattle to be returned. Bride-wealth, paid and unpaid, is a restraint on the tendencies which go to split a marriage before it has become established. It may not be much more than that if the couple really dislike each other or one party is determined on divorce.

CHAPTER X

Christians as a Community

THE CHRISTIAN CONVERT is not in practice a member of a Christian community. In a few areas Christians form the majority, but in general he is probably isolated from any possibility of a corporate Christian life. In some ways his situation is comparable to the position of the Christian in a Western town, surrounded by purely secular activity; the difference being for the Sukuma convert that he is surrounded not only by an increasing amount of secular activity, but also by the remnants of a traditional system based on magico-religious practice in which religion, the state, and the individual were bound together. In the present situation he can believe and practice his faith or reject it; he can follow the fragmented religious practices of his forefathers in whatever way he wishes to interpret them, the agnostic materialism of the modern world divorced from all religious practice, or his Christian denomination.

His trouble comes not so much from the difficulties inherent in any all-embracing socio-religious system, but because he has to balance himself between alternative systems. He probably feels that, whatever he does, there is something lacking, that he has failed to follow the necessary ritual for his particular difficulties, as he would have felt had he been following the traditional system. In a world of religious alternatives available to a people who are naturally religious and who have an uncertain livelihood, there is a strong temptation to try as many rituals as possible in order to get the right result.

There are few covert tensions between Christians and traditionalists. The Sukuma have a natural respect for religious activity of any sort, and organized objections to some religious activity do not seem to be traceable to objections to Christianity as such;

it is the practice of the traditional religion which is repugnant to some Christian priests and Sukuma Christians, rather than the reverse. Personality clashes between a priest and some prominent local personage, or, for example, the choice of sites in regard to which the community has some underlying objection on the grounds of history, legend, or some localized superstition, are in fact matters that are not directly brought to the notice of the priest except by one interested party or another. Often the points at issue are not apparent to the priest until it is too late to avoid tension and open disputes.

Little trouble comes from a Christian's open refusal to take part in a traditional ritual, provided that it is done tactfully. The trouble over a Christian's noncompliance in the community's ritual for rain, for example, was that the very nature of the rite, to be fully efficacious, required everyone's attendance—thus he was deliberately preventing the community from benefiting. Conflict between these two viewpoints has been eased by the Christians' praying together for rain and their pointing out to others that both approaches are directed to God and for the same purpose.

The earlier missionaries were very much preoccupied with the question of which Sukuma traditional customs were contrary to Christian morality and with the necessity for Christians to remove themselves from these rites and, if possible, to set up an alternative system within the Christian subcommunity. This has always run into considerable trouble because the Sukuma community is knitted together by a complex system of reciprocal obligations and interdependent social organizations. There is always stress on conformity and compliance, not so much that there should be an economic return for the duties performed, but that the mere attendance of each individual may visually demonstrate the unity of the community. These earlier missionaries, who wanted to neutralize the bad elements, did not understand the interlocking nature of these activities nor grasp that their functions could not be separated from that of the community as a whole.

The importance of these binding elements in Usukuma has been shown in the readiness to organize small social groups for every type of activity, including herbalism, dancing, cultivating, hunting, and worshiping, but Christian activity has probably been

more successful in reducing the influence of these societies than in
the creation of Christian organizations to replace them. The Sukuma are great joiners, and usually no difficulty is experienced in
starting a specifically Christian group, but to the Church's way of
thinking these groups require constant supervision and direction
to keep them going, and they die out as soon as this is withdrawn,
which means that they never contained the Sukuma seeds for their
own viability.

The priests' attention, for example, was often concentrated on
the work parties (*kisumba*), of young men and women, who carried out cultivation and other tasks for the community members,
in return for beer and meat, and who often slept away from home.
They were also concerned over twin and marriage rituals in which
there were obscene elements in gesture and song. For the Christian to withdraw meant not only that he was breaking the village unity, but that in return he would be depriving himself and
his family of many opportunities for mutual help.

The position is even more extreme with members of the African Inland Church, as they are not permitted to use beer for the
payment of such work, without which it would be difficult to get
a work party to come, and indeed, in rejecting alcohol they cut
themselves off from traditional communal life completely, as well
as further unbalancing a diet which fluctuates widely in food
value with the time of year and the success of the harvest, some of
which can be balanced out with grain beer.

Most missionaries have reached the conclusion that once the
Christian joins the work-party organizations he cannot avoid immorality. He would be required to work on Sundays and to attend
their feasts even when under an obligation to something else.
He would have to listen to the immoral songs with which they usually accompany their work, and have to take part at the end of the
day in the mutual washing of young men and girls.

The demands of such associations are indeed another reason
for the conversion of those who are in paid employment. They
cannot always be taking days off to carry out obligations to the
associations of which they are members. Since they have no tradition of regular paid work they do not regard this as an excuse, but
baptism provides an acceptable reason for noncompliance.

Attempts have been made to organize purely Christian groups but, without sufficient numbers in one neighborhood and the necessary social gradings within the association, the members seem to lack both the incentive and the discipline to make them viable, for they are, alas, trying to function without the magico-religious element which existed in purely traditional societies. The Christians are thus sometimes isolated by their beliefs and have been left to harvest and winnow their grain alone, without the assistance and excitement provided by work parties.

Christians as a minority group in Usukuma affairs do not appear to have attempted to express themselves politically or to have specifically voted for a candidate because of his religious beliefs. Even in the earlier formal councils, Catholic chiefs did not appear to have grouped themselves together to express a Catholic viewpoint on their affairs; they were too much divided among themselves on almost every issue.

CHAPTER XI

The Individual
Christian's Tensions

THE SUKUMA CHRISTIAN, in his attempts to follow the faith, is subject to the least pressure on his beliefs when he is in church; he can believe there and, if it were at all possible, could forget the world outside. Even there the Christian can be subjected to the pressure of belonging to his community—of being like everyone else. The Christian cannot morally receive Communion if he has no intention of giving up a particular sinful practice, but when everyone else goes up to the altar, how can he remain behind? He becomes the isolated one, the person who stands out from the rest, which is the last thing in the world that is wanted; possibly this is more common among women than among men.

Once outside he is in a world which is not based on the categories of the commandments, and enormous social pressures build up for him to conform to what is going on around him. He may not go out to seek sin, but sin comes to him, as in a two-day cultivating party with the girls staying all night. He cannot leave without excluding himself socially from the group, with all the penalties which that involves. His father wants some work done on a Sunday, so he cannot go to Mass because his father's control has far more implications for him than does disobeying the Church's law. The Sukuma have very limited freedom, possibly no more than freedom to join this or that social group, certainly not freedom to abstain. It is not so much a question of why so few Sukuma are good Christians, but of how so many do manage to lead such faithful lives under the social and economic conditions surrounding them.

Their preoccupation with children and the continuation and expansion of the family and lineage makes Christian marriage the main ground for conflict. This expansion is one in which the family must occupy ground, and in which its size is seen as a prerequisite to political authority, economic success, and ritual identity in contradistinction to other families in the immediate neighborhood, which are under similar pressures to expand, or suffer under the sorrow of diminishing size. Be fruitful and multiply is the theme of Sukuma family life and under such compulsion it is difficult to love your neighbors once your family's expansion must be at some other family's expense.

In the peripheral areas of Usukuma it is still possible for a family to expand in numbers and in land usage by taking up new land which has never been occupied before. In theory a man can love his neighbors because they are not a menace to him; their boundaries are not contiguous, and he is not hemmed in. But in the overcrowded areas of the lake shore and in Mwanza and Kwimba the best land has been fully occupied for years, and Christianity's commandments clash with Sukuma ideals.

The Church has the concept of original and actual sin, while analysis finds that conflict built into any social situation cannot be resolved in moral terms. The resolute Christian man or woman, with his acceptance of Christian moral obligation, can split the lineage of which he is a member. Refusal to divorce for infertility, desertion, adultery, infection with venereal disease, the use of magic medicines, refusal of conjugal rights, physical cruelty, impotence, or the lack of maintenance, becomes an issue in which a Christian is pulled one way by his Church obligations and another by obligations to his own lineage and family.

Members of the family badger him to remember these obligations and they live around him all the time, and the Church does not. They are there all the time, living their obligations, however indifferently from the point of view of ideal Sukuma standards, while the Church is not present either as a community or as represented by priests. In fact the appearance of the priest may be solely for the purpose of reminding him of his Christian obligations, while he ignores the economic and other satisfactions of mortal sin. The Church may too often see the individual as being in default when he has been subject to social pressures that members of European or American nuclear families are rarely subjected to in urban and industrial communities. In crude terms, he has to sin to survive.

Although the absence of children and the resultant compulsion toward polygamy will impose the greatest strain on any marriage, divorce is a troublesome business and best avoided, for the man has an acknowledged right to extramarital liaisons and there is status in being the head of a polygamous household.

The woman isolated in the home is easily tempted into adultery and once her children are no longer physically dependent upon her, she has no social rights to them which might restrain her through the thought of losing them. She has special problems from her inferior status, and until her human rights are recognized Usukuma must be regarded as a man's country; the priest can take specific action in support of women's rights only at the peril of losing influence over the men. Her inferior status is so ingrained into her as she grows up that her docility to the beatings of her husband and her refusal to complain make it an almost impossible task to accept her as a Christian equal in the absence of any wish from the woman to assert herself.

The problem is not one of nuclear households with closely defined rights and responsibilities and necessary concern for the growing child whatever happens to the marriage of his parents; he has already been well adjusted to possessing classificatory mothers and fathers who have given him as much affection and guidance as he can require. The very close connection between grandparents and grandchildren may balance the disciplinary role of the father and the lack of kindness often associated with the patrilineal kin, while the mother and other matrilineal kin with their institutionalized kindness may restrain the patrilineal side of the family. The child should not be regarded as a dependent of his natural parents alone or as having sharply defined loyalties to the nuclear family.

Another general cause of conflict is the Sukuma conception of the causation of misfortune and disease. The search for a cause is often still in terms of the traditional life, in which, if blame cannot be attributed to a relative or neighbor, the malevolence of unremembered ancestors must be the reason. The overseas student who has had a nervous breakdown through overwork, the infertile wife who is perhaps the unhappiest person in Sukumaland, and the man who has suffered repeated material misfortunes, may turn to traditional explanations. To a people who have never disputed immediate causes of misfortune, the explanation that it is God's will cannot give them the satisfaction provided by the traditional system, which provides explanations, or alternatively the reasons for their failure to get an explanation.

The Christian view may seem to them to be a counsel of resignation and despair, while their tradition has always been to seek for a cause with great persistence regardless of the cost; in that sense they are a pragmatic people. At the present time a person in misfortune is more likely to turn to divination than to the obligations of ancestor propitiatory sacrifices for the relief of his anxiety.

The obligation to propitiate the ancestors is always a family affair in which all possible family members should be involved. The affair may no longer be a sacrifice, but it is probably a name changing, the search for a particular medicine, or the joining of a society that may be necessary. The Christian who openly refuses to come or makes excuses which both he and his relatives know to be specious is guilty in their eyes, not only of breaking family unity, but of contributing by his absence to the possible failure of the sacrifice or ceremony and thereby to the continuance of that individual's and the family's misfortune.

A by-product of the decay of these traditional rites attended by many members of one family has been that Christians no longer know as many members of their own lineages as they might have done in the past, with the result that non-Christian relatives at marriage negotiations have to supply the necessary information to prevent incest according to Sukuma custom.

Another consequence of this development of a nuclear family which may accompany conversion is a practical break in the social functions of grandparents; they were much nearer to the children than the parents themselves, the recipients of confidences and, particularly for grandmothers, responsible for the instruction of their granddaughters in marital and sexual practices. This can lead to serious consequences, as when a girl comes to marriage and the prenuptial investigation discovers that she has not menstruated for six years and that her parents have not known this.

The solution to many Christian difficulties is for the family concerned to move into another area as far away as possible from where they were previously living, so that they can be relatively free from interference. The difficulties are particularly serious in matters of divorce, where the couple are never in a position to work out their own troubles; both man and wife are still so much a part of their own families that often the trouble may be provoked by the in-laws. A married woman undergoing instruction for baptism, on being asked, "What would you do if your father did not like your husband any more?" replied that she would do as her father wished and leave her husband. It requires exceptionally strong character for them to be able to follow their beliefs while being geographically a corporate member of an extended family.

The traditional ideas of causality have been only overlaid by Christian instruction and baptism, and misfortune, if it does not cause a return to traditional practices, can be best answered by emigration, a flight from the sorcerer. The death of a child or a long illness will start a move. The isolation of a Christian family may make them move to where there are others, and also the need for schooling, but it is not an easy thing to do, involving much expense and the creation of new neighborhood ties, which at their best cannot replace the all-embracing values of their own families.

It does not seem that the Sukuma Christian or non-Christian can conceive nondeistic beliefs, and the lapsed Christian does not say that he has ceased to pray or that he has stopped being a Christian, but says that he has an obstacle to the sacraments or that he has ceased to receive them. Even in a situation of disbelief they still express themselves in terms of belief; others confess, but say in the confessional that they cannot receive absolution because they do not intend to try not to commit a particular sin again.

PART THREE

RITUAL
AND
THE CHRISTIAN SUKUMA

CHAPTER I

The Function of Ritual

THE FUNCTION OF RITUAL for non-Christian African communities is well known, but the study of a revealed religion, conducted by a priestly caste, has often been inhibited by the tendency to presuppose ends rather than to proceed according to the evidence. The function of Sukuma traditional ritual in its historic and current form has already been described, but the conversion of Sukuma men and women to Christianity, to the African Inland Church, the Anglican diocese of Central Tanganyika, or Catholicism, has shown wide variations not only between these three groupings but between the inland areas and the lake litoral. Some explanation must be sought other than that of "conversion to something different" as a part of a general process of social change. It is necessary to stress again that Christianity in Usukuma is a religion of the converted in which there are always problems which stem from their traditional religion, with which, in one form or another, it is paralleled. This problem of the convert does not really exist in Europe or America.

Whether the parallels of Christianity and traditional religion continue or converge depends entirely on whether Christianity can supply the needs of persons who are no longer satisfied with traditional practices. Van Gennep[1] states that "the critical stages"[2] of the life cycle—birth, puberty, marriage, parenthood, and death—were socially defined; secondly that the entrance and exit from these critical stages were always marked by ritual and

---

[1] *Cf.*, Arnold van Gennep, *The Rites of Passage*. Trans. by Monika B. Vizedom and Gabrielle L. Caffee. Chicago: University of Chicago Press, 1960.

[2] For the phrase "critical stages," see Meyer Fortes, "Ritual and Office in Tribal Society," in Max Gluckman, ed., *Essays on the Ritual of Social Relations*. Manchester University Press, 1962.

that these rites of passage were usually of a more or less standard pattern. He did not distinguish between primitive and Christian rituals, considering them both to obey these same attentions to the critical stages.

Although his model has been acclaimed for the insight it gives into various ritual functions, it is necessary to consider more deeply the concept of these critical stages and their existence in Sukuma life, so that the coincidence, or failure to coincide, of traditional religion and Christianity, and indeed other alternative ritualistic solutions, can be examined.

The fact that Christianity is a revealed religion may have little relevance to its sociological function and its success in the creation of Christian communities. Also, if an individual convert is sustained in a religious life which is largely at variance with inherited religious practice and tradition, it must be the result of Christianity's providing a comparable ritual, at least as satisfying as the traditional ritual in its historic form which it has replaced, and in line with his present-day problems.

It has been shown that, whatever the motivation for conversion, the Christian Sukuma becomes involved in a religious way of life which impinges almost everywhere on his traditional conceptions of religion and society. Despite the detailed instruction given before baptism, there is no doubt that the Christian concepts conflict with traditional ones and that his enthusiasm for the various parts of Christian ritual and his ability to follow Christian doctrine are in direct proportion to their coincidence with traditional customs and beliefs, particularly at the critical stages.

Van Gennep pays great attention to the physiological passage through life, drawing his examples from a wide variety of societies, but the Sukuma do not, in their traditional observances, pay equal attention to all these stages. Puberty has almost no ritual attached to it and death very little, whereas there has been in the past and remains now a great concentration of ritual surrounding parenthood, birth, and marriage, all involving the fecundity of the Sukuma as a person.

The lay researcher talking to a practicing Catholic Sukuma about the rituals of the Church can measure the man's interest by the length of time he talks about a particular subject, and also

by what he remembers. With one, the Church marriage was remembered by the ring because the priest had to provide it himself,
and by the Kiswahili prayer which made reference to the fertility
of the marriage and the successive generations which would come
from it. The participant could remember nothing more and yet
he went on to talk for half an hour about the preceding traditional arrangements. It might be said that he ignored the Christian ritual; it existed, he passed through it, and he obtained the
wanted prescriptive right for his marrige in Church terms.

In this man's case the inadequacies of the Church ceremony
had been balanced by the satisfactions of the traditional activities
preceding and terminating it. He was not a young man and marriage must have taken place twenty years before, but he did not
remember until he was reminded that his was the first Church
marriage of a pupil from a particular Catholic school and that the
pupils attended and the school band performed outside afterwards. In plain terms the overlay of the Christian marriage had
not taken much away from his traditional identity, or even replaced the traditional ceremonies. He was an urban railway
worker and the ceremony may have been more convenient and
less expensive away from home than going home for an expensive
outlay which he did not wish to afford. It must be assumed that
he could have got leave to go home for his first marriage if he had
wanted to, since by his own admission it had required much
planning in advance.

Another Catholic, describing his baptism as a boy of twelve,
spoke of the lining up so that the process of baptism could be gone
through efficiently and quickly, and mentioned water, oil, and
salt. For these acts he had the reasons somewhat confused, but to
him it was a necessary ritual and it gave him the status for which
he had asked.

In both these cases the ritual was important as ritual, and it
appeared to make no difference what form the ritual actually
took provided that it was ecclesiastically legal. In the former case
the Church ritual obviously did not complete the necessities for
such a critical stage, while in the latter the young boy, possibly
feeling the need for social rather than religious recognition, was
baptized in a ritual associated with puberty, whereas no such ritual

had previously existed in Sukuma life. He was gaining access to a satisfactory closed group, with some additional status and theoretical equality with his peers and possibly elders at an age when he was unrecognized socially in his own traditional group.

People's awareness of those coincidences which give satisfaction is not verbalized and is shown only in the success of certain rites and in the reactions to innovations introduced by the churches as corporate bodies or through the experimental work of individual missionaries. It is these which must be examined, as well as the marked lack of such coincidences in other activities.

Thus it is seen that Church marriage does not appear to satisfy the needs of this critical stage, while school baptism satisfies a need of socially immature persons not recognized by traditional society because they have not yet reached a critical stage recognized as such by the Sukuma. This is not to say that baptism while in school should or should not take place, but rapid change is taking place in society and in their lives. These boys and girls apparently do feel specific needs, but it should be recognized that this is an adaptation of these Sukuma to the services provided by a relatively exclusive group, the Church, and their willingness to be baptized may not mean that the Church has succeeded in attracting them by its doctrine. In line with the Sukuma liking for societies they are seeking membership.

In any comparison between the complex of traditional ritual associated with the critical stages of personal fecundity in children, crops, and cattle, and that offered by the Church, the latter's total effort seems to be almost insignificant. This comparison cannot be explained away by the decline of an out-of-date traditionalism. The traditional religious ritual associated with these critical stages may have declined, but they are still critical stages for the majority of the Sukuma and will be just as critical for decades, if not centuries, to come. If Christianity cannot help in the crises of its adherents, they must seek their satisfactions elsewhere. They look to Christianity to solve their problems and if it does not they will go elsewhere. There is no doubt that the Church cannot respond, by means of religious ritual, to the whole of their anxieties and needs concerning these critical stages, but there is equally no doubt that it should attempt to orientate itself to these Sukuma needs. If it is unable to satisfy the Sukuma on a wider scale than the purely religious in the Church's terms, schism is almost inevitable.

CHAPTER II

Sukuma or Western Christianity

THE IMPORTANT RITES of passage associated with pregnancy and birth in the traditional culture have not been replaced by Christian ceremonies stressing the importance of a woman as the link in the development of the family. Christian prayers for pregnancy and the completion of a safe birth exist, but they are rarely used, so that these events are not covered by any Christian ritual comparable to their Sukuma importance. The Church has worried over moral issues in this context, but whether such pregnancy rites can be related to differences between wed and unwed mothers seems to be irrelevant to Sukuma needs and indeed to charity. Similarly, many priests have been reluctant to carry out the ritual for the churching of women because it implies that a woman incurs impurity in childbirth.

This may not be biologically true, but to the Sukuma and in innumerable other cultures childbirth does require ritual cleansing; in fact the belief is so strong that the Church must either adhere to their ideas in the absence of any direct ruling from the Holy See, or gather into the churches persons who, for want of cleansing or the fear of an alternative solution, are regarded as impure. The remark made in one parish that it would take up too much time seems completely irrelevant to the theme of adaptation. All too often the Sukuma is left to use various traditional practices to underline the importance of such things, while feeling that such activities have been prohibited in part or whole by the Church because of their pagan associations.

One priest, thinking over this issue, considered the possibility of having Masses twice a year for the women of the parish, itemizing their classes of difficulties. Such adaptation does not necessarily involve extra work for already overburdened priests. In fact, such days could be organized at each out-station to coincide with clinics or social workers' visits, so that the spiritual would precede and introduce a day devoted to women's problems.

Many priests have commented on the unfortunate lot of the infertile woman, aware that she is the most unhappy person in Usukuma and that an infertile Christian marriage has very little chance of surviving. If monogamy is the aim of the Church, then those who are in the greatest difficulty over this fundamental issue must receive the Church's ritual attention because they are receiving it in traditional forms in every case in which a woman considers herself infertile or feels that her fecundity is menaced, whether she is a Christian or not. Pious counsel in the parish office is no substitute and verges on the futile, for the importance of this issue in Sukuma life is well recognized.

The priest, when questioned about this issue, will suggest to a woman that she should go to the hospital for a physical check-up, and only if that is unsuccessful in disclosing a cause would he resort to prayer. The physical and the spiritual areas are so closely related in the Sukuma's mind that an answer of this nature is tantamount to rejection by the Church. It is not only recourse to traditional practices in the case of such a failing marriage that alienates the Sukuma from Christianity; in such affairs a condemnation by implication is extended to much of what they consider essential ritual concerning the critical stages of their lives. This feature in the Christian Sukuma's life accounts for much of the underlying separation of the laity and the priesthood in the matter of the direction and maintenance of a specifically Christian individual, family, and community life. Well versed though the priests may be in the exactness of moral theology, they are nevertheless creatures of the cultures of their upbringing, be it American, European, or of the African seminary. Even though the Church may not condemn, the face and voice of an observing priest may indeed convey a ruling on the value of a particular practice, which on reflection he would deny having given at all.

The priesthood as a whole is at the moment particularly sensitive about the issue by virtue of their strong reaction to the implication that such condemnations have been made in general and in particular. Some explain carefully the rules by which they judge a particular issue, but nevertheless, in the eyes of the Christian and non-Christian laity in most places, the Church appears to have condemned even the simplest herbalist.

It is not suggested for a moment that the Church has officially condemned traditional rituals as the laity suggest, nor is it germane to the present situation to discuss whether the fault lies with the priest, the catechist, or laymen, but the situation exists and the concentration of such activities on Sukuma crises shows how important these are to them. The point is well dealt with in the Maryknoll Spiritual Directory, which states, "If it is asked what is good and what is bad in the customs, observances and cultural developments of a people, the answer is not far to seek. That is bad which has been pronounced bad by the Holy See, and everything else is good, or at least innocent and indifferent, and is accordingly to be respected and, if possible, strategically utilized by the missioner." [3]

Individual priests often go very much further than this wise counsel directs. They see social customs which, they consider, impede Christian values and they get overconcerned about it to the extent of expecting from the faithful what they have no ecclesiastical right to demand.

The son-in-law's subservience to his father-in-law, the practice of leaving much of the bride-wealth unpaid, the attitude toward women, claims on the ownership of children that ignore the rights of the Christian family, and so on, are all customary. Those without pastoral experience in the poorer parts of their own countries may well imagine that the ill treatment of wives, including occasional beatings, and their inferior position are peculiarly Sukuma; they are applying their own values to conditions which indeed may have more parallels elsewhere than they are aware of.

In fact it goes much deeper than this when the priest, with his scientific attitudes toward disease, immunizations, and cures, looks at much of his pastoral role through the eyes of culturally trained scientists. Nevertheless he is dealing with a people who see such scientific facts as only one facet of the complexity of life. The priest

---

[3] James E. Walsh, M.M. *Maryknoll Spiritual Directory*, Maryknoll, N.Y.: Field Afar Press, 1947, p. 64.

from overseas has known communities in which crime and the morbid pathology of much of Western life have not in fact been greatly solved by science, and there he may have stressed spiritual values as the only way out of these terrible problems. Once overseas, the realities of Sukuma life possibly become too much a question of the sulpha pill and the penicillin injection rather than a real appreciation; for example, the recognition that witchcraft exists for the simple reason that the Sukuma know, not just believe, that it does exist.

This difficulty has perhaps arisen because in America and Europe the scientific aspects of social work are undertaken by other agencies. In Usukuma the priest attempts to be a functioning part of every conceivable type of social work just because there may be no one else doing such work and because, as well, he sees the element of science as a short-cut to the social-welfare standards of his own country. The evangelical missions have perhaps arrived at their policy of no nonreligious work because of this difficulty. "The Church has become in this respect the handmaid of science, and when Church leaders speak in denial of witchcraft or *abosom* [lesser gods], they do so as men of culture rather than as Christians. . . . We should be able to recognize that the spiritual world in which the African believes is a reality." [4]

Many priests stress correctly that the purpose of the Church's social activities is not to obtain conversions but to help the individual as a human being, although they hope that such charity will cause a disposition toward practicing Christianity. They state that the Church does important work for women in prenatal, maternity, and child welfare works. They may not realize that insofar as they help the Sukuma woman through her crises, which are as likely to be psychological as physical, these activities are virtually devoid of any religious significance.

The use of medicines of purely herbal content and of particular plants and trees in traditional rites, which has been and is so common and not necessarily associated directly with ancestor worship in a morally objectionable form, is a particular case in point. Su-

---

[4] E. A. Asamoa, "The Christian Church and African Heritage," *International Review of Missions.* Vol. 44, No. 3 (July 1955), pp. 298 and 300.

kuma Christians have been unable to distinguish the one from the other and have usually taken the whole of such herbalism to be under a cloud. Christian ritual is thus deprived from the start of valuable elements from traditional life which could support Christian rites and make them more readily understandable to the laity. The use on altars of certain flowers and leaves and the use of certain woods for Church purposes would seem to be a way in which the laity could better express themselves traditionally within the Christian idiom because it would not be the relatively simple flower symbolism of Western usage.

Although the comparison of traditional ritual with that of the Catholic Church shows that the latter does not cover as much of Sukuma social life as the former, it is obvious that the simplicity of non-Catholic ritual, apart from other factors militating against Church membership, must fail even more to replace traditional rituals to the satisfaction of the Sukuma. In the same way, religious practice based on the interpretation of the Holy Bible may serve as an incentive to literacy, but leaves the individual Sukuma depending on this single source of reading matter and would seem to lead, in an illiterate or partially literate people, to institutional rigidity; it is easy to quote the Bible and retire behind the quotation as a reason for not adapting to change. The quotation becomes proof of a religious equality which leaves a person to choose much of his own destiny, when socially, religiously, and economically he is attuned to mutual dependency.

In sum, it must be admitted that the Church has not adjusted its work to Sukuma crises and where attention is paid to them, it is more likely to be the action of science rather than the comfort and guidance of religion.

CHAPTER III

The Role of the Christian Priest

TRADITIONAL RITES have usually been performed by ritual specialists, while the disturbed persons have subordinate roles. None, other than these ritual specialists, ever tried to conduct their own ritualistic lives, so that there is nothing difficult about the priest's celebrating Mass as a complete stranger to the life of the parish. He is doing so by invitation, as in tradition. He is fulfilling people's needs, and is separate from them during his ritual office.

Another measure of success which should come from this essentially "neutral" rite, which only the priest can perform, is to provide the opportunity for compromise. As neutral rite the Mass is seen as a ceremony in which the priest and congregation are united in the same church and centered around the same ceremony but are functionally separate.

Up to the recent changes in the liturgy, the priest and congregation were seen to coincide for only small parts of the Mass if the ritual was examined as a time and motion study. Most of these coincidences involved only minor movements—standing, sitting, praying at regulated intervals—which for most Catholics are virtually automatic. A further class of movements were irregular and broke the isolation by requiring the churchgoer to watch and act, as in putting money into the collection and going forward to receive Communion. Vocal participation was entirely voluntary and a high proportion of churchgoers might in fact never speak during Mass.

The priest and congregation should jointly participate, but it can be seen that, in fact, their joint activities might not be as much as ten per cent of the Mass and even less if the Mass was lengthened by a sermon or announcements of details of the following week's services. This left both the priest and the churchgoer to their private intentions. The former could pray for sanctifying grace, while the latter could pray for, or think about, rain on his fields, more calves, and another son from his wife's current pregnancy. The congregation was not required to participate actively, and they were left alone to interpret the ceremony as they wished, to put in or take out whatever they wanted, and as such this arrangement had immense value. This was in fact an almost ideal situation—a working misunderstanding with which both parties were essentially satisfied. How the recent changes and those still to come will affect matters will be treated later.

The role of the priest as a leader is important, apart from the danger of his being used as a scapegoat for unpleasant decisions, for he is the only person not completely committed to the Sukuma group involved. He should exercise his ritual office so as to make compromise in disputes possible, rather than for making decisions; whether he is Sukuma, American, or Dutch, the position of the priest in this respect would be essentially the same. He is the holder of ritual power, he can never be like other men and, in that position, he is potentially using his power all the time, whether he is conscious of doing so or not. The clear-cut, one-sided decision is against Sukuma practice, and decisions must take account of the fact that the disputants have still to live together in the same community, whereas the priest just does not have to do so to a similar extent. In a sense no Sukuma dispute has an end; the compromise is no more than a temporary solution and a new one can be called for at any time.

Just as he can use his ritual power to aid compromise, the laity can see this same potential power as a reason for giving way toward a compromise solution. But in fact it is vitally important that he should not be a decision maker. Every social role, the priest's included, has built-in checks and no one has unlimited power. To the Sukuma, who are aware of the checks and balances, possibilities of their own society, the priest appears to be in just such a position. They cannot see the bishop's power or the consecrated functioning of the priest's conscience, they see only that the priest can make decisions apparently without regard to Sukuma concepts.

The Sukuma magician and diviner is interdependent with his

patients, relatives, and apprentices, but the priest may well be seen as practicing ritual in isolation without the necessary assistance of subordinate ritual workers; he can even celebrate Mass without servers and in an empty church. Concelebrations would appear to be a far better adaptation to Sukuma ideas, since the practice of ritual groups of elders is recognized, but a single celebrant with altar boys in attendance is not. To them independent authority is mobilized incontrovertibly behind the priest.

Priestly costume and vestments, the intoning of prayers, and the use of a different language present no particular difficulties to the Sukuma, for these things represent much of their own culture, but mere ritual is not enough for them and it has no particular validity of its own. In Mass, only the priest acts out a symbolic role, followed by a prayerful but hardly collaborating, congregation. They do appreciate the ritualization of roles because, for the majority there has been no great fragmentation of social relationships. As in a monastic community, religious values overlap into every part of their lives.

It has been noted in business and in the preindependence civil service that one of the main advantages, or difficulties, which came with service overseas was that responsibility was given at an earlier age and to a much wider degree than for equivalent positions and ages in the home countries. This was not a conscious policy of any organization but the result of a combination of factors, such as the difficulty of communications and a shortage of staff to deal with problems covering thousands of people and wide areas. It was necessary to give responsibilities to the people on the spot or face a slow-down in all the work which was to be done, had matters had to be referred to a superior.

An almost exactly similar process has occurred in every missionary order. Parishes are widely spaced and priests are scarce. Most priests may expect to be in charge of a parish within five years of ordination, whereas in England or America the equivalent period would be fifteen years. It was interesting to learn that this was apparently not an issue known in advance which could have had any particular bearing on missionary vocations.

There are other administrative parallels which appear to have similarly resulted from the isolation of the parish rather than the

isolation of the bishop from the priest. Some spoke of themselves
as face to face with practical problems for which diocesan institutions were unrelated to the facts as they saw them. This has not
quite led to the sort of administrative division in which the department might regard the head office as quite out of touch with
reality as the man in the field saw it. This is a trend, not a split,
because any variations which are practiced are done "in conscience," and this is a difficult issue to argue at any time.

This came up particularly in discussing baptismal procedures.
Perhaps the diocese wishes for as many Christians as possible to be
baptized in any year. Morally, on the other hand, it is quite clear
that each baptism is that of a distinct and individual person, and
represents an individual moral problem, and there is social pressure to provide high figures of baptisms in order that mission action may attract funds. The diocese, for all its religious and social
work, is almost entirely dependent on money provided by charitable persons and organizations in Europe and America.

There is an immense and vigorous competition for these funds.
A very considerable number of the ordained priests in any order
are out of pastoral work altogether and engaged in promotional
work. Indeed the personality of the priest may be an important
factor in getting money; but more important is the reputation of
the order itself as doing good Christian work. Unfortunately, to
the layman, or indeed the social scientist, this is extremely difficult to demonstrate in numerical terms. The mission's annual
reports give figures for those who go through Christian rites, but
this is not necessarily any indication of the expansion of Christian
values. Numbers mesmerize the reader unless he is very careful,
and particularly in the mission field they may indicate almost
nothing of real social and religious significance.

Varying attitudes about baptisms may also be due to difference
of age. The older generation accepted liberty of conscience but
did not practice it to the extent of questioning whether the person entering the Church does in fact know enough to make an
intelligent conscious choice. The younger priests accept far more
readily the practical aspects of this liberty of conscience, and consider it necessary to give individuals more opportunities to accept their Christian obligations in full knowledge. The priest in

the field, while recognizing this problem, cannot see his way in conscience to baptizing those who will not, in his opinion, stand a reasonable chance of following their faith, or of being properly supported or instructed by their parents afterwards.

During the short period of this study there seems to have been a gradual change in the views of the priests themselves toward baptism. Initially few questioned the multiple baptisms of school children, infants of non-practicing Catholics, or those born into mixed marriages. Now there seem to be strong feelings that the real issue in baptism is the possibility of subsequently getting a Christian. In spite of this change of heart there does not seem to have been any direct movement toward altering a policy.

Priests, just as much as other people, talk over their business and indeed probably discuss very little else when they are together; particularly as a religious community they have very limited social contacts with the world outside their parishes. By this process of interaction a consensus of opinion on any issue comes into being; the conservative priest is urged forward and the progressive one is restrained. This consensus seems to have a surprisingly uniform effect; they feel the need for a consensus and are dependent on it to a considerable degree for the motivation toward a particular stage in the development of their work. It seems also that this consensus in an entirely American missionary order stems from a need for stimulation by means of discussion and is not as common in orders which are more international in composition or whose members have at least a part of their religious training outside their country of origin.

CHAPTER IV

The Catholic Mass
and Its Development

ALTHOUGH the Church uses the same word, *kitambo,* for the Mass as is used for a traditional sacrifice, most Christians do not see it as a ceremony in which there are many parallels to these rites with offering, consecration, and communion present in both, although it is much easier to relate the Mass to these activities than it would be in Europe or America, where few, if any, have ever seen a sacrifice. Sophisticated analysis of the two cultures by an outsider can rarely bring either side to a greater understanding of the other because he essentially remains the only link between them. Similarly, the reservation of the sacrament has a parallel in the way in which the sacrificial animal stays the night, tied to the center pole of the house of the family who are to propitiate.

These similarities brought out in analysis account for the ease with which certain practices are assimilated while others are rejected. The knowledge or the explanation of similarities or dissimilarities to the people concerned will almost certainly have little influence on their future activities, which are based on a multiplicity of origins. Perhaps it can be said that the Mass is a development of previous rituals to which those practiced by the Sukuma have a practical affinity. Certainly the occasional convert is struck by the parallels between the two rites and the majority of adult converts understand the meaning of a blood sacrifice and that it is done to obtain something from God.

An important feature of any sacrifice, and of the ritual separation of one family from another, is the possession of ritual equipment (*shitongelejo*). It is usually required that this should be destroyed upon baptism and that its place should be taken by

Christian objects, just as the spirit houses and ritual areas for worship near the traditional house have to be replaced. Although their existence can be abolished, the idea behind them cannot be so easily eliminated.

Outside altars and roadside shrines would seem to be particularly suitable to Sukuma ideas. Sukuma culture is very stong in the association of places with events, not just with the names of first founders. Apart from their household shrines, there are numerous semisacred or semifeared places which could be occupied by Christian symbols. It is possible that they see the church itself as an enlarged shrine, a memorial to a compact made with a spiritual force and as such accepted naturally as having traditional values. Although they may come to Mass in a cotton co-operative store, it is probably because such a store has no parallel in their traditional life that they feel able to do so. But Mass inside a house is a direct clash with traditional practices and would be reluctantly agreed to on the priest's insistence.

If a traditional house and a Christian one are compared, it seems that the latter is less interesting, not so much to the visitor but to the Sukuma himself probably. The practicing traditionalist is surrounded by his religion, while the Christian may have only a cross on his roof. A special place for an outside altar in a grove of cassia would be a distinctive feature of the Christian household, a shrine of one's own when his house cannot culturally contain one, and a permanent invitation to the parish priest.

The need is there, since little of their traditional ritual took place indoors but it seems that, in their desire to show some signs of Christian permanence, the Church and the priesthood have concentrated on buildings—after all, in Europe and America the weather scarcely permits outdoor services. The need for buildings is easily understood; they are the external form of Western Christianity and social welfare and show well in the photographs so very necessary for the raising of funds, but they do not fit in with Sukuma traditional ideas. The Sukuma always tried to have his traditional sacrifices early in the morning, to avoid the heat and thus the tendency to have early Masses coincides; but many churches do not have them outside and to do so would coincide.

The Church is thus left with the task of incorporating what is really a new ritual in a new form and place into Usukuma life. This puts an altogether new stress on their ritual activities, apart from the fact that most young Sukuma may not have seen traditional rituals and thus may be unable to appreciate the niceties of adaptation. It has already been suggested that ritual supplies satisfactions which are not necessarily religious and that this need for ritual can be satisfied in other rites which conform to their needs, political adulation, co-operative meetings, and so on.

Ritual, then, in the Mass may supply these satisfactions, provided that the Mass itself is in conformity with their important needs. The ritual of the Mass must be related as much to a sense of religious and community well-being as to personal and communal misfortune. In this the Mass is admirably suited in that it is a "neutral" rite in which the priest can make current allusions and into which the laity can induce their own private intentions, without any prearranged changes in the ritual itself. The Mass becomes effective because the ritual commits it to nothing more than the generalities of Christian intention and the physical presence of the laity.

When the Church considers the participation of the laity, there will always be the fundamental division between the priest's role and the laity's; the latter cannot encroach on the former's functions. One priest asks, "What are they going to do during Mass?" They cannot use a prayerbook as most are illiterate, the priest is facing them or with his back to them, and they sing foreign melodies; they are always receiving, never giving anything. He is upset because the congregation is not with him in any concrete sense. All the same, there is the same passive experience at a traditional sacrifice, which is usually well attended, and there is no playing to the gallery by making major alterations in the parallel patterns between the types of sacrifices. There is no singing to attract them and maybe they would consider it sacrilegious.

In considering ways of making Christian ritual more acceptable or understandable to the laity, the Church will be able to make only minor changes in the Mass, tinkering here and there while leaving the ritual centrally as a mystery. These minor changes can never have their anticipated effect simply because the Church cannot change the core. For all the efforts to encourage participation, the new forms of Mass usually, practically or verbally, distinguish the priest and the congregation; the Church is stressing the changes but it does not seem that there has been any fundamental difference.

In a sense, the Church has so concentrated on its central rite that it has blinded itself to the social facts of life around it, and it surely must be inexplicable in terms of this life. The absence of cow ritual among a cow-conscious people has already been commented on. Although this is now changing, it might perhaps be regarded as symbolic that the priest used to say Mass not so much with his back to the congregation as with his back to the Sukuma.

In fitting the Mass into the liturgical year, it seems that the Church is frequently drawing attention to saintly persons of very limited interest to the parish. At least the Sunday Masses should be announced as being said for intentions intelligible to those attending. The whole cycle of the year for peasant farmers and cattle herders, together with national and local elections, the visits of national figures to the locality, the school year with its examinations, council meetings, self-help schemes, and so on, provides opportunities for tying in the Mass with the Christians as a community. The church notice board stating that it is the feast of a virtually unknown saint, with nothing applicable to the locality stated underneath, is encouraging a ritualism in the laity and not a living ritual.

In attendance at Mass and the reception of Communion, the laity are able to see who are and who are not guilty of mortal sin; those who abstain may have valid excuses but there is still a separation. Admittedly, this has not the force of the insistence on attendance at traditional rites, but at least it is a passable adaptation, in which moral failure has a social expression, with the virtuous rewarded and the sinful physically delineated. Similarly, the Church's insistence on attendance at Sunday Mass, subject to reasonable excuses, is a valuable asset in that it conforms exactly to traditional requirements.

The current reemphasis on the liturgy as the collective act of the Christian community as a whole tends to clash with Sukuma ideas that participation in sacrifice varies with the organizing groups and their intentions. Although the Church would stress that the rule of attendance is directed at the individual, the laity must presume, as they did in the past, that a rite to be successful must be collective. Priests report that much of this attendance is not really connected with the service at all, with a proportion of those attending loitering about around the church door. But the parallel to the traditional sacrifice is there, for then only a few are actively preoccupied with the ceremony, while the remainder appear to stand around, showing interest only at the more important points. The bell at the elevation underlines the parallel.

The Church has always emphasized that the laity should participate in the offering of the Mass and stressed that the regular reception of Communion is necessary for the maintenance of the Christian life, but this participation has almost always been taken to be singing during the service, and the promotion of this singing has been the subject of much difficulty. There seems to be no parallel to this in traditional sacrifices, where only the ritual leader speaks, while those attending act out a part of the ceremony. Congregations have been reported as liking a representative family to bring the offerings to the altar, and the reading of the Epistle by laymen.

It is impossible to find any parallels to the use of children as Mass servers; socially they have no importance at all and yet they are given this position of great ritual importance. In traditional sacrifice, children have no role and their use here would seem to reverse many values, either upgrading the children or downgrading the ceremony. There would seem to be a case here for the use of adults at Mass to singularize the devout and to stress the gradations in ritual knowledge which are so much part of their lives.

While one of the functions of ritual is to assist in the creation of an identifiable community, which is served at least in part by Church attendance, another equally important function is to delineate the family. In this the Church has not been successful, as families do not sit together in Church, and, even if they did so in the fashion of America and Britain, they perform no collective ritual act which could give them an individual identity at the service. This reluctance to sit together at the services must be because such mingling is not a part of their social practice, and indeed at any traditional rite the nuclear family does not identify itself separately; it merges into the larger groupings which divide the patrilineage from the affines. The Mass then cannot be expected to support the family as a ritual institution unless it can be celebrated more often in the compounds or houses of Christian families, or better still, offered by prior arrangement for the special intention of a particular family. It might thus be possible to reactivate the practice of the whole family gathering for a ritual purpose.

CHAPTER V

No Ritual Concentration
on Sukuma Crises

CHRISTIAN RITUALS in Usukuma, because of the demands on the few priests both in time and distance and the difficulties of adaptation, tend to be brief, if not perfunctory, and do not appear, therefore, to be either ritually complete or satisfying in themselves, apart from the fact that they do not concentrate on Sukuma crises.

The significance of these crises has to be underlined by ancillary social rituals, which the priest himself cannot promote or conduct. This danger of replacing a complex traditional rite by a much shorter and less complex Christian ceremony has been recognized since the beginning of missionary activity, even though the core ceremony may well be liturgically complete in itself.

The Venerable Bede quoted from Pope Gregory's letter to Mellitus about the conversion of the English that "because they are accustomed to slaughtering a great number of oxen in sacrifice to devils, some solemnity must be given them in exchange for this. . . . They should no longer offer animals to the devil, but in their feast let them kill cattle to the glory of God. . . . In this manner while they retain some outward signs of festivity they may more readily consent to inward joys." [5]

This early perception of the necessity of taking heed of the dominant values in existing societies seems to be absent in one obvious direction. The conversation of almost every priest is heavy with references to the devotion of the Sukuma to their cat-

---

[5] Bede, *Ecclesiastical History of England.* Trans. by A. M. Sellar. London: George Bell, 1907, p. 67.

tle and the manner in which this hinders the development of
Christian marriage, and yet the cow is totally absent from any
Christian religious activity. Priests recognize the commercial
value of cattle to their owners while appearing to ignore their
sacramental importance; yet for the Sukuma, cows sanctify marriage, are their only means of social and religious immortality,
and are used in ancestor propitiation ceremonies as symbolic of
the family's lineal obligations.

The Church ignores this, whereas the social situation would
seem to presuppose the immediate success of an approach like
that of St. Francis to a people who see spiritual values in their livestock. Even if it is argued that the modern Sukuma looks at his
cattle in purely economic terms, there is still no case for excluding
his worries on this account from the consolation of Christianity.
The farmer has the consolation of a harvest festival; there is no
need to presuppose that the trader should be deprived of parallel rituals associated with his distinctive problems.

Also care must be taken to see that their existing values are not
upset; the rich man has no desire to exhibit his full herd in one
place for reasons of jealousy. Similarly, ritual attention to bride-
wealth cattle might well raise additional difficulties, although
there seems to be a parallel between the symbolism of the blessing
of the ring and the passage of bride-wealth cattle or money from
one family to another. Even the crudest cash payment can surely
be graced with some religious significance; the coin used in the
wedding service to symbolize the maintenance of the marriage
can symbolize other aspects; the coins once provided by the father-
in-law in the marriage of an Englishman to a Spaniard appeared
to have great significance for a series of their family marriages.

The blessing of cows symbolic of the herd, at some time of the
year, would seem to be a very necessary rite. So often discussions
on these issues eventually end up in considering the partiality of a
particular innovation. The priest is naturally concerned about
the solemnity of the service and the cows can be troublesome; it
could of course be done in the home, but then there would be no
solemnity connecting the cows with the marriage. Such ritual
blessings would not only assist the Christian in a matter which
has always been particularly sensitive to Church interference, but

it would also bring the unconverted within the paraliturgical orbit of the Church in a way nearest to their hearts.

Similarly, the blessing of tools on St. Joseph's day has attracted
large congregations drawn from the whole area and every occupation. The blessing of cow-bells would be a start as a direct adaptation from the remembrance of ancestors through specific bell-
hung cows and goats. Surely the Hospice of St. Gothard found a
way to incorporate its dogs into Christian ritual, with a crucifix
over their kennels and medallions around their necks, with
quite as much justification as the Sukuma would have for similar
acts, since they have done so for their religiously significant cattle, goats, and sheep for many generations past.

The Church has also had an annual blessing of pets in other
countries with far less justification than in Usukuma, where the
cow is very near the center of their lives. Possibly if a Mass were
said for cows in just the same way as for seeds, a few representative cows would appear at the church or, much more conveniently, the ceremony would concern only cow bells, which could
line the sanctuary steps. Such imaginative use of liturgical opportunities would be far less time- and labor-consuming than the creation of the paraliturgical spectacles usual on the major feast days.

Another important critical stage in Sukuma life has been similarly neglected. It would not be too strong to say that the Sukuma
live in a state of almost permanent agricultural crisis. The soils of
Usukuma are not particularly fertile, surface water is inadequate for most of the year, and the rainfall is irregular not only
in its gross fall but also in its distribution. The average Sukuma
cultivator lives from one year to the next in a condition of fluctu-
ating hope and anxiety, both increased by the mounting desires
for what money can buy to alleviate his hard life. A Presbyte-
rian minister from Scotland, describing the indifference of his
former parishioners to any Church activity, commented nevertheless that few missed the annual harvest-festival service. It is difficult to believe that the Sukuma, who are just as involved and even
more dependent on the harvest, would not react similarly.

Some priests have described prayers in times of drought and
implied that they were not particularly well attended, possibly
because the prayers were general rather than particular. Usukuma

rainfall is notoriously uneven, or conversely, Sukuma effort to co-incide with rain is irregular, but possibly the prayers should have been directed at particular areas or people. Rainworkers' activities in the past were prompted by individuals or groups in trouble, and only rarely was the crisis sufficiently general for everyone in a chiefdom to be involved. Anyway, in the past the chief was involved every year in a cycle of ritual activities necessary for maintaining the welfare of his chiefdom.

It can be presupposed that a harvest festival would be successful, just as the St. Joseph's day blessing of tools is, because every person would be there bringing his offering, something personalized. If these offerings are retained afterwards for parish charities, possibly they would not respond, but if at least part of their offerings were to be taken home to sanctify the stored harvest, then there would surely be intense personal interest within a traditional idiom. In any case, the Sukuma surely cannot be left to the vagaries of nature without consistent religious support.

Similarly in some places the annual blessing of the seeds on All Souls' Day has been an outstanding success. The seeds alone would interest them and the ritual, with its parallels from the past and in combination with a church feast, for the ancestors, is in accord with what used to be carried out traditionally. Christians flock to the service, even those who have not been to Mass during the whole of the previous year, as well as numbers of non-Christians. This blessing of the seeds has been so popular that non-Christians have sent their seeds to the service with the Christians or begged some from them afterwards.

Priests readily accept in principle the need for this attention to critical stages or conditions, but then they have doubts, for when the Christian Sukuma has seen the practice of magico-religious rites in his own community, he may see in these Christian rituals a parallel magical action. They fear that *ex opere operato* will be carried too far and far too generally for the Sukuma, so that the whole of Catholic ritual to them becomes a magical system. They look for spiritual understanding and development, not mere ritualism; perhaps this can be overcome by having these special blessings as a part of a lengthier and more comprehensive service.

We are thus faced in Usukuma with a situation in which the rites concerning critical stages, which were previously centrally important to communal and family life, have been downgraded, or are entirely absent in Christian ritual, with the Church concentrating its religious practice on the Sacrifice of the Mass as the central rite of its observance. Some priests, questioned about their attention to the Sukuma critical stages, state that they have never been asked for such ceremonies. They admit that such ceremonies are available and refer to them as gimmicks—they are utterly wrong. These events are the very core of a Sukuma's life and the Church cannot afford to forget them.

The changes inaugurated by Vatican Council II have put the Church into the lead again in some directions. The whole movement of Christianity is one of leading toward a better spiritual and physical life and it should not wait upon requests for action whenever the Sukuma should get around to expressing them. Sacrifice, while occurring in most of their traditional rituals concerning rites of passage, was certainly not central to them and occupied such a position only in the propitiatory rites which were occasional rather than regular in the lives of most Sukuma. In recent years these rites have depended more on misfortune and the need to regain ritual neutrality than on regular observance and propitiation for the development and maintenance of a satisfactory spiritual life.

Some priests recognize the importance of these matters to the Sukuma but say that they should receive no special significant treatment from the Church since these problems will change with time. This again is surely entirely wrong; it is to fail to support an individual in his present problems on the grounds that they will disappear and presumably be replaced by others. It is not suggested that anything fundamental should be changed, merely that the Church should emphasize what the Sukuma emphasize.

Surely it is this separation of the Church's practicality from the everyday problems of little people that makes Christianity unreal to them. Most priests would agree about harvest festivals, but millions no longer harvest but do business. The annual striking of the firm's balance of profits and loss is analogous to the harvest, and if the community survives through plastic cups and curtain cloth, then the associated problems need the blessing of the Church. No priest would question that Christianity is the answer to life's problems, but may he not be taking it as the answer to his problems and negating its applicability on a wider scale? It seems that the Mass must be so orientated that it serves the needs of the people; it should not be a question of the people's considering the need of the Church for a particular type of devotion.

CHAPTER VI

The Problem of
Christian Exactitude

SINCE THE RITUALS of the Sukuma are not written down, the exactness of Church rituals is a constant source of difficulty. There are few, if any, actions in customary rites which have to be done for the validity of a ceremony, and an examination of Sukuma coronations[6] showed that the variety of the composing rituals had been greatly diminished over the years and yet the chiefs concerned were still considered to be validly installed. In fact, Sukuma ritual is so haphazard to our Western way of thinking that any such injunction would be impossible to carry out; the necessary man is suddenly sick, someone cannot obtain a particular ingredient, another forgets a section of the ritual, and another cannot pay the fees. There is just not the functional ability there for exactness.

Marriage in this sense alone is a head-on clash, the question of monogamy apart, between exactness in time of the Church ritual, and the Sukuma necessity of allowing ways to be kept open for the solution of future conflicts. There is no clash in other rites of passage; in infant baptism or the social incorporation of the child into the family in the traditional name-giving ceremony, the ritual is only a preliminary to the slow development of the personality either socially or spiritually, despite the assumption of the Church that there has been a fundamental and immediate change.

Similarly in burial ritual there is in fact no exactness either, although it is the burial or social end of an individual who is no

---

[6] R. E. S. Tanner, "The Installation of Sukuma Chiefs in Mwanza District, Tanganyika," *African Studies,* Vol. 16, No. 4 (1957), pp. 197-209.

longer capable of exercising his role. Rather it is the preliminary
to the development of the social roles of those inheriting the positions of the dead person. This explains the relative unimportance of the burial itself and the far greater importance attached
to the later ceremonies, in which these new social positions are
defined. No one is bound socially by being baptized in infancy,
or buried, or by participation in these rites; in the former the
child has little social importance in its own right and in the latter
the distribution of the property has far more importance for all
than the actual burial.

The baptism of the child and the burial of the deceased Christian may be social opportunities which the Sukuma, with his understanding of the intricacies and balances of relationships, may
be very loathe to forego. The following of Christian ritual ensures
the benevolence of the Church and it may be cheaper and involve
less time-consuming organization in the home. The graveyard
burial may leave obligations of remembrance to the parish rather
than to themselves, and at least it gets the dead out of the way and
decently disposed of, which might in their opinion fulfill traditional obligations in a more binding manner.

Christian burial may serve its religious purpose in underlining
the prospects of eternal life for the deceased, but its concentration on the dead makes it of little use to the survivors. The ritual
of death in traditional life was a function of the survivor's social
life and more attention in Christian practice should go to the relatives of the deceased. Even with the family in decay each family
has its acknowledged head for whom a ceremony of blessing might
be indicated.

Few Sukuma can easily accept the notion of a ceremony as
complete in itself, but the point is not an issue in either Christian
or traditional baptism and burial. But it is difficult to find the
exact moment of a traditional marriage, and it is safe to say only
that at any given moment the couple are rather more than less,
or less than more, married than at a previous time. The Christian
ceremony is exact and the net has closed on a couple who have
only minor social importance. Such exactness is alien to the flexi-
bility in social relationships which has always been fundamental
to their communal life.

This exactness, not only in time, but in the liturgy itself, must also give rise to considerable tension. The Sukuma must draw a distinction between the orderliness of the Church, dependent at all times on writing, and the disorderliness of their traditional rituals, in which there is an observable cohesion to their cultural patterns but a complete absence of exactness. Ceremonies for the same purpose are similar but not exact replicas of each other as is the case with Mass.

It is not suggested that moral exactness should be relaxed, but that the exactitude in ritual should be relaxed and that minor movements and proportions should no longer be the subject of deep and protracted centralized discussion and decision. There are, of course, grave dangers that this may lead to schismatic activity, but the obverse is just as valid: that the Sukuma may see the ritual inexactness of schism as more to their liking in the face of all that the Church may do.

In the anointing of the abbot of a Catholic monastery, the ritual is both so long and so complex, in order to stress its importance to the participating community and to their guests on the periphery of their communal life, that the ceremony requires little social support other than that the latter should not be sent hungry away, but this is a religious community in action, a situation in which the religious and secular activities are so closely interwoven that they are undistinguishable. This can now exist only in monastic institutions and to a certain extent in communities relatively unaffected by Western man.[7]

The Church continues with its exactness, as the Sukuma sees it, at a time when he is separating his political life from his religious life for the first time. Furthermore, possibly he is tending to see his Christian adherence in opposition to his life in the community as an independent African in his own country. This does not appear to be the appropriate time for stressing both the centralization of ritual changes and adherence to a fixed set of ritual rules.

---

[7] *Cf.* Emile Durkheim, *The Elementary Forms of Religious Life.* Trans. by Joseph Ward Swain. New York: Free Press, 1965.

CHAPTER VII

The Need for Sukuma
Christian Ritual

THE SUKUMA RELIGIOUS system in its historic form as a series of largely corporate acts of family, clan, and chiefdom has been in decay for many years and has been replaced by individual secretive acts for retaining health and property. Its corporate function has gone forever and the success of Christianity must lie in the provision of something satisfying for the individual and his family, even if it may no longer be able to do so effectively for the larger groupings.

The narrow margin between disaster and success in Sukuma life, the very shortness of life itself, must be remembered all the time, and religious activity must be concentrated on the points of tension in their lives, plain survival in terms of fertility in family, cows, and crops. Rituals concerning factors peripheral to these dominant preoccupations are found to be peripheral to their religious interests.

This change to Christianity of individuals and families may not be so dangerous for the maintenance of harmonious relationships within each community as might be surmised. The practice of traditional ritual was diffused among large numbers of individuals, depending on their political, social, and economic positions corresponding to their ownership of stock, their cultivation of fields over a wide area, and their age, marital relationships, and surviving children. There was no concentration of ritual in a few hands directly related to the survival of the community and its effective unity, such as might be expected in a village depending for its existence on a limited supply of water, where conversion would be much more disruptive.

It is possible that in Sukuma life, just as corporate religion has decayed, the family has suffered a comparable decay, because of cash crops and labor migration, and Christianity may never be able to provide a satisfactory community ritual against these trends. Its only chance of success may lie with the individual rather than with the family, with those who may see in Christianity of one sort or another an antidote to the growing impersonality of their lives.

Sukuma traditional religion was once an important factor in the need for harmony within the family, clan, and chiefdom. It typified a unity both symbolic and actual when there was no alternative to their existing way of life—religious, social, or economic. Christianity provides an alternative to the traditional religious system, but it is now only one of many socioreligious alternatives which a Sukuma can choose, not only for life in general but within Christianity itself since outside their area there are different Christian groups, run from missionary centers, as well as some purely African separatist churches. Even the Catholic Church, now in every part of the area, has not now, and is not likely to have in the future, a ritual association between itself and the general welfare of the community which would necessitate universal participation for the maintenance of success and the prevention of failure.

The result of this diffusion of alternatives is that the community is no longer able by means of traditional ritual to enforce the conformity of divergent individuals or to control problems which threaten their apparent unity, and Christianity cannot function this way either, and indeed would not wish to do so. The Church does little ritually for the community as a whole to express either their joys or their problems. The observer tends to feel that the Church offers itself to the Sukuma on its own terms, that the Church must be approached by the Sukuma and not the other way around. Where the Church has been successful it can be regarded as God's grace, but it should at the same time be examined on purely analytical grounds, to discover what the Church has done which the Sukuma like; time enough later to consider whether their replies have religious or purely social significance.

In no sense is a cynical approach suggested, for example, that

the Church should be run on the lines of a management consult-
ancy, but surely the early suggestion of Pope Gregory quoted by
Bede remains valid. The occasion of independence was celebrated religiously almost everywhere, but ritual action for rain
shortage, harvest success, plagues, and famines seems to be more
noticeable by its absence.

Bishops have indeed for some time had the power to change
the dates of the Ember Days, which correspond in Europe to the
agricultural cycle, but apparently they have not done so. Individual priests have obtained permission for changes when they asked,
but it appears that the majority "follow the Missal for want of a
better day," a curious lack of perception. Even so, the Missal itself
provides votive orations for many situations, including those for
rain, in time of famine, etc. Furthermore, the Prayer of the Faithful, recently added to the Mass, is meant to include the very particular intentions of the local community.

The success in most parishes of the Corpus Christi and Palm
Sunday processions and the Easter festivities shows that the Sukuma welcome opportunities to celebrate religious occasions and
that to have such celebrations in the parish gives a more personal
incentive and pleasure than seems to be the case with nationwide
festivities. It has been said that the Sukuma welcome any opportunity for a holiday, but this is perhaps natural, since few are in
regular employment and the majority look after their farms and
livestock and cannot therefore have the regular holidays of the
wage-earner.

Despite the changes in community life and the ritual associated
with it which are typified by the removal of all Sukuma chiefs
from executive roles, which had been indistinguishable from their
underlying ritual position in the eyes of the people, the need for
such ritual is still felt and particular disasters call forth communal
explosions badly in need of control through appropriate ritual.
The mass murders of old women suspected of being "witches" in
the Nassa district of Mwanza in September 1963, triggered by the
sudden death of a child, showed mob action which could have
been controlled only by the chief supported by the ritual power
of his office, which was responsible for the general welfare of the
chiefdom.

From discussions with some of those involved it seems clear that the overt action of the Church amidst these dreadful occurrences was purely secular, the humane actions of sheltering or removing menaced persons, the same actions that would have been taken by a government official doing his duty in the face of mob violence. No one mentioned any Church religious action for the purpose of drawing attention to the moral dangers in which these parishes were standing. Special, well-advertised Masses for articular intentions would have increased the moral strength of the Church in an issue which many of the Sukuma concerned must have known to be wrong, and in which they had no one to guide them. The secular activity was understandable but seemed to be mere reaction to the forces of evil.

In the absence of any possibility of Christian communities of similar ideology, the most the Church can hope for or aim at is the creation of Christian families, but it does not seem that there is much emphasis to ensure family participation in such Christian rituals. Family prayers and the possession of devotional objects in the house are encouraged, but such activities are not subject to religious sanctions. This failure to support and require external signs of family unity, particularly outside the home, except as a function of the individual seeking interior grace, means that the family, still the most important unit in their present-day life, has been given no definite Christian expression in ritual in regard to adversity, conflict, or success.

The compulsion or need to attend or create Christian rituals is so loose that ritual does not serve to express unity or to delineate socially approved or accepted divisions in the family. For example, the inevitable split between father and son, which used to be symbolized by the son's using fire from his father's house for the first fire in his own, is ignored by the Church. The son starting his own social life as a family man is without the support of appropriate Christian ritual. Since traditional ritual was in the hands of family heads, the transition to family prayers would seem to be easy, but this has not proved to be so. Traditional ritual was individual, with prayers related to the family's ritual paraphernalia, whereas there is no such individuality in Christian family prayers. There is little in them to enhance the status of the family head.

In the Musoma diocese, adjacent to Sukumaland, during 1956-58, in the months of May and October, there was a daily procession through the streets, with a statue of the Blessed Mother and the recitation of the rosary. On the first night the procession left from the Church, and on the second from the house of the Catholic family to which the group had progressed the previous evening. Neighbors came to say the rosary at the little private altars which had been set up in the homes of Christians to which the statue was brought in procession. The rosary was led by the head of the house if he was able and willing. More imaginative use can be made of this need to reconstitute the identity of the head of the family as one having ritual power.

In the change from one form of religious practice to another, the Church must evolve rituals in which the laity participate, but which they do not necessarily have to comprehend in order to be satisfied religiously, because most rituals provide satisfactions which are not intrinsic to the rites themselves—in fact, a series of what might be termed "theological fringe benefits," benefits which the Church itself will not regard as essential to the purely theological work for the salvation of individual souls.

A Christian service without a certain amount of nonessential ritual is at a disadvantage in attracting the Sukuma, who, although they may not have practiced traditional rites themselves, have witnessed them or have some private conception that rituals must be complicated if they are to be efficacious. A bare Church with a celebrant who may be indistinguishable from themselves contains little that will be in harmony with their traditional culture. It is only necessary to remember that the magician dresses differently at his rites, that he robes in private before carrying out ritual activity, and uses paraphernalia which he himself can usually explain but which his followers do not have to know in order to be convinced of their ritual values. In the performance of a family ritual, nothing is secret, in the sense that it is not carried out secretly. The family is standing around for most of the time rather than participating in the worship, but the rite is nevertheless secret because only the celebrant knows the full key to potential success.

The current stress on the laity's understanding the ritual performed at the altar may well be a move destined to a large measure of failure. The individual practices his religion because it gives him satisfaction and relief, but this may be totally separate from any intellectual perception of the rites themselves. Belief that a religion is divinely revealed is of far more value to the strength of a church than any degree of understanding of doctrine that does not relate to believers' needs or aspirations.

The dialogue Mass may in fact be totally irrelevant to the needs of those practicing their faith, and the dangers of doctrinal explanations of the Mass are obvious where the Mass may appear to be a human sacrifice and cannibalism in allegory. Non-Christians have remarked that when the Christians eat their God every Sunday, it ill behooves them to comment on disgusting traditional rituals. It may well be argued that Sukuma converts are not taught this and that we are dealing with a theological mystery that cannot be explained. They receive *kwegela*, the Sacrament, at Mass with the idea of nearness, and it does seem that the essential directness of Catholic dogma in Latin on this issue may have been missed in translation.

In summary, the Church, while not neglecting conversion and the problems of the catechetical class, should plan its activities around the essentials of Sukuma life. Explanation of Church teaching and the immense effort put into homiletics are ancillary to the fact that the Church itself does not attract as much as it should if it has in fact a doctrine of practical moral value to all men of all ages. The Church indeed has a plan for the salvation of souls, but souls are in human bodies with individual and cultural needs, and what is needed is a consideration of these rather than a purely religious approach. Secular planning, in fact, is required, so that the Church may control the moral values and the essential rituals.

PART FOUR

THE ADOPTION OF
CHRISTIANITY

CHAPTER I

Christian Ecology

THE SUKUMA have a culture in which the extent and uniformity of their habitat, allied to its unattractiveness to outside cultures and economic influences, have combined to make them, if not resistant to change, at least slow to succumb to outside influences, if compared to the Chagga and Haya. These two tribes, living in well-watered areas, attracted outside influence and interest and, as a consequence of the accident of their geography, are not only progressing economically but have acquired a high proportion of the positions requiring education, because of the concentration of schools in their locality, which has increased rather than diminished with the years.

The Sukuma, living widely spread out on a steppe almost devoid of surface water, have not had many schools and for the same reason mission activity has been widely spaced and available to relatively small numbers of the people. The impact of Christianity on the Chagga and Haya was both immediate and universal, so that "paganism," a word widely used to cover any traditional religious system independent of both Islam and Christianity, ceased to exist many years ago.

Any Christian activity there automatically came within the walking orbit of thousands of people, to whom the very newness of this faith, combined with economic attractions brought in its wake, brought them to an interest in receiving instruction. Whether they went as far as baptism was relatively unimportant in terms of total social change, because Christian social ideas became the background to their new way of life, which was brought about more directly by external economic and political events; so-called pagan activities became probably no more influential than they are in Europe and America. Those who turned away from Christianity began to have the same ideas on Christian social matters as those who had actually become Church members. Traditional religious ideas, as a social force, had almost disappeared.

The Sukuma, on the other hand, except in the small areas which could be reached from the few missionary centers, remained almost untouched by the appeal of this new faith which was combined with opportunities for Western education and medical facilities. Even in recent years, the movement toward Christianity in the north has not had any parallel activity in the south. In the former areas a fair proportion of those signing up for baptismal courses now have some peripheral knowledge of Christian principles; they know at least that Sunday observance is not too strict and that the Catholic Church does not prohibit so much as the Protestants.

It was not only a shortage of missionary staff but a shortage of initiating and maintenance money that made missionary stations few and far between and accounted for the concentration in them of all available staff and funds. This attention to material progress, without incorporating the laity into responsibility for decision making and for financial and physical support for the work, probably with the best of intentions to hurry on progress, has meant in some places that Christians often feel that the parish belongs to the priest and not to them. They realize only too well that most missionary priests tend to want everything done in a hurry, so that they have only to remain patient and the priest will get the work done himself, with the help of charitable contributions from his own country, without getting any commitment at all from his own parishioners.

It is only recently that Catholics, through the availability of American priests and funds, have been able to create two dioceses and to subdivide parishes, and thus make Christianity geographically available to larger numbers of Sukuma than had been the case when the area was administered solely by the White Fathers.

Thus the initial problem in considering the adaptation of Christianity to Sukuma conditions has been one of coinciding with the limitations imposed by their social ecology. Here the priest in charge without an assistant may be a greater power for the creation of a Christian community than an almost monastic community of several priests, isolated by distance from real contact with large numbers of Sukuma.

It is probable that the White Fathers' rule of three priests or Brothers at each mission station, imposed when transport between churches was not easily possible by motorcycle, is still necessary for providing continuity over times of leave and sickness. Furthermore, the necessary tolerance for living with one's fellow priests and Brothers may well have been a valued support in their times of difficulty as well as a restraint on too strong an individualism.

The Maryknoll missionaries, with their policy of more missionary stations with smaller staff, are better adapted to the conversion of these people and their retention within self-supporting Christian communities, although it imposes a serious strain on their priests. Someone may not be suited to such isolation, not so much because of his family background but because of his seminary training. Living in a totally alien environment brings personality problems, which can be allayed to some extent by a community life at the mission station; isolation in a foreign country and without the constant support in faith and in companionship of one's own kind is a constant strain. Humanitarian as well as spiritual considerations suggest that it is not wise to have parishes with only one priest.

Comparable studies among the Hangaza of the West Lake region have shown that viable churches, whose faith and practice is dependent on the use of the sacraments, can exist only where priests are available, irrespective of whether there is a nucleus of believing Christians or not. In Usukuma, the erection of a church with a resident priest automatically means that a Christian community will become centered upon it, and that itinerant priests, circulating by motorcycle and car, no matter how devoted and hardworking, will not have the same effect. The out-stations without doubt have been a success and their absence from the African Inland Church's program contributory to the small size of their following, and they have meant that most Christians can come to Mass once a month.

It is only necessary to stay for a short time in a parish priest's house to realize the difference his presence must make to his parishioners, not only for the regular provision of the sacraments, but for comfort in distress and advice in indecision. It is only human for the circulating priest to be drawn to his home, and that his attention is centered there. This is supported by the fact that short-term intensive campaigns for converts have been no more successful than the results of long-term personal contacts. Admittedly, large numbers sign up for instruction, but as soon as the personal element evaporates, so does the interest of the majority.

Sukumaland presents an enormous geographical challenge which the Church cannot effectively cover without increases in the numbers of priests before an increase in churches. The dioceses appear to be dangerously overextended through some failure to fully realize these geographical limitations. They have hurried to occupy non-Christian blanks on the map without realizing, possibly, that they are being drawn on more by a desire of the people for their social services than anything else, and that the subsequent shortage of staff would largely preclude the continuity of pastors that is essential for Christian communities.

CHAPTER II

The Priest and His Own Culture

BESIDES THE PROBLEM of geographical adaptation there is that of the adaptation of the missionary staff themselves, who come from Western Europe and America, to the cultures in which they have to work. Throughout their lives they have learnt and lived their own cultures and these have coincided with the prolonged training they received in the seminary before they were sent abroad for pastoral work. It is difficult for them to distinguish between the fundamentals of Christianity as a faith of universal appeal and what is just the social practice of their own cultures. There is nothing wrong in the priest's practicing his own culture, and in doing so, propagating it for the Sukuma to select which aspects they prefer and which they reject. He is then an element in a never-ending process of social change, but it could be expressed as enforcing an alien culture by implied religious sanctions.

Perhaps the greatest difficulty which this missionary priest has got to overcome is the feeling that his parishioners are not people but Africans instead, which makes it necessary for them to be given special treatment, the "we must always remember that they are not quite there" attitude which insidiously creeps into his consciousness from his constant battles to reconcile two different cultures. Few priests really accept or even consider the close parallels between individual Christianity and parish practice in Usukuma and in their own countries. It is as if Sukuma marriage problems were something entirely the fault of the Sukuma themselves as opposed to the fact that these problems predominate in church work everywhere, or that lack of cooperation were something peculiarly Sukuma.

It is too easy to reach facile conclusions as to these characteristics seemingly associated with one order; perhaps an order containing the nationals of only one country is more prone to adopt these attitudes than one in which the seminary and postordination training involves close contact and possibly adaptation to other national attitudes. They expect to find in Usukuma the signs of cultural values which are probably just as absent in their own cultures.

A priest says that it is impossible to hold an intelligent conversation with a Sukuma; "It is just cows, fields, wives, and local politics." Everyone anywhere in the world talks about the matters in which he is deeply involved and the conversations of his own home town would be just as barren to the outsider. If by intelligent conversation is meant conversation which is not personally involving those present and their problems, he will have to go into very select and highly specialized groups indeed; or does he mean that what interests him does not interest the Sukuma and vice versa? This is a serious matter for more personal consideration. Priests talk well and earnestly about their parish problems, but the question as to whether this or that does not equally occur in an Italian, Polish, Southern, or other American parish often seems to be an entirely new idea to them.

In addition, the status of the missionary as opposed to the African clergy has undergone a very radical change over the period of national independence. In theory his position was always separate from that of the colonial civil servant; in practice he was seen as the same. He may not have had a privileged position by law, but in fact he was treated with the deference accorded to most Europeans. Now, within a few years he has become an alien, tolerated, indeed, for the services which he is giving but nevertheless generally not particularly welcome; in effect he is on sufferance for the services which he may or may not be able to provide. It is essential to realize that the personal devotion of many colonial civil servants and the good which may well have been done during the colonial period have been overlaid by a political folklore of oppression that has made the average Sukuma prejudge the potential work of any European or American whom he encounters, while still treating him somewhat in the old-style manner.

This is perhaps the broad political picture, but at the parish level the priest may indeed appear to be too paternalistic and will be severely criticized for his attitude to the new African. Unless he puts the administration of charity in the hands of his parish council or a special committee, he is forced into paternalism by the incessant begging to which he is subjected with a servility of approach that no Sukuma would attempt with one of his own kind.

The new priest comes to Sukuma full of the enthusiasm of his calling and finds himself dealing with basic situations of which he has had no previous experience, and which are against the fundamental everyday policies of his own culture. Americans adhere to a certain forthrightness in personal contacts and do not appear to be devious in attempting to get what they want; the Sukuma, who live under different conditions, carry face-to-face politeness to excess. They are a polite people who have a natural dignity in their community life and rarely speak their minds; anger and irritation are not externalized.

Priests have remarked on the formal courtesy with which bitter enemies treat each other outside the courthouse, where villification is accepted; they also notice that non-Christians who have acted strongly against the Christian members of their family are nevertheless always polite in talking to the priest. This is not deliberate deception but the normal way of downgrading tensions which would otherwise disrupt their lives. They talk out disputes so that a compromise evolves in which both win and lose something and are able once more to live together. If the priest in a dispute of any sort feels that he has won his point, he is either misinformed as to what the final decisions amounted to, or he has forced a situation on the participants which will leave nothing but resentment behind. He must balance his participation in any dispute so that he has cards to throw away as well as retaining a hand that will gain him a reasonable number of tricks but not an overwhelming victory.

The newcomer is also disorganized by the fact that the Sukuma do not follow the time; the priest has lived by the clock for years and the Sukuma have few watches. Time changes with the weather; on rainy or overcast days the morning starts later and on hot days the early hours are shorter because more has to be done in that time. When it is not possible to measure time, it is therefore impossible to know how long work takes and accordingly how much time to plan for. It is not possible to arrive on time because the time of leaving is not determined.

The whole question of exactness is foreign to the Sukuma; he has no measure of distance and no measure of weight and volume in his own culture with which to attempt to standardize values; possibly the four-gallon kerosene tin is the nearest thing to a universally accepted unit of measure. So all these values expand and contract according to those involved and the problem involving them. Time, for them, is making the most of an adventitious opportunity; the unexpected shower means immediate planting activity and the available life in a car makes it necessary to visit a distant relative.

The missionary in his own culture has clearly defined personal rights, not so much according to the legal rules accepted by his country, but through everyday practices which no one in his own community would ever question. It appears to him in Sukumaland that everyone wants something for nothing, but this is in fact the cultural response of anyone who is not visibly economically equal to his neighbors. No amount of explanation that it is demeaning to beg will have much effect, and the only answer is to have nothing to be borrowed or begged. Some have found that the only solution of the problem of being asked for loans is to have no money on their persons, so that they can turn out their pockets in public or, alternatively, attempt to borrow from an incipient borrower.

The Sukuma's idea of personal privacy is apparently not related to areas, but rather to and from certain persons. He may have certain rights to land or to his compound, but that does not give him the feeling that he can prevent people from passing over or through it. His house is not a privileged private area, entry to which must be by invitation, but it would be closed to certain classes of people. He would not enter if his mother-in-law were inside and vice versa. The Sukuma just do not have exclusive rights in which someone can say "this is mine" and no one else has any direct or indirect influence on what can be done with it. So he has difficulty in understanding the priest's obvious conviction that he has certain exclusive rights over property.

Privacy as a European or American understands it is possible only at night, when the Sukuma do not move outside their houses and their compounds. It is fruitless to expect them to respect a priest's privacy during the day; the very fact that he is there means that he is available for them to approach. The Sukuma, from their experience of trying to contact Europeans in their homes, know that this is an area of special difficulty and mutual tension, so that if there is any real acceptance of his ideas of privacy, he would seem to have lost contact with his parishioners in an important way.

In the priest's own country it is possible to assume that there is an area around each person, according to his status, in which he is free from being jostled or crushed. The higher the status, the larger this area becomes; the rich and important certainly have these areas of privacy around them. The Sukuma do not express importance in this way, and the traditional chief never expected or received any such treatment. If anything, status is shown in one way by the presence of many people near the person concerned. A chief was almost lost in the crush at his coronation and on every public occasion at which crowds were present. In the Sukuma's everyday affairs there has never been any of the spatial separation on which Europeans and Americans overseas place so much importance.

The missioner has been brought up to be independent and to stand on his own two feet and possibly this is a fundamental American and European cultural value. Dependence on others would be classified as weakness or lack of character, but the Sukuma value interdependence rather than dependence, and this is not so much a desirable cultural trait but rather the basic system by which their society holds together. They do not see mutual give-and-take as a series of independent events having little or no bearing on each other, but as a continuum in which people are bound together by debts and demands over a period of years and possibly even over generations.

These interrelationships make each individual very dependent on the communal will or consensus. It would be almost impossible for him to live without the community's agreement to his being there; without it he could get no help in sickness or to bury his dead; he could not build his house or harvest his fields without some measure of help; no one would answer his alarm call for help, and his cattle might be driven from the water and his wife and children denied companionship. The fear of boycott still makes the Sukuma conform to his community's wishes, and makes the boycott an effective weapon for local control.[1]

Also, the Sukuma have a very fine sense of what is reasonable and unreasonable in these relationships and they have many indirect ways of avoiding unwelcome attentions which in themselves do not give offence but which are stylized for overcoming difficult situations. Few Sukuma will give a personal answer concerning their property, and the priest, when he refuses to be personally implicated and puts charity in the hands of the parish elders, is not being clever, he is merely behaving as a Sukuma would behave in similar situations. In their lives there is not a single political, economic, or social activity in which unilateral action is readily accepted or possibly even permitted.

It is also necessary to recognize that it is just as essential to grasp the everyday implications of these basic differences; the Sukuma cannot apply American or European values to changes in their lives. For example, the lavatory is not a feature of their lives and when it exists their culture has not yet allowed the surrounding social usages to be created, so that no one has the obligation to see that it is clean. The missionary should be wary of laying this obligation on particular persons.

They would borrow from the priest or beg from him, but these actions become offensive only because they are taken out of the idiom of Sukuma life. People know from experience that the priest will not take payment in Sukuma terms because it would inconvenience him at the best or be unpleasant for him at the other extreme. If the priest did exact repayment, by living with the households which have used him, then there would be a better understanding of the mutual obligations involved and possibly also the priest's closer entry into their lives. The difficulty comes when value judgments are made that inhibit the Sukuma from

---

[1] Cf. R. E. S. Tanner, "Law Enforcement by Common Action in Sukumaland," Journal of African Administration, Vol. VII, No. 4 (Oct. 1955), pp. 159-170.

making their own choice, when the priest says that this is the correct way of doing a particular thing.

Some priests have come to realize that disorderly processions at Corpus Christi are as the Sukuma like them and that no disrespect is given or intended, while others expend great efforts to line everybody up. Some struggle to get small Sukuma organizations to reach decisions and develop individuals as leaders, because that is the way of parish organizations in their own countries. Others now realize that the Sukuma do not function this way, that there is no failure to their characters just because their society works to distribute decisions among many rather than to create leaders, and that the build-up of Christian social organizations will have to take place on their terms and not on the terms of alien cultures.

Others try to inject vigor into the congregational singing of a new melody by conducting in the aisle. It would be hard to find a greater contrast than between the Maryknoll Fathers, from an order largely composed of youthful priests bounding with physical and spiritual energy whose motto might well be "Come on, fellows, let's go," and the Sukuma with their alertness to linguistic nuances and their slowness to move from patterns laid down by their own traditions.

Despite the former's concept of the divine, he typifies Delavignette's "Man must put the world in order. This determination has the compelling power of a religion and the European is its prophet." [2] The Sukuma know the compelling drive of the European and the American to get on with the job; there is no essential difference in its effects whether it comes from a government official or a priest. They can see what the priest may want and, if it is what they want as well, they have infinite patience and they know that they have only to stall long enough and the priest will do it himself. This has to be stressed again and again, not because the Sukuma does nothing by himself, but because to him the parallel is between the Church's drive and the government's drive, an invidious comparison for a spiritually backed organization.

---

[2] R. Delavignette, *Freedom and Authority in French West Africa*. London: Oxford University Press, 1950, p. 17.

Another more specific problem, particularly for the Maryknoll Mission, is that the priests are almost entirely from urban backgrounds and yet their life's work is with farmers. Goodwill and the wish to learn is absolutely no compensation for the farming knowledge acquired in a farming family. They can observe and intellectually understand the seasons, soils, and seeds, but they cannot feel and cannot think from the same basic assumptions that a farmer accepts unquestioningly.

There is then the double problem of different cultures and different economic backgrounds. From this difference in background the priest can fail to give the advice and genuine encouragement which anywhere is a part of their Christian service. The popular literature of the Church is full of pictures of priests participating —from cardinals dancing to curates playing baseball amid the happiness and appreciation of their parishioners—but in Usukuma the participation is minimal, nothing at all or mere attendance at some function. These priests were born and ordained apart and they remain as far apart as when Christianity first entered Usukuma.

Another aspect of this apartness which gained special notice from the Council is that collegiality is not something for the hierarchy alone to consider and practice but for the priesthood and people as well. Christianity cannot in practice be a question of set principles which the priest does his best to administer; there are the real moral problems of practice, which require the contribution of the laity to the knowledge and understanding of the priesthood. This has to be listened to, absorbed, and utilized. It cannot be a question of telling them, without ever listening to their needs. Otherwise the result in most parishes seems to be that, along with the propagation of the faith, the priests teach the social practice of their own cultures. By their very presence they are sweeping instruments of social change.

Priests' knowledge of the Sukuma culture in which they work is severely circumscribed by the requirements of their mission work. As the years move on, they learn a great deal about the marriage customs because Christians' failings in this direction become preeminent in most Church activity. In other fields their knowledge depends more on the personal inclinations of the missionary than on the requirements of his Christian administration of the parish. As Luzbetak says, "A missionary who studies native dwellings, agricultural techniques, wedding and funeral customs 'photographically' may be given credit for having an innocent and a partially useful hobby, but he certainly would not be following a scientific approach to the understanding of his people. [They] must be studied in all their details but *as they are functionally interlocked with the infinitude of human ways.*" [3]

There is also a real danger in these relatively untrained anthropological enquiries of their becoming either implied criticism or uncritical praise. It is extremely difficult to enter another society at any time without causing some sort of cultural disturbance; whether he likes it or not the newcomer is the one person who does not fit in. It is best, of course, to wait until the group becomes used to him, and they can become used to him as a parish priest but not as an enquirer.

He has divided his life quite clearly into two parts, pastoral office and the need to learn about the people, but to the Sukuma there is no division—he is just a priest making enquiries. They do not understand his need because they do not experience any such desire to be inquisitive about his country's way of life.

Very few persons have the patience, even if they have the time, to wait until the knowledge comes to them, and if the enquirer comes upon something that attracts his interest, he tends to start probing. It is almost inevitable that what excites his interest will be something that is strange to his own culture, such as witchcraft and magic, marriage customs, and so on, all subjects that are antagonistic to Christian ideals and rulings. It will be difficult for him to remain entirely neutral in his enquiries once they become specific rather than general.

When any enquiries are made, the first answer is almost inevitably what the answerer considers he ought to be doing; it is usually an historical answer which may be as much as 25 years out of date and possibly the views of the elders of a particular community who have a special interest in bringing the past to life again. Certain reports of priests about the workings of the traditional religion of the Sukuma contain interesting and knowledgeable accounts of what the Sukuma thought they did in the past, but the recorders have recorded all this as present practice. The priest who is looking around for the same happenings in his parish, is expecting to find a particular practice, and the Sukuma are on edge almost at once because, although they cannot express it, they worry over the difference between their present and past lives and the enquiries must be a source of tension to them. He is treading on disturbed ground.

It is a strange experience to read these detailed and dedicated recordings of a corporate religious life which may not have existed for half a century. They take no account of all the changes that have taken place recently, and give the impression that there is still a battle to be fought with "paganism"—a term still used by the authors for various customary practices.

When the enquirer gets further into his subject, he will tend to take the replies of one man as generalities, to consider some particular thing to be Sukuma custom, whereas he has the statement of one man, who sees himself as giving evidence which may be used later, not necessarily against him, but he would not be human if he did not turn the explanation of local problems to his own advantage. It will no doubt be a very lucid tale and the man himself will be speaking the truth as he sees it, but it is only one side. The priest is rarely in a position to find and record the other side of this story; he may not have the required contacts in the one small community, nor the scope. Perhaps it would also be dangerous for him to press his enquiries so that he could gain this rational understanding; he would be interfering and becoming a factor, even if only a small one, in local power politics, and might lose his pastoral immunity.

Another failing of these partial investigators is that there is an almost automatic concentration, not on what is going right in the everyday life, but on what is going wrong or has gone wrong; if not this, on the abnormal elements in the communal life, out of proportion to their frequency and importance. For example, they are concerned about the supposedly large numbers of illegitimate babies in the parish, which is dysfunction from his cultural viewpoint, but even if what he supposes is true, the situation may be no more than one of the external signs of a change in Sukuma customary morality.

He is applying a set of answers to a different set of facts; between these two sets there is no relationship which could be useful in practice. Another example would be the missioners' interest in a certain Sukuma nun, who took her final vows against the fierce opposition of her father. They are entirely right to admire and support such a woman in her devotion to her vocation, but nevertheless it should be quite clear in their minds that they are supporting the abnormal behavior that is out of balance with Sukuma values and practices.

If this is accepted, with whom do they have contact and how can they learn Sukuma customs? The Church at the best, and certainly at the moment, is an independent power on the fringe of Sukuma life and the people are only too pleased to put onto the Church all the problems for which they themselves cannot conveniently find solutions. After all, if they were satisfied with their own culture, they would feel no need of Christianity at all or of anything else outside this culture, so the Church gets the poor, the sick, and probably the abnormal, as mendicants and maybe as informants as well.

It is not that the missionary priest has any specific feelings in this respect, but simply that he is more liable than the cultural anthropologist to become misinformed. He wishes devotedly to be, for the rest of his life, for the Sukuma and therefore looks for ways to transfer practices from his own to their culture; these get plastered on top of Sukuma practices but do not necessarily replace them and the actual function of the latter is overlooked. Thus it seems that while they are in the midst of Sukuma life, priests are often, in a quite remarkable way, not a part of it and often substantially ignorant of the local way of life except when a breach of morals is involved. When one of them seeks for knowledge and understanding he is, in fact, being dependent upon those who want him to be thus dependent.

Even when there is an interest in Sukuma life it seems to be more in the nature of an enquiring mind's searching into the customs, rather than an understanding mind's getting a knowledge of the function of each custom as a part of the whole which goes to make up each localized Sukuma community in the neighborhood. This nonfunctional approach to the understanding of Sukuma life is typified by the questionnaires on Sukuma customs that have been distributed in some parishes in the past. This, of course, solidifies particular customs in the eyes of the recorder and the subsequent readers, although in fact the responses almost always represent a process of compromise.

Good intentions, youth, and energy, alone or together, are not enough to create and maintain Christian communities in what are still largely traditional environments, unless they are accompanied by an understanding, not of what people do, but of why they do it. The widow agrees to be inherited so that she can remain with her children; the witness is not put on oath, for it recognized that he will speak in his own interest and it is pointless to expect anyone to tell the truth just because he is under oath in the government law courts.

The alien missionary, for alien he is, must adapt himself or herself to the Sukuma way of doing things, and it will never be enough to apply in Christian charity the social doctrines of their own cultures, or to go to the other extreme and become a Sukuma-phile so that much must be changed as soon as possible because it is European and not Sukuma, as may happen when the priest thinks that it is his own culture alone that stands in the way of understanding the Sukuma and bringing them to Christianity.

The intermingling of African and non-African clergy in the one parish would appear to be an essential requirement to a more human realization of Sukuma problems. A group of non-African clergy will unconsciously take an "us and them" attitude to the difficulties of their pastorate, while in a mixed religious community the issue must be submerged in a greater realization that these difficulties may in fact not be failings, but the ordinary day-to-day functionings of another viable culture.

It is not only in these various ways that the missionary priest is fenced off from full knowledge; there are, besides, the added difficulties and complexities of Kisukuma, which is a tonal language. Some priests have noted the contrast between the flow of language between Sukumas and the simplified usage employed when the Sukuma talk to them. The learning of a new language by any adult must at any time be a prolonged and difficult task, but it is strange that language problems have come up hardly at all in discussions concerning pastoral work. The translation of philosophical terms from one language to another is a difficult task, but no one seems to have questioned semantically the use of certain key words in Kisukuma or the use of Kiswahili words in the Kisukuma religious vocabulary.

There are any number of words which must suggest important considerations to any priest. The Kiswahili verb form that allows the phrase "to love one another" to be translated by one word (*kupendana*) seems to suggest that community or togetherness might well be a much more fundamental idea than it is in the Christian English-speaking West. The concept of ritual states (*busebu* in Usukuma) was found to be almost unknown to priests and in one parish "to sacrifice" was being translated as *kwikinja*, a verb that has mainly Moslem connotations.

It is difficult to expect the Sukuma to have a spiritual understanding of Christianity rather than a merely ritualistic use of it if the very core of their language has not been examined carefully and used with as much discrimination as would be used by a minor papal official in drafting a decision on a case involving canon law.

Another aspect which must be carefully considered before Kiswahili comes fully into liturgical use is the structure of that language itself. Kiswhahili is an expanding language from a center of largely Moslem culture and linguistic practice. The scholars of this language look to this center repeatedly for grammar and form, but the practice there is increasingly archaic, partially un-understandable to the majority of its users. In translations we must look for the simplified everyday usages, grammatically correct but not abstruse.

There is another interesting point, which may show that the transfer to Kiswahili may not be as difficult as has been suggested. The Church has trained its priests in Kisukuma at a language school or expected them to learn it within a specified period while working in a parish, and thereby Christian practice in Kisukuma has at least partly been carried on by its own momentum. But when there have been no Kisukuma-speaking priests available in

a boundary parish containing numbers of non-Sukuma, Kiswahili has been accepted by the faithful readily enough. Perhaps
the Church has been far too conservative in this respect; the
colonial government carried on most of its business in Kiswahili
in Sukumaland without any serious difficulty. Kisukuma became
an issue in politics only when it was used by people as a means of
asserting themselves politically in local government meetings; in
this way they forced the government official to use an interpreter,
thus demonstrating that he was the odd man out.

There is a considerable difference between an adequate utili-
tarian knowledge of a language and its use for religious purposes.
To be at one with people of another nation one must use the language with a lightness of touch that the listener appreciates as a
sophisticated use of his tongue. Both Kisukuma and Kiswahili
contain a wealth of proverbs, nicknames, and specialized words,
which are often far more useful for holding attention and creating confidence than any number of regular phrases. Yet there
seemed to be no one who was interested in these languages, which
are exciting in themselves, in spite of the fact that priests' working lives would be spent using them.

Perhaps in a subtle way they were not yet totally committed to
the separation from their homes and from their own language
and culture that is implied in a vocation to missionary service.
And furthermore it is not so much a Bantu as a Sukuma philos-
ophy that would merit serious consideration. However, an objection to Kiswahili that may well arise in due course among educated Christians is that its use in religion takes away from them
the English that they use to support their position.

Even if the priest is very fluent in the language, as many old
missionaries are, he is still not in a good position to learn the customs of the people, because as an alien and a priest he cannot mix
in village gossip, dancing, and the many other social ceremonies
that go on in the parish and in which both Christians and non-
Christians participate. Even the family visit is a special occasion
on which the missionary can only hear but not see what is going
on. If the priest's visit is known in advance, the family concerned
may resort to hide-and-seek with the devotional objects of Christianity and those of traditional religion. This might be the case

particularly when a priest comes to administer the Anointing of the Sick. The African priest is at an advantage here because he probably has had the experience of seeing such deceptions during his childhood.

There is also possibly the forgivable tendency to feel that one must put things right and that the Sukuma must change in order to absorb Christianity into their own culture. Theologically it would perhaps be truer to state that the consciousness of God existed in Usukuma before the missionaries arrived and that the priest's role is to develop this theological truth, rather than to plant something new. Protestant theologians would go further and state that Christ existed everywhere prior to evangelization: "We do not only go with Christ. We meet Christ in those to whom we go. . . . It is the very height of impiety to imagine that in any situation, or in any meeting with my fellow man, I arrive before God." [4]

The priest is supposed to exemplify Christ's injunction to "give all and follow me." The Sukuma may not have been able to discern this in the lives of their priests—African or alien—who, in their priesthood, appear to enjoy a standard of living immeasurably better, possibly, than even the richest of their parishioners. It is not so much clothes and cars which bring the priest into the category of a rich man (nsabi), and the rich Sukuma does express himself in this way, but the house. Some priests have said that when they moved from the more humble houses used when the parish was first started, the small gifts of food from the parishioners were not so readily forthcoming. The overseas priest has given much, but not in Sukuma terms, while the African priest may appear to have gained economically. In this context arises the very important question of how the priest is to be maintained by his parishioners.

This support can be in kind or in cash. To some extent it seems that the decline of parish visiting and the growth of administrative rather than pastoral functions in the priest's lives have moved them beyond the most obvious means of getting parish support. Less hierarchical and institutionalized religious systems

---

[4] Canon Max Warren, *Perspective in Mission*. London: Hodder and Stoughton, 1964, p. 21.

have their priests supported by their neighbors without any obvious strain on their pockets or consciences. Buddhist priests go
out to beg their food and Hindu priests receive it in offerings; perhaps only the Christian Church away from its European and
American focii expect this maintenance to be almost entirely in
terms of cash, a commodity which the Sukuma do not have much
of and which they traditionally regard as being available only for
the things that they cannot produce themselves. This economic
and social distinction between cash and kind has been suggested
for other parts of Africa[5] and there is no reason to suppose that
the Sukuma are fundamentally different.

By concentrating on cash contributions the Church is seemingly
putting itself in the category of things which are not naturally
a part of Sukuma life. It is not hard for the Sukuma to see that this
distinction is very valid; the priests are not dependent on them,
and the social aspects of contacts of priests and laity that are natural to an American or European parish are to a very large extent
absent. There is just no regular social contact between the parish
house and the parishioners.

Hospitality is as fundamental a feature of Sukuma life as it is
with most Americans and to a lesser extent English communities.
It has a moral connotation which few Sukuma would dare to
break—they do not think twice about feeding the stranger without the gates. They do not feed their priests because they do not
see them very often outside the church or parish office. Pastors of
the Anglican Church, whose stipends are infinitesimal and who
cannot, by reason of education or poverty, run such an institu-
tionally complex parish organization, are in fact maintained because outside church they carry out their pastoral duties in the
homes of their parishioners and have meals there as often as they
need or are needed. The Catholic priest seemingly is not similarly maintained, simply because he does not want to be.

Even the smallest parish of Catholics can feed a priest according to their own simple standards should the priest visit every
Catholic household once every quarter. Perhaps it would be too
crude to state that all he would have to do is function as a parish

_____
[5] Cf. Conrad C. Reining "The Role of Money in the Zande Economy," *American
Anthropologist*, Vol. 61, No. 1 (Feb. 1959), pp. 39-43.

rather than a church priest. The White Fathers in their early days were often maintained in this fashion and the growth of the Church as an institution has prevented priests from being supported by the parishioners, who would never deny such an obligation. Their rule that two days out of three must be spent on the mission station so that they can enjoy their community religious life prevents the use of this idea to its fullest extent, but other orders have no such rule. With the White Fathers, the rule of three meant that there were always two at the church and that in difficult times no one would be alone too long.

There is no danger that overseas priests, with cultural as well as biological views on eating, would carry out to excess the practice of eating at parishioners' homes. A priest may not like their food, but he can learn, and being hungry is one of the easiest ways to learn such an appreciation. He may fear infection, but it would be a foolish man who would predict that he is adequately protected in his own house and automatically infected outside. Water away from home can be sterilized and the food served is cooked, not raw.

These are hard things to suggest, but the Church was originally one with its people, and there were not two separate and parallel social systems. The Council has been stressing that the parish must be an organization of priests and people working together. This is not a counsel to practice asceticism but a counsel to have the same standard of living as the parishioners. The moral problems of Sukuma with full and empty stomachs are very different, and those who have no personal experience of the difficulties of survival and well being in this locality cannot truly understand this difference.

The pastoral literature of Christianity is full of experiments by which the Western priest in his own country can get near to the core of the separate problems besetting the Church. Even leaving aside the still continuing experiments with priest workers, there have been priests specializing in drug addicts, juvenile gangs, and down-and-out drunkards, and they have been able to get a measure of spiritual as well as material success only by identifying themselves with these special groups by making a conscious attempt to adapt, if not adopt, their mode of living so that they can experience and understand it. The parish priest is often an island of expatriate living and cannot really be regarded other than as an alien in intent as well as in fact.

A further difficulty of regular, defined contributions apart from their direct parallel to government tax collection is that this method separates the "haves" and "have nots" although they are of equal significance religiously. This is so even if written receipts are given to those who really cannot afford to pay so that they need not be embarrassed in attempting to continue their Christian practice. Receipts are given and become an issue—who has paid and who has not? And it seems most undesirable that the priest and the Church should be a demanding agency. As has been suggested above, it may be right to demand and expect in Sukuma terms but wrong to do it in other ways. Possibly the Church has got to make up its mind to be supported in Sukuma terms, since it does not require much imagination to suggest that it will never be accomplished otherwise.

The African clergy and Sisterhood are in a parallel, if not more complicated, position. The acceptance of their vocation has meant that they have been removed from their own communities, probably during adolescence and, through their long novitiate and seminary life, have become members of another culture. While the missionary may well never bother to consider whether his own or the Sukuma culture is a more suitable vehicle for the propagation of Christianity, the African religious has unconsciously been taught and has accepted the idea that Western practice of Christianity is superior to any local adaptations.

African priests and religious have become of high status in their own society, on a par with the highly educated as viewed by the common man. Apart from their superior knowledge of the language, the local priest or nun is often not the best informant, or even the best acquainted with local customs. He not only weighs the Sukuma culture against the Western-orientated seminary culture of his training period, but also in terms of his relationship with the priests with whom he is living and associating, so that even with a knowledge of his own culture, he may be subject to as many cultural prejudices as the overseas priest. Perhaps, within the bounds of Christian charity, he feels that he has risen above the need to consider seriously Sukuma practice, as opposed to Western Christian practice, as meriting attention.

Adaptation, to the African priest, may appear to be regression, and an unconscious resentment may contribute to his reluctance to consider these problems. At home he might be served food in a gourd and this may appear out of date even there, so he would be in a difficult position in a committee of priests if some of them suggest the replacement of the chalice by a gourd. Also for him there is none of the novelty in the Sukuma way of doing things that attracts at least the eye if not the mind of the missionary. Nevertheless, the long period of religious training, while obliterating the practice of another culture, will not have destroyed his perception of himself as an African, nor indeed his African reactions to the problems of his pastorate.

If he does adapt, there may also be "the risk of his action being interpreted as the African priest's discovering after all that the missionary priest was not telling the truth and that it is now time to go back." Some think that a possible consequence of the promotion of an African clergy will be their overruling of the recent changes in the Church's liturgy. Although his seminary years have made him a conservative toward liturgical adaptation, this training will not have made the African priest into a pale imitation of his European church superiors. The first few years in parish work will have made him undoubtedly African again in aspiration.

Although the Church made an immediate start in training Africans for the priesthood and the first Sukuma priest was ordained in the thirties, it cannot be assumed that as the number of Christians increases so will vocations. In the early days the priesthood provided almost the only channel for the ambitious and intelligent African to rise to a position of authority and responsibility—a channel, moreover, in which his race was an advantage rather than a liability. It also provided clear economic advantages, a visibly higher standard of living in relation to the Sukuma, although the White Fathers had a notably ascetic way of life. Some of the initial motivation for vocations may have come from seeing priests with their Mass stipends and motorcycles. Perhaps it would be unfair to question the purity of such vocations, considering that many missionary priests have been drawn to their vocations by the excitement of going to Africa.

Nowadays the priesthood is no longer the only channel of advancement, and the same class of person can choose any number of careers which have easier and more attractive surroundings for learning than the seminary. It no longer provides a higher standard of living as compared with that of other educated persons, although it is still higher than that of the average peasant.

Nevertheless, if education is the only means toward economic and social success and secondary-school places are in short supply, there will be no shortage of applicants for the junior seminaries. Similarly, those who fail their examinations see there another chance to succeed. Perhaps the decline in vocations is also due to the fact that the Church, and some orders in particular, have not adapted themselves to the modern world. They give an out-of-date image—the job just does not seem to be exciting enough in terms of modern Africa. The center of change is in the towns, while the center of missionary activity still remains in the countryside and even the politicians have a limited interest in that.

CHAPTER III

The Circle of Catechists

THE EARLY MISSIONARIES went to considerable trouble to abstract converts from traditional dancing, work parties composed of both sexes, and rain ceremonies, and to modify birth, marriage, and death ceremonies, with the result that converts could no longer function as full members of their own communities. Adaptation to Sukuma practices, or reversion as it would be in their eyes, when they have not yet entirely freed themselves from the internal as well as external subordination of the colonial period, would in any case be tied for its execution, not so much to the clergy, who receive directions for adaptation or who initiate adaptations themselves, but to the catechists. They have had a special social power deriving from their pastoral duties and would be required to make the major effort to disseminate and popularize whatever adaptations are intended.

Many Christians see the catechist as a teacher but also as an enforcer of Church discipline through his relationship with the priest. Who used who for what moral purpose in the past is a fruitless line of investigation, but it can be seen that the catechist was in a strong position to gain economic advantages, which may have been hard to resist. An English text from a thoughtful and devout university student used the word blackmail for some of these situations. Certainly the catechists are the people who keep the priests informed of what goes on in the community. It is not that they are informers, but they understand what the priest wants to know, and the idiom in which he asks. The average parishioner cannot make the same linguistic or cultural assumption and gives literal answers to literal questions; the priest finds out later that he has not been told the whole truth, just that part of the truth which he himself had inquired about. "Are you married?" brings the answer "no," but the man has been living with a girl for five years and has been separated from her only this week. The Sukuma certainly do not see such an answer as a lie.

Up to the time of the present radical changes, these catechists have come to comprise an entrenched class; much more so than the average convert, they were committed, not only in their teaching work but also in their administration of church out-stations, to as few changes as possible in ritual practice. Semiliterate by modern standards, they made great efforts and sacrifices to learn Church doctrine and teach it to their less privileged neighbors. They learned to be different from their fellows and in the majority of cases have devoted much of their lives to the preservation of this very difference. For these reasons catechists are often poor informants on custom. In discussion, if not in practice, they see a Christian moral issue in almost every facet of the traditional birth, marriage, and funeral ceremonies and they report what ought to be, in their interpretation of Christianity, rather than what is the normal practice.

There is a tendency for them to be easily scandalized and, as part of the fight against the "pagan" influences surrounding them and in support of their own position, many cut down the rites of passage to comply with Christian ritual and the bare necessities of the physical situation. The priest, with considerably less of this face-to-face challenge, tends to feel these days that he is not yet in a position to judge particular customs. This removal from the rites of passage of many traditional acts which did much to delineate their importance and added to their excitement became the sign of the active Christian, a conventional dullness. It is easy to see how this attitude to traditional practices, many of which were not in fact contrary to Christian morals, would encourage a wide social rift between the Christian and coincidently the more modern minded, and the traditional elements in each community, and that it would be used as a means for self-justification in a situation of social revolt.

It is not only in ritual that the older catechist may feel a reluctance to leave the practice in which he has grown up. There has always been the temptation, at the very least, to be right when others are wrong or, more definitely, to point out to others that they are wrong. The Pauline Privilege and relaxations of the marriage bond of like effect have always been a difficult issue and the Church appears to have become more lenient in its attitude to those who in their traditional lives have not stayed with their original spouses. They have now lived for many years in their current marriages and it is felt that it is better to leave them in that state than to start accusing them of living in sin. The older type of catechist may find it very difficult not to make observations about "living in sin," thus stirring up social as well as religious difficulties for that couple.

Although there may be convincing reasons for having catechists, it is difficult to avoid the conclusions of many Sukuma that the groundwork for the salvation of souls requires paid functionaries. But few feel the obligation to spread Christian and Church doctrine as a part of their acceptance of Church membership, now or in the past. Gluckman has recorded that "some field workers have noticed that the evangelical drive among Africans has passed from most established churches . . . to sects," and "Africans now tend to leave paganism and the established churches for the 'unions' and the separatist sects; so did British workers in the early nineteenth century." [6]

Priests have stated that these catechists have played a vital role in the establishment of the Church and that even now they are essential for the initial contacts with those who want to consider baptism: "Without them we would get no one." This statement, or its parallel, came from several parishes, and at the least it is a striking illustration of the weakness of the Church when, by their own admission, the priests require such a link for the extension of their influence, and the former system has been changed, in the recent abolition of paid untrained catechists, not for moral but for economic reasons.

The catechist is also essential to the priest in that he has a house to which he can come in order to initiate contacts with the people, while the people themselves look to the house as the place where they can get in touch with the priests. It is probably more

---

[6] Max Gluckman, "Malinowsky's 'Functional' Analysis of Social Change," in *Order and Rebellion in Tribal Africa* (collected essays). New York: Free Press of Glencoe, 1963, pp. 212 and 223.

important that the catechist should be regular than that he should
be a good teacher; catechumens may come a long way for their
weekly lesson and if the catechist fails to appear, they will not
come the next time and the whole class has to be started up again.

These old-style catechists were paid small sums monthly, more
honoraria than salaries, and often the amount was only enough
to pay their tax for the year. According to the labor laws, however,
this was employment, involving the payment of minimum wages,
severance pay, and the right of the employees to become members
of the national trade union. It was on these grounds and others
that a start was made on giving catechists more intensive training,
paying higher salaries, and providing housing, when candidates
became both catechists and social workers.

In one diocese, the title at Mipa of the Leadership Training
Centre sounds as if it were directed more to modern social welfare
than to catechetical training. In one parish it was said in appreciation of its own Mipa-trained catechist that "he appreciated our
logic," and yet it was this same catechist who raised the question
of the disparate standards of living of the priests and the catechist
doing the same pastoral work. Faith there may be, but it seemed
that he considered himself an employee in search of equal rewards
rather than a worker dedicated to his faith. It would seem that
these catechists now have two roles which are necessarily in conflict; in the former they must lead by example and in the latter,
organize action.

Whatever role the catechist plays and has played, he has to get
something out of it even if he is not paid in monies. Elsewhere,
choir boys have outings, and these men should be rewarded with
similar irregular but anticipated jollifications, which in some
places are quarterly beer parties, elsewhere annual retreats and
monthly meetings at which food is provided. It is not suggested
that payment and faith necessarily exclude each other, but payment changes a socioreligious relationship into one in which economic values are constantly being assessed between Sukuma poverty on the one hand and the Church's apparent and visible wealth
on the other.

A difficult problem was not so much the recruitment of these
untrained catechists but getting rid of them again if they were

not doing their work or if their lives were scandalous. It was interesting to hear that although the idea of 30 shillings per month, or whatever it was, as a salary was denied any connection with minimum wage rates, some priests spoke of sacking catechists, a curiously inappropriate term. Other priests who were more sensitive to their relative positions got around this problem by giving such catechists "leave" from their duties and never recalling them.

The Church now aims at having no paid catechists other than the limited number of fully trained men being produced by their catechetical schools. Where this change has been completed there has been no significant loss of catechists who work on an entirely voluntary basis. They teach one hour-long class per week and in the absence of a priest lead the community prayers on Sunday. The catechist of either sort is under the additional obligation of entertaining the leading Christians of his area and those with problems that require prolonged contact; this probably involves no costs except for food, but it may well further impoverish a present-day catechist, who is getting less and less status from his catechetical role. Nevertheless he is an intermediary, particularly when he is a salaried servant of the Church stationed in one area for any length of time.

This is a particularly difficult problem because the catechist appears to be a success or failure not in specifically Christian terms, but because he is or is not a good Sukuma by traditional standards who happens also to be a Christian. If he is bad in Sukuma terms then no amount of ecclesiastical expertise will make him into a successful catechist. Perhaps bad is too strong a word and it would be better to say close-fisted, impatient, too ready to make decisions and too quick in making them.

The catechist in Sukuma terms has acquired some ritual specialization in the Church's doctrine, and the gaining of social prestige from its manipulation in the Christian context has a parallel in their traditional practices. The people have no talent or liking for extemporary Christian prayer, and in their love of competition, success may well seem to come to those who know more regular prayers than others. It would be asking too much of human nature to expect this occupational class to initiate or to assist very actively the adaptation of the existing ritual to Sukuma tradi-

tional forms, particularly since they have in the past, and probably in the present as well, derived religious status from their personal and privileged association with Europeans rather than with
priests as such.

Also, in the eyes of the laity, there would be a basic contradic-
tion if these same catechists who have worked constantly to change
Sukuma traditional customs, regardless of any specific Church
ruling, and who "threatened and victimized the laity for participating in ceremonies which were not contrary to morals," reverted,
and said that adaptation is good. The laity might even say that
the catechists have abandoned Christianity.

Although great importance is attached to godparents the trend
for it to take on a greater social than religious significance is very
marked. Since the majority of Christians coming to baptism belong to the younger generation, there is a shortage of suitable
older Christians who are eligible for this role. Under these circumstances the catechist is the obvious choice either at the request
of the priest or of the catechumen. Priests are aware of the economic obligations which go with this spiritual role in Usukuma
and warn any catechist against taking on so many godchildren
that he would not be able to carry his burden. Nevertheless there
are catechists who have well over a hundred godchildren, with
their wives being responsible for nearly as many women.

It has been suggested that Christianity can be looked at as a different avenue for getting social advancement and perhaps this
is another aspect. The Sukuma are dedicated not so much to the
maintenance of their families as to their expansion through children, cows, and cultivation. They do not see themselves as a series
of unitary families loosely gathered together in localities, parishes,
or chiefdoms.

The old-style catechist in his efforts to obtain a new form of
social power had to give up some Sukuma values in order to gain
Christian acceptance. Much of Christianity's problems in Usukuma are related to marriage, with the possibility of polygamy
always at the back of people's minds as a means of gaining social
and economic power, an insurance against infertility, and compensation for the untimely deaths of children. To the Christian

this is prohibited from the beginning, but he is still a Sukuma and the obligations to godchildren enhance his status under quite obvious religious sanctions.

Godparenthood is as much liable to the intricacies and long-term consistencies of reciprocity as any other Sukuma relationship. The godchild involves the godparent in his social life, such as consultation before marriage, possibly direct financial help, or contributions to the food required for guests. It is not likely that this contribution, whether in kind or just in advice, is regarded as an isolated event. It must be repaid, although this is too crude a word to describe the web of long-term obligations that godparenthood can initiate. The godchild will feel obligated to help his godparent when the latter is in some difficulty. He may not fulfill the obligation, but it exists and it would be un-Sukuma not to feel this pull.

So the Christian debarred from some forms of family expansion by his adherence to the Christian faith may well see godchildren as an extension of his own lineage, even the creation of a clan with himself at the center. Possibly this was at the back of the trouble in one parish, where the catechist claimed the out-station (*kigango*) church as his own and relied upon his neighbors and godchildren to give him social support for his separatist activities. He was not successful, for the relationship was not strong enough to supply the full religious and social needs of his followers. Perhaps the Church's wish to restrict the number of godchildren stems more from a realization of the spiritual difficulties than from any knowledge of this sociological use. Certainly these centralized groupings around a particular man are not in the interests of the Church, since they facilitate schism and give a Christian power to which he is not religiously entitled.

It may of course be that religion cannot be abstracted from the general facets of Sukuma life and that Christian roles cannot avoid this economic and social interpretation, just as the head of the Buchwezi cult in the Nyegezi area uses his religious power to benefit himself economically and his assistant uses his economic assets to increase his religious importance. Godparenthood can also be a means of evading the Church's supervision when a godparent is chosen simply because he lives in the same locality as a mistress and the religious relationship gives the new Christian a legitimate reason to be in that place.

There are also clashes within the catechists themselves between Christian and Sukuma values which are more destructive of the unity of the parish than the inattention of the laity. It is nothing so simple as a straightforward reversion to traditional religious practices, but cases such as the disappearance of the catechist's married son on a prolonged work migration, when the daughter-in-law is sent back to her people and the children are kept by the grandparent with the remark, "They are my wealth." Catechetical work would seem better done by voluntary workers, trained separately from those who intend to do social work, for which a totally different training is required. There seems to be a case here for Sukuma lay brothers to take on the pastoral work.

CHAPTER IV

The Priest as an Adaptor

THE PROBLEM of adaptation is further complicated because the missionary, attempting changes which have not been ordered or detailed by the Church, is working in isolation. Whatever his own keenness and success, the hierarchy must look at his work as experimental. Successful attempts would be tried out elsewhere, or under different direction, to see whether there are indeed universal applications for such changes. Failure turns back upon the initiator and lends support to those who see no virtue in change and even less in experiment.

Success also brings with it the problem of the singularization of individual clergy, something that is anathema to religious communities dedicated from their foundation to humility and charity in their practice and membership. Here again there is some conflict with Sukuma traditional ideas, where the relative success of any particular ritual is related to particular individuals and their ideas, not to ideas without individuals. It is difficult to consider successful any Sukuma activity that is not related to this individualization, and it is possible that the hierarchy's concern over such individualization of the clergy in a Sukuma setting may be overdone, since it is traditional whether in a religious, economic, or social setting, and is not essentially charismatic.

The Sukuma have never developed prophets or religious leaders standing apart from their traditional social organization. The very fact that adaptation is considered suggests that it is the priests who must initiate; perhaps this is so in the liturgical field but it certainly should not be so outside the field of specifically priestly functions. It is a very human failing in Usukuma as elsewhere to see change initiated by oneself as good and to be rather resentful of anything initiated elsewhere. This is more than true in regard to the Church, and the priest must have a sensitivity to what is practicable in Sukuma terms.

By its nature experiment in adaptation has its source in individuals, the progressive liberals or the "lunatic fringe" of the Church according to the views of the onlooker. The Church member sees the experiment as the product of an individual rather than as a stage in the development of the Church. If the experiment is attractive to him and his fellow Christians they become in some ways personal followers of a particular priest rather than better members of a universal Church. Even if they do not relate changes to a particular priest, there is danger of losing the essential universality of the Church and its central rite of the Mass under a load of paraliturgical gimmicks. The priest with a personal following because of his popularity or success in adaptation creates difficulties not only between members of his own order at the time of the events, but makes it doubly difficult for the priests in surrounding parishes and for his successors in his own parish.

In considering change a religious order is in a very different position from that of a political party or business organization. It is constitutionally self-governing and external forces have little direct bearing on its internal practices; it is not subject to external scrutiny and has an establishment of senior clerics. The balance of such power is likely to be toward conservatism, while the forces for change lack the numbers, seniority, years of service, and personal authority to carry the requisite number of votes. The older priests will likely see the order as the *raison d'etre* of their lives, while their juniors may consider that the order is a means to greater ends. A research report on change records:

> Once the means have become ends, to change any of the rules or regulations becomes tantamount to changing the image of the religious community itself and even to threaten the essential concept of a "religious." The total commitment of the members of religious communities to an organization constituted not only a life's work but a *way* of life. . . . If persons oriented toward the collectivity have found their source of security in the present organizational structure and have shaped their own self-image through the organizational patterns of behavior, then change in the structure would mean change in their own personal perception of attitudes and

values. There is less likelihood of change originating from the members of this group.[7]

Perhaps also the older the order and the wider the geographical spread of its organization, the less the potential there is for change; head offices have their problems as well that tend to put the urgency of one particular area into a wider perspective.

The constant references that have been made to adaptation insinuate that the Sukuma is the main problem to be considered, but it seems, now that so much change has arrived, that there is an equally good reason for considering seriously the problems of adapting the clergy to the present activities of the Church in Sukuma. No priest mentioned the aspects of rapid change that involve them: the basic differences in seminary training between priests ordained a decade apart, and a spirit of individuality that was not required before but may be useful now. There is also the problem of the priest who has been encouraged to develop a particular talent from his seminary days and finds that there is no possibility of carrying on with this work in his parish.

Yet the new individuality may coincide with the frowned-upon singularization resulting from some measures of adaptation if they are successful. The talent of the Sukuma for the creation and running of large numbers of individual but interlocking societies for every conceivable purpose makes this singularization their inevitable reaction to attractive adaptation. When parishioners start calling themselves followers of a particular priest rather than Christians, the way of the innovator becomes even less easy. Dedicated opponents materialize both within and without the hierarchy, who oppose his work and intentions not only in charity but in the full armor of their own faith.

The missionary may be able to approach the problem of adaptation free from any detailed knowledge of the society in which he works. His main difficulty is to clear away from his intentions ideas based on the functioning of his own society. The African clergy are in no such easy position of being able to attack the prob-

---

[7] Sister Rose Anne Murphy, S.N.D. d.N., "Organizational Change and the Individual: A Case of the Religious Community," *Sociological Analysis*, Vol. 25, No 2 (Summer 1964), pp. 92 and 94.

lem with a clean slate. Even though they have spent many years away from their own communities, they are still family men with close relatives who see no reason for excusing him from considering their family problems just because he has become a priest. He is not working far from his home, and his material success in life, as opposed to the material abnegation of the missionary, will mean that he is constantly under pressure from his relatives to give them help. In their eyes his vocation may well be incidental to the benefits he is receiving from his status.

The African priest does not, and indeed cannot, consider adaptation purely as part of the process of a worldwide ideological struggle. He may accept wholeheartedly the concept of a universal Church as the ideal to which all his religious and social activity is directed, but at the same time in the Sukuma context he may feel that this universality in practice is Western-oriented. The political neutralism of the nation may appeal to him as a better exemplification of this universality than the present situation. He wants the Church of his nation to be left alone to work out its own salvation locally as a part of an ideally universal Church; this is one of the main points apparent in any study of East African Christian separatist churches. The political ideal of nonalignment may well fit in with the Sukuma's moral conception of goodness as God's leaving them alone to work out their own destiny.[8]

To him, every question, without calling into question the purity of his faith, can be related to family and tribal circumstances, the individual pressures which affect his consciousness as a member of various functioning social groups. Perhaps the simplest example of these pressures must be the Church's continuing discussion and past rulings on the number of cattle to be paid in bride wealth and the conditions under which it is paid or returned. The African priest with more sisters than brothers may not readily accept the idea of limiting the cattle to be paid, while another with more brothers than sisters will press for just such limitations, because of the immediate advantages to his family. Possibly such problems are not consciously considered, but they remain the background of their thoughts because of their origins. When

---

[8] *Supra*, p. 7.

their opinion is not directly affected by the family situation, they tend in discussion to ally themselves with Africans of similarly high education rather than to their own family background.

From another aspect the Church cannot take up the position of attempting to guard the Sukuma culture when the Sukuma themselves are in the process of rejecting a large proportion of it. Adaptation in this context was described as "looking out of the window for a custom in order to save it." Everything that the Sukuma did in the past was a product of the conditions existing at the time and served a function. It is not possible to abstract a particular item and use it in the Church, expecting it to have the same results from a totally different function.

Thomas Merton wrote:

We cannot reproduce what they did because we approach the problem in a way that makes it impossible for us to find a solution. We ask ourselves a question that they never considered. How shall we build a beautiful monastery according to the style of some past age and according to the rules of a dead tradition? Thus we make the problem not only infinitely complicated but we make it, in fact, unsolvable. Because a dead style is dead. And the reason why it is dead is that the motives and the circumstances that once gave it life have ceased to exist. They have given place to a situation that demands another style.[9]

Although adaptation may be either to the past or the future, the overseas priest in Usukuma is surrounded by a state of affairs almost entirely related to the past, while having no parallel knowledge or appreciation of sociopolitical trends and the religious ideologies of the national leaders. He is naturally more related to these movements in his own country and there seems to be a hiatus between his diocese in Usukuma and the diocese of his own home. He sees the latter's adaptations as clearly unsuitable for Usukuma and almost by default he may tend to see in the traditional customs of his Sukuma parishioners the ways to which he must direct the changes that are necessary within the Church. So it comes about that adaptation so far is directed much more to

[9] Thomas Merton, *The Sign of Jonas*. New York: Harcourt, Brace, 1953, p. 86.

the past than to the future, as in recommending the round Church when most Sukuma want square houses, the gourd and water pot for baptism when they see the practical utility of metal, and so on.

The creation of an African personality as a political abstraction has shown itself popular and important, but the creating of a tribal personality with the support of the Church would be taken as reactionary and would almost certainly cause unfavorable political comment, from which so far in Usukuma Christianity has been surprisingly free in view of the clashes that have occurred elsewhere. It is possible to see the occasional clashes as more thoughtless than deliberate, as when a Sunday morning is used for an important political demonstration. Such a time is well established as allocated to Christian services, so much so that on one occasion those involved pitied more than resented the official's mistake.

When a clash has occurred, it seems to have been confined to a few government and party officials of low rank who have not received much support from their superiors, except when there has been a particular case in issue in which the Church may have been at fault; for example, when the priest is too physically energetic in his condemnation of moral faults. When a clash of this nature is attached to a particular person, it appears to be the convention for the government to ask for his withdrawal and the diocese to accede to this request on the grounds that from both the parties' points of view, further publicity would be undesirable.

Tribalism limits not only the extent but also the possibility of adaptation as an expression of a universal Church. The same view in another form is the idea that the good practicing "pagan" was more valuable in the eyes of some than the average present-day Sukuma. This may be a concept in a discussion of the relativity of morals, but it has no relevance to present-day Christianity, which is dealing with people who have more in common with the future than the past. Much of this viewpoint develops from the excitement and stimulation of face-to-face contact with another culture at a particularly susceptible time in the new priest's ordained life.

Even if the priest practices, in his parish administration, an American or any other cultural approach, he does so consciously

aware that the Church has nearly two thousand years of development behind it and that its ritual is an amalgam of many different
cultures, and that the Church's official language has no present-
day connection with any existing nation. The Sukuma do not see
Christianity as affected by such an historical evolution, but merely
as a religious system brought in from outside. These historical developments are unappreciated by the majority, although catechumens may accept them as supporting the validity of the priest's or
catechist's arguments.

Adaptation at this crucial period in the history of the Sukuma
is being attempted by the missionaries, passively accepted by the
African clergy, and rather dubiously followed by the laity, wherever it has been attempted without considerable prior consultation. The leaders of the parish Christians will be the real initiators of any successful adaptations which have been suggested to
them by their priests. The optimistic suggest that the force for
adaptation may be expected to come from the educated African
laity rather than from the African clergy, for although the former
are also of high status, they are more conversant with the customs
of their people than the latter. There have been no signs in Usukuma, however, that any particular group shows a tendency to
initiate. Impetus for change usually comes from the outside.

CHAPTER V

The Attack on
Traditional Religion

THE FIRST half-century of Christian activity in Usukuma has underwritten the present resistance to ritual change and supported the conservatism of a people who have never at any time been ready to change. The initial impetus of the colonial period soon died out amidst the ecological difficulties of the environment, and when the development programs of the final years of colonialism were tried, they met with little success. There was little spark from within the culture except for the development of cotton as a cash crop and co-operatives to get Indians out of the cotton trade. The development plans of the independent national government seem to have met with no more success so far; both attempts were from without and not from within.

The early missionaries, saintly and devoted men and women, saw their task as the conversion of the Sukuma from "paganism," without inquiring too closely as to what this "paganism" meant and what its function was; it was a brash, vigorous, insensitive evangelization. Paganism was so vigorously attacked all over East Africa that "pagan" became a Kiswahili word for a person with no religion and, by implication, one of lower status.

In Usukuma this was a misnomer—certainly so if meant in the dictionary definition of "one of a nation or community which does not worship the true God." It is the opinion of priests who have known them for decades that they believe in God and are a God-fearing people, who could not by any reasonable understanding be described as pagans. A Sukuma uses the phrase *Nati na dini* ("I have no religion") to describe himself as a traditionalist who has not been converted either to Christianity or Islam; the same phrase occurs in Uganda, and in no sense is the person intending to describe himself as one who does not believe in God.

The goal of the early missionaries was to convert the people, provide them with the opportunity to have the sacraments as often as possible and, through the authoritarian structure of a missionary Church, subordinate them to existing Church practice. Inquiries into local customs were incidental to this task and missionaries may not have approached their work with any feeling of the practical necessity to adapt rather than to use local customs.

Perhaps in the use of the word "pagan" by the lay Christians, when priests prefer to avoid it because of its strong overtones of inferiority, there is still a feeling of exclusion and the attitude that they alone are right. A priest would refer to such a person as one who has not been baptized, while the lay Christian states that he is one who has no religion. Another defines a pagan as a man who worships another God, or who does not recognize that God exists. Others define a pagan as someone who does not believe in the word of God, or who believes in evil spirits, or who worships an inanimate object. Then there is the traditional definition that he is the Sukuma who believes in the powers of the ancestors and that there are sorcerers.

All these definitions are apart from the basic view that a pagan is a backward and ignorant individual, and those who hold it consider that they have escaped this state, probably by their own personal efforts rather than by any acceptance of the grace of God. It is much more a status classification than a religious one. It indicates a break with the past by those who do not think of themselves as having any investment in the past, a break they must retain for economic or social reasons.

Some priests are not conscious of their use of this word or its use by their Christians, but certainly to the laity it has a basic use—it distinguishes us from them. Other priests deny that it is a valid term and yet minutes later in the same conversation they bring in the word seemingly as a part of their way of speaking; it is still very much an everyday word in religious circles. When someone comes to the priest to discuss a marriage, the answer to the question, "Whom are you going to marry?" brings the answer, "He is a pagan." The question does not bring out the name in the first instance. Even asking a Catholic woman, "Who is your husband?" brings the similar answer, "He is a pagan."

A situation is now arising in which children come to instructions knowing nothing of Sukuma traditional beliefs and who are in effect "pagans" and have to be taught the reasons for the existence of God. This was never the case with the earlier adult converts. These new catechumens know a few traditional customs—that some people go for consultations with a magician and that others spit when they see a chameleon—but they have no knowledge of a coherent system; it is really a close parallel to the neo-paganism of Europe and America.

The early attack on "paganism" meant that there was a continual pressure in regard to the external symbols and activities associated with traditional practices. This attack, associated with European overlordship and social and economic change in general, meant that many more were affected than those actually in the process of conversion. In the Sukuma environment the result was that more people were aware of what the Church was against than what it was for. The priest could speak and explain in terms which to him were clear, but in the gossip groups at markets and meetings and around the evening fires, only particular words and phrases would have impinged on their memories and only these would be argued about and casually and unconsciously distorted.

The removal of amulets upon conversion and the absolute prohibition of wearing them afterwards meant that there was a tendency for them to be worn wherever they could not be seen. People still felt a great need for these personalized ritual objects; the widespread use of the cross as a neck ornament, even by non-Christians, and the pleasure in possessing a rosary seem to be universal trends, but this is not personalized enough to replace what went before. The missionary was justified in requiring the destruction of amulets before baptism, because they represented a non-Christian, flatly "pagan" reality, but the difficulty is that something physical has been exchanged for something spiritual; it is not a clear exchange and there is a gap in the home.

In some parishes the cloth used at baptism is retained for years, as just such an object, but there is a lack of such Christianized objects which people can treasure and use. In their type of mud and wattle housing with few shelves, cupboards, and corners, there are few places for the Western type of devotional objects. The traditional sacrifice in the open, attended by as many members of the family as were able to come together, has tended to be replaced by secret rites of single individuals, unassociated with family commitments and unwitnessed by the community, which previously exercised some control over the nature and purpose of these rites. The common divination ceremonies, which almost everyone made use of to guide them in their conduct for the future solution of their troubles, and which always took place in the open, now tend to be done out of sight.

The result seems to have been that this pressure on the external aspects of traditional religion broke an essential link between the individual and community control. It assisted in an unexpected way the pressure on the individual in Christianity to ease himself out of kinship control and obligations. The manner in which missionaries were able to ride so easily over traditional religious practices has meant that they have been faced more and more with the problems of its creeping back as a secret cult. This attack on traditionalism is still very much in the minds of most priests. They seem to see Christianity as a battle of numbers, in which conversion and baptism is Christianity, in which one parish does better than another, and in which the individual is looked at in relation to his practice—good, bad, coming along or going backwards, his or her intrinsic worth forgotten.

One priest was deeply concerned over this attitude to numbers, saying, "Pope John did not categorize. What would he have done?" It is necessary to stress again and again that no custom anywhere can be abolished or be made to disappear in the same way that a material object can be destroyed. Change takes place constantly and pressure on a particular custom which a community or individual still finds useful means that its uses and satisfactions will be transferred to some other part of the social system and survives in some other form.

The Church must ever consider this pressure on traditionalism, in relation not only to semisecret, backward-looking cults such as the Buchwezi society which flourishes as vigorously now in the

Mwanza area as it did ten years ago, but also to separatist Christian churches, which are common on the northern and eastern shores of Lake Victoria. Sundkler states, "Magic, on the other hand, does not give way to the pressure of modernism. It is driven underground—it is revitalized and it reappears in the Zionist Church . . . the actual belief in witchcraft is vital to the Zionist Church." [10]

The attitude of the Church toward traditional religion has swung away from the uncomplicated condemnation of the early missionaries to the present view that traditionalism and its administrators or priests represent no threat to Christianity. Priests now see its decline more in terms of expanding education than in the expansion of Christianity; they may associate education with Christianity, but in conversation they stress the former.

This may be a grave misassessment of the situation; the decline or transformation of these traditional practices depends very little on education. If the situation is related to Christianity, the test will be which system helps the Sukuma through their crises. The expansion of paganism and traditional religious activities and their comparison with exotic practices in Europe and America is not related to education but to the failure of Christianity to provide for the crises troubling the possibly deviant persons who indulge in them.

It would be a mistake to assume that the traditional religious practitioners are living on the fears of their followers; it would be more true to say that they are living on their hopes. Indeed the closely integrated religious system of the past has already gone and not simply because of education, which has been and still is a sparse commodity in Usukuma. The Sukuma may well see in the ritual itself the defenses which they crave. The cutting open of a goat and the smearing of the mother of twins with the dung is usually revolting to the non-Sukuma spectator and horrible to his imagination; the Sukuma may see it quite differently and view some European and American practices with a similar moral horror. They see the physical religious acts as spiritually effective.

---

[10] Benkt G. N. Sundkler, *Bantu Prophets in South Africa*. London: International African Institute, 2nd ed., 1961, p. 261.

The traditional cult of the ancestors presents many opportunities for the incorporation of such religious acts into the Christian ritual, much more so than a simple transfer to hagiology. The early missionaries were very probably much too strong in their condemnation of ancestor worship. The use of the word "worship" presupposes vigorous objections, whereas the Sukumas' ideas of the powers of deceased ancestors have never overridden their fundamental belief in monotheistic power.

It is probably true to say that the Church made no official statement condemning Sukuma ancestor worship, but surely no priest could afford to show tolerance to a religious system that was organizationally, if nothing more, in opposition to his own insistence on Church practice. Any priest understands that the Catholic life as a religious system is all-pervasive and the Sukuma system was equally so. Similarly the priest could not ignore the fact that ancestor worship was primarily a function of fear that the anger of the spirits would harm one's relatives. He must stress that Christianity is the religion of love, rather than hate, a semantic problem in itself, since the Sukuma do not appear to think in these abstract terms or to draw comparisons.

The fact that so few Sukuma have doctrinal difficulties or even ask questions during instruction suggests that they do not see Christianity as a natural development from their own traditional religious ideas, but as an entirely separate system. Once the convert is determined to become a baptized Christian the content of the doctrine is relatively unimportant. To attract and develop the spiritual virtues of the Sukuma, a much more personalized remembrance of the ancestors might well be developed. There is a real need for connecting Christian ritual with the deceased in particular and not just in general, as in the case of All Souls' Day, so that it is fully understood to be the remembrance of particular deceased persons.

Masses for the dead in their own homes, the development of family shrines, and the use of personal relics, would all seem to be opportunities for building upon the traditional propitiatory system. It is perhaps unnecessary to stress the negative aspects of the traditional practice; one should rather concentrate on the all-pervasive understanding of the interrelationship of the living and the dead. Sacrifices in propitiation of an individual angry ancestor are usually directed at all the ancestors—name no names or other ancestors will start trouble. A Mass for the repose of the individual's soul would be contrary to Sukuma practice and would not be as successful as Masses for the souls in purgatory.

CHAPTER VI

Old and New Christians
and Adaptation

ALTHOUGH the Churches have aimed at an indigenous clergy from the start, they have only recently seen and acted on the need for a Christian ritual based more on traditional practices, which would make the Church independent in faith and practice of its specifically European initiators. The accelerated promotion of African clergy has been only one aspect of this program and one of the easiest to accomplish, despite the length and difficulties of their training.

In the adaptation of ritual the European clergy have been the initiators and in the postcolonial period popular opinion may well be that, divorced from the protection of the colonial government, they are merely adapting in order to maintain their power and place in Africa. The laity may be suspicious of what appears to them as sudden change and they are not prepared for radical changes in their accustomed rituals. Many Sukuma may interpret "this reversion to adaptation as mere propaganda of the helpless missionaries, who want to pretend to identify themselves with the Africans, so that they may remain here perpetually after the colonial white man has been overthrown."

This changing situation is difficult enough for the overseas clergy, but the Christian in his social life is also faced with problems which he cannot sort out in the quietness of his parish church or in conversation with his parish priest. He is asked by non-Christians, who may be his own relatives, "What did your European talk about this morning at Mass—that agent of the colonialist who still remains to deceive us?" Or alternatively, "When is your Eu-

ropean in the mission going away, or is he still continuing his lies
so that we shall have mercy on him and permit him to remain?"
If he defends the priest he is likely to "isolate himself from the
progressive elements as well and thus he will be paying too much
for his religion." The intermingling of African and non-African
clergy in the one parish seems an absolute necessity in offsetting
this trend, for the danger of anti-Europeanism as attached to Christianity appears to be much more than just antipathy toward Europeans as a group, which may well be remedied by the passage
of time.

There is also an ideological split between the old-guard Christians, who made some specific sacrifices for the faith and who
lived as a small isolated elite group in close association with the
early priests—those from the period of missionary paternalism
and rather pious receptivity—and the mass-conversion Christians
of recent years, who have not suffered such pressures and who do
not see the Church as giving them satisfactions such as the former
gained from their subordination. The former, in their attitude
to the liturgy, probably say to themselves that this is what is done
by the Church and the good Christian will do it.

Possibly in the present atmosphere of change it is easy to assume that the laity may not understand the essentials of their faith
because these have become hidden under an accretion of liturgical
ceremonies. But enough of the Mass is understood for them to realize that a sacrifice is going on; they may agree in due course to
peripheral changes but not to changing anything they consider
fundamental. It is extremely hard to find out what they consider
to be fundamental to their Christian faith and one is inclined to
feel that the Church's and the average Christian's feelings are
widely divergent. Authority in ritual is an asset which they appear
to appreciate and obey, not because they are deeply involved in
liturgical appreciation, but simply because they are not involved.
Their satisfactions come from factors incidental to the content.
The fundamentals for the majority of Christians may well be social practices—not interfering with drinking is an obvious example—which are not essential parts of Christian doctrine.

A further problem of adaptation is the effect this slanting of the
Christian mission activity has had toward alien social practices.

The practicing Christian has indeed had to pay in the past as well as the present for his faith and devotion by a considerable amount of social isolation. The compensation for this isolation has been a code of religious practice almost totally different from anything that he or his fellows have ever known before; and a code, furthermore, which from the time of his conversion has been a personal thing to him alone in his religious practice. He has accepted an alien faith and, leaving aside the question of faith and its mental satisfactions, this very alienness has been the prop of his life, and his interpretation of it an important element in the defense of his own social isolation—the satisfaction of being different.

Whatever he was seeking by his conversion, it may not have been Christianity in a dominantly Sukuma framework. He wanted a different religion, not one which attempted to be as Sukuma as possible—this would have been no recompense for the isolation imposed by the moral requirements of conversion. Since conversion has been much associated with prohibiting and controlling previous patterns of Sukuma conduct, the average Sukuma may be inhibited from considering the adaptation of Christian ritual as anything more than a reversion to practices closely allied to what their priests used to call paganism.

There is also another very fundamental difference between the past and present Christian Sukuma. The first Christians were tied closely to their priests, so that ecclesiastical obedience may have coincided or appeared to coincide with lay obedience in the social and political sphere. The priest was able to change or innovate as he thought fit after careful consideration and in due prudence; the crisis of decision must have been largely one for his own conscience; the laity would be obedient because it was a form of authority which they understood. The new Christians may have no such personal relationship with their priests, while their concept of ecclesiastical obedience has changed along with their political development. Bishop Blomjous says, "What is called obedience is not obedience in our sense any more." [11] It has to be considered whether the laity will in fact accept the Church's moral and liturgical leadership, for the Church's institutions are in com-

---

[11] Bishop Joseph Blomjous, "The Role of the Layman in East Africa," an address to the clergy and others, Easter 1964. Unpublished.

petition with community and state institutions, which during the colonial period never existed in potential opposition to Christianity. Something more that must be taken account of is "the beginning of thinking of the Church as a voluntary association in which everything is done by common consent," as in fact it was traditionally done in their not so recent past.

In Usukuma the current wave of experiments in adaptation have been both aided and inhibited by the fact that the Sukuma number well over a million and inhabit a vast area. The universality of the Church as an aspect of its doctrine seems to have been lost in the desire to make the liturgy more attractive to this enclave—in crude terms, to support a specifically tribal element among the laity. In the nearby diocese of Musoma, where there is an amalgam of several local tribes and immigrant communities, the clergy are noticeably less keen on adaptation and see the universality of the Church's doctrine as a positive asset in creating Christian communities out of these divergent elements.

It must also be remembered that stable communities, in which the majority of families and individuals remain in one place for even a generation, have not existed in the past and are not likely to exist in the future; the countryside gives only an illusion of stability. Most Sukuma have traveled outside Usukuma, and the rural communities have much migration over relatively short distances. The constant movement associated with the towns and their problems is so obvious that the observer forgets that all this movement is to and from the countryside, spread out maybe, but just as disturbed and in effect just as unstable.

The convert, as indeed any African, stands at the meeting place of two worlds. Probably for years the activities of aliens in word and deed have convinced him that his own culture is second rate. Even as a citizen of an independent country he may still feel the same thing even though he might not be willing to admit it openly. Too often the attempts at adaptation have been teaching him to perpetuate his subordination and to continue the second bestness of his own culture, as if the European-backed way of practicing Christianity were too good for him.

CHAPTER VII

Church Administration

IN THE ADMINISTRATION of Christian practice there are also problems peculiar to Sukuma society because the shortage of priests in all denominations, in areas predominantly illiterate, has meant that the Christian administrator and the pastor of a Christian flock have in too many cases been the same person. He is the administrator particularly of property held under a Western concept of ownership. The colonial government required missions to hold land titles, and as their work expanded so did the number of their buildings and land holdings.

There can be no doubt that this property is used for Christian purposes in the abstract, while the Sukuma Christians see it in relation to their own communities and to the priests who minister to them. It seems that the nationalist politician does view Christianity and property as virtually synonymous. The nationalizing of church schools and other institutions is an obvious, if not inevitable, part of their political thinking. This may not be the result of any careful weighing of the advantages and disadvantages but is rather an instinctive assertion of their national right—or natural right—to control their own educational or medical system.

It might almost be said that the legal rights of occupancy under which the Church holds its landed property are a constant provocation to politicians who cannot really be called extremist. As a "voluntary agency" the diocese administers a large number of schools which it legally owns, but what does this amount to in fact? The government pays the salaries, often not through the priest or even the local authority office nearest the school; the syllabus is nationwide, and school expansion, repairs, and alterations are in the hands of educational committees of the area. The Educational

Secretary of the diocese may have difficulty over teachers' transfers and penalties involving moral as well as work failings, and the local priest may have no say at all in such problems, and neither does he determine which child goes to which school.

In the abstract the diocese has a responsibility, but in fact this appears to amount to very little. The main concern of the diocese is that the children should have access to the Christian truths; apparently there has never been any difficulty over this and all schools of whatever denominations have periods set aside for religious instruction. The Church would lose nothing in this respect if the schools were under direct state administration. In addition, every new African government looks at church schools with suspicion, but this does not in any way affect their acknowledgment of the great part the Christian churches have played in initiating education in Tanzania or elsewhere. In their opinion the Churches have divided the country, and their existence perpetuates division, and they see a state educational service as essential for the unity of the country.

If the administration of church schools does not in fact exist as a lively and useful function of the Church and is tied to the political idea of the Church's interest in property, to wait for their nationalization seems to be politically inept. The overseas publicity will damage the nation and the Church will appear in some ways as an injured party in moral opposition to the government. It would be far better to propose a plan for turning over primary schools progressively to government control, and thus to appear to be in advance of obvious intentions of the government, assisting it almost.

Possibly only with schools immediately adjacent to churches should the diocese try to negotiate some special agreement to ensure that the school and church are able to live administratively in accord, since they use in almost all cases the same facilities—a headmaster acceptable to the diocese, participation of the school and staff in worship, and so on. Whether the Church owns or builds and gives to the nation, it is still nevertheless enmeshed in buildings; it appears as a property owner and whether in Christian charity or not, it has legal rights which the buildings bring with them, and these are in conflict with the simple life of Christ, which is nearer to the Sukuma way of life.

Some priests feel that they ought to withdraw from this problem of Church buildings and the conflict involved, because they cannot bargain with their parishioners and neighbors in essentially non-Sukuma property-owning terms. In describing a self-help scheme supported by Church funds, a priest observed that "if they put just one brick into the building, they think it belongs to them," as indeed it would if they were working according to Sukuma tradition, according to which each man's work gives him an equal share in the profit or results.

Building by the Church in these circumstances is achievement or progress only when it is related to social services, such as hospitals or conference centers, which cannot be paid for by local effort and so must be built and maintained by outside efforts. When buildings are related to the priests and Sisters, the Sukuma make a clear distinction between what is necessary for ordinary people and what is apparently necessary for priests, Brothers, and nuns. The standard in some places is too high. Apparently the White Fathers were able to build up resistance to disease and environment, but American priests find this more difficult.

In Europe and America these two roles of priest and administrator are kept more separate and the pastor is possibly more able to give his primary attention to his flock. In Usukuma church schools have to be inspected, the headmaster helped with his administration, and parents' meetings attended. Money collected from dispensaries has to be accounted for and drugs collected and issued, and so on. A priest who has no pastoral obligations can control and administer without difficulty, but it is impossible for him to carry out both these roles in the same place and with the same people. It is futile to expect a personnel manager in a factory, who hires and fires, to have the confidence of the worker.

To the priest trained to the regularity of seminary life, or to any person whose life is lived by the clock, Usukuma meetings are both tedious and unproductive. The time arranged is nothing more than an elastic period related to a particular day; meetings started with a reasonable quorum have continually to go back to the beginning because a latecomer wants to make his speech and they often end, not because a decision has been reached, but because those attending are hungry, their bicycles have no lights, or they have to walk a long way home. The fact that a meeting was called for a specific purpose may appear to them to be totally irrelevant to the need for unanimity; it is often a test of endurance as to how long the priest or the laity can hang on before the matter under discussion becomes irrelevant or the opportunity is lost. This is not something specially put on to exasperate the priest unless there are some unusual circumstances, but the normal way of doing business for people who have to live together and who cannot afford to quarrel.

A meeting is also the occasion for some entertainment in their otherwise dull lives. If they have to go to a meeting, let it at least take as long as possible, so that they can hear as many speeches as possible and, even better, some violent and necessarily short-lived disagreements. Cotton co-operative meetings, no matter how important the visitor or how small the agenda, may well last more than eight hours. School committee meetings, although not potentially providing as much excitement, for there is not so much money involved and therefore probably attract a less important audience, can hardly be expected to last much less. There seems to be little doubt that the priest could with perfect propriety read his breviary or write up the monthly report for his bishop without really upsetting the steady onward movement of the meeting, provided that he is alert to the right moment to interject the correct and apposite remark.

Even allowing for these Sukuma characteristics, Oldham has questioned the whole committee and meeting system:

> The practice of passing resolutions and making pronouncements is beset with dangers and may often be a sheer waste of time. . . . Reliance on mistaken or futile methods of procedure cannot but weaken the influence of the Church for good. . . . Pronouncements which do not have behind them a solid body of considered and convinced opinion can have little or no effect on public action. . . . Secondly, the habit of passing resolutions carried to excess defeats its own purpose. . . . Where opinions are easily, cheaply, and glibly expressed, they are accorded little public attention. . . . Finally we

have to take account of the immense amount of valuable time that might be expended much more fruitfully in other directions, which is often spent in the passing and debating of resolutions.[12]

Welbourn questions even more strongly this involvement:

A fundamental character of the missionary culture is its conception of the Church as a highly organized institution with a specialized ministry, specialized buildings which, with gross etymological (and indeed theological) inexactitude—steal from the worshiping community the name of the church, diocesan offices, hospitals, schools, enactments of ecclesiastical law and international co-ordinating committees. This is the complexity—though of a different type —against which the early reformers—Peter Waldo, Francis of Assisi, John Wycliffe—made their primary protest. It is something very different from the small circles of readers gathered around Mackay and Lourdel in the early days of the Christian Mission to Buganda. It is different, I suspect, from the Church in Corinth, visited by letter and in person by Saint Paul.[13]

The newcomer to Africa will soon realize the limitations that a nearly total illiteracy set to the running of any system which depends upon writing. It takes far more than the simple ability to read to be able to use reading and writing administratively to even the simplest degree of efficiency. Furthermore, to use writing as a means of ensuring that commitments are met in such a society is not sensible, for those who cannot read have no check on the writing, and Sukuma society functions essentially through the spoken word and has as yet not given much value to the use of writing in customary law.

In Usukuma the great distances involved, not only between churches with resident priests and pastors but also between church out-stations, hospitals, schools, and catechetical centers, and also the wide spread of country between one Christian or non-Christian household and another, have meant that priests are involved

---

[12] W. A. Visser 't Hooft and J. H. Oldham, *The Church and Its Function in Society.* London: Allen and Unwin, 1937, pp. 224-225.

[13] F. B. Welbourn, *East African Rebels: A Study of Some Independent Churches.* London: S.C.M. Press, 1961, pp. 211-212.

constantly in time-consuming traveling. Whether or not there are technical Brothers available for doing car repairs, the priest in Usukuma, in terms of the time involved with his transportation, might without levity be called an ordained driver. This is probably unavoidable, but it is time spent out of contact with his parishioners, while the priest on foot will meet and be met with more Church problems in one day than he will ever meet in a car on a road.

The old colonial administrators used to say that they lost touch with the people when they no longer had to walk to meet them. Although standards of living will always be disparate, walking in the long run means shared hardships and experiences and provides many opportunities for increasing knowledge and sensibility, which cannot be done in a car or even partially so on a motorcycle. Even if he has riders as he travels from place to place, once the car stops the priest goes one way and the passengers another; they have shared nothing personal other than the knowledge that the priest can afford a car and they cannot. This vehicular traveling consumes much time, effort, and money; it is an expensive use of men with sacramental powers, too few as it is.

Another aspect seems to be that the relative affluence of one order of missionaries in comparison with another has led, not so much to the higher standard of living which has already been commented on, but to a higher mobility. The more affluent are always driving. Driving within the parish is an acceptable use of time, but beyond this they seem to be constantly on the move in what can be called parasocial traveling. Possibly it is a case of its being easier to drive to a place than to plan.

Although religion may cover a much narrower range of human activities than the civil service, it seems to involve much more and regular face-to-face confrontation. Even accepting the stimulus of personal contact with fellow priests as a necessity, the civil service was apparently able to cover a much wider and more comprehensive variety of work with minimal communication with superiors and equals other than by letter. It is possible to question whether a priest, who has a far higher degree of dedication than any government employee, needs such a number of days away from his station; the civil service did not allow an officer to move out of his district except in an emergency or without the permission of his superiors. The weekly visit to get the mail or for shopping is a luxury—or a chore—which effectively takes a day out of the working week; it is not rest.

It is doubtful whether some orders would feel that they could afford a yearly retreat and a purely secular leave. The need of priests for relaxation is quite obvious, but with a much higher sense of vocation than could ever be attributed to a civil servant or overseas aid worker, a tighter rule might possibly be justified without causing any loss in efficiency. The urgency of the Christian situation would seem to deny much of such activities any essential part in the priestly life; the time might possibly be better spent in acquiring local knowledge, related to pastoral work concerned with East African if not Sukuma problems. Perhaps a time and motion study of the costs of missionary activities would indicate that movement alone in terms of distance and time lost is eating into the ability of the Church to fulfill its primary functions.

In an industrial country the work of the parish priest may well be reasonably even over the year, the same indigent persons, the same marriage problems, and maybe more visits to the sick during the winter. But in Sukumaland the fluctuations between harvest time and six months later are often extreme. The fees paid for medicine may go up ten times after the cotton harvest, and during the same season there is a corresponding increase in the problems of supply and demand for other ancillary Church facilities.

The Sukuma is tied to the agricultural year for his money, even for his health, and probably for his morals as well, and the priest therefore must have additional work during the harvest season because of the presence of money. Indeed there are other periods of tension, such as the school-year opening in January, when money and even food may be scarce and parents worried over the new year's planting and rainfall, but again this involves administrative, not pastoral work, a loss of time in the limited working life of a priest able to administer the sacraments.

The priest, whether alien or African, lends money to those in need but there is little realization that this is totally divorced from his priestly functions, so those who have borrowed money stay away from the church. As the apparently richest person in the com-

munity, he is the natural focus of any person who cannot get his
financial problems settled by family, shopowner, or the co-operative. It is not that the priest is personally wealthy, although the
laity are clearly unable to distinguish between the personal funds
and belongings of the priest under the rules of his order and the
funds and property which he is able to utilize as a result of overseas gifts.

In a similar way the shortage of literates, not so much in the
sense of their being able to read and write, but in their ability to
administer church funds and business in a proper manner, has
meant that the priest or pastor is involved in a perpetual round
of committee work and supervisory duties not directly related to
his pastoral office, which must remain the most important part of
his duties. It may well be that the Church would be glad to be rid
of all these material obligations in order to concentrate on the
essential pastoral work, but it is likely that the government has
not the staff and would rather that priests were occupied with
nonpastoral duties. There is a utility in school and hospital work
which is a recognized part of national development; the care of
souls has not so far received similar recognition.

In the past some dioceses have been highly centralized with
funds administered, vehicles registered, and persons employed
through the bishop as head of the organization. New legislation
has defined minimum wages, severance pay, and other obligations
with the result that the Church had to pay out large sums for part-
time catechists. Accordingly the Church has retired many catechists and taken on a few full-time catechists—a radical change in
catechetical approach.

In a similar way it has proved difficult to carry on with the missionary practice of having the diocese manage its own building
projects, with the inevitable involvement in disputes and union
negotiations, wherein the diocese is treated as an abstract body
with overseas financial assistance and becomes the target for labor
troubles. So building work goes out to contractors, and missionary
Brothers, while still doing useful work in the maintenance of
vehicles and buildings, may well change over to secretarial work,
for which there is a need. In another direction, at least one diocese
has arranged that any salaried Christian worker is an employee of

the parish council where he works. The council has responsibility under the law and must organize for what it wants without sheltering under a diocesan blanket.

The priests have never been unaware of the need for initiating change, whether in the form of experiments with minor liturgical variations or in extending the work of the Church into a wide variety of social fields, but it is almost always a question of inability to find the time. By the nature of his calling a priest has to perform his sacramental duties before branching out but, in the use of his remaining time, energy has to be combined with prudence and the encouragement of the laity in order to disguise direction. He is not a corporation manager, with a prescribed and limited field and a short-term conception of profit and loss.

These great difficulties have meant that family visiting has perforce been relegated to a subordinate role, and it is generally agreed, not only by Christians but by pagans as well, that such visiting is most welcome and initially essential. In areas in which the Christians are a very small minority, family visiting is of fundamental importance; not in any sense to discipline Church members who may have lapsed in their practice, which is often the reason for a priest's appearance if there is no regular visiting, but to remind them of the wider Christian community of which they are members and to strengthen them thereby. Priests who are organization men may well direct Christian activities, but this looks like a very poor substitute for lasting personal influence in a more limited field.

Often the reason given for the failure to follow up a possible fruitful line of Christian development is that the priest has not enough time. It seems necessary to question seriously the use of time by many priests, in that they are not allocating their work to the primary needs of the parish. It is of course not possible to cut down the time involved in sick calls and other time-consumers which are clearly moral obligations.

Another way in which the priest can become involved to the detriment of his main work is by becoming too readily helpful to persons for whom he has no moral responsibility. He wants to help—it is a good intention for which he can get nothing but praise—but he may be asked to take someone to the hospital and he cannot be sure that this is wholly agreed to by the family; through being too ready to help he may find himself the center of a family quarrel and this is damaging to his position and difficult to explain away.

Time should be planned for its maximum utilization in relation to the basic Sukuma concerns of family, field, and livestock. Anything that is not germane to these problems should be ruthlessly excluded from the week's schedule. In many matters the priest has only himself to blame if he becomes a soft touch. He is not the only person in the parish who can sell stamps, deliver letters, take people to the hospital, have money borrowed from him, act as a shop for religious articles. This is usually totally unnecessary. Most persons in authority from the West seek in everything a measure of efficiency; if they do not find it they try to instill it, imagining that it is latent in any Sukuma organization in which they are involved. Perhaps the situation of most priests can be summed up as one said it: "What really gets me burned up is the lack of efficient cooperation"—though all would readily admit that this is not a particularly Sukuma problem.

This involvement in minor chores comes from an impatience with the working of the social system as they find it in comparison to what they wish for. As another priest explained, "You learn patience or you go nuts." Priests accept money for school fees and have to accept the responsibility of handling such money; if it should be mislaid the Sukuma are very much quicker to demand restitution from the priest than they would ever be to demand it from their own people in similar circumstances.

If the priest is to have any relief from a mass of functions which are essentially lay rather than priestly he must incorporate the laity as much as possible into the running of the parish. Some priests are experimenting with parish councils (*ibanza lya bato 'ngi*) with varying success and enthusiasm.

It is certain that any form of council based on Western precedents must be foredoomed to failure. The British administrators put in years of work to attach an essentially English system of local administration onto Sukuma roots. It may well have been a valuable educative experience one way or another, but it was not a

success and is being increasingly rejected. In the colonial period
the District Education Committee would hold one meeting in a
year at which decisions would be reached on which the Church
could take action. After independence the same committee would
literally meet for months with no agenda and no minutes, so that
it was impossible for the Church to know what was planned or
agreed. It was difficult for the Education Secretary to attend so
many meetings and complete his other work, and yet there was an
obligation to attend as often as possible in case an issue came up
which was vital to the diocese.

Any Sukuma parish council must be created and run on lines
which conform to Sukuma principles—the first of which is simplicity, not so much in the sense that the matters to be discussed
should be simple, but that the procedural foundations beloved of
literate nations should be abandoned. It is not that the Sukuma
will state that they mistrust the written word, the constitutions
and rules which may be produced with infinite care by their
ecclesiastical authorities, but the apparent keenness of such authorities to get this sort of thing all worked out in advance
awakens memories of the past and this for the Sukuma bodes ill.

The more complex the machinery the more difficult becomes
the possibility of complying with Sukuma ideas. Members become
accountable in a Western legal conceptual sense, and inevitably
the result is that the priest ends up having to control more than
ever before because the members will evade the very issues which
he wants settled. What the priest may take as a decision his parishioners will regard as a general predisposition to agree to do
something, provided that no other factors interpose between the
date of the meeting and the time the agreement has to be carried out.[14] Any attempt to prevent them from compromising with
subsequent and to them more relevant events will mean the fading away of the council.

This was shown only too clearly in the parish where the priest
avoided the written agreement and tape-recorded the agreement
of parents to the conversion and church marriage of their daugh-

---

[14] See M. Whisson, *Change and Challenge* (Christian Council of Kenya, 1964), p.
149, for a similar opinion concerning Luo Christians.

ter; the tape was played back to them, and agreed to be correct, and yet two months later she was married by traditional rituals alone.

The choice of members presents many difficulties. Even if members are voted for they will have no more controlling power over the laity than if they had been chosen by other means. There are no real advantages in having large numbers of councillors, if they *are* councillors and not legislators, and three to four would probably be as near ideal as possible if the priest is looking for cogent advice. But there is no limit to the numbers which may be included if the council is to be used as a sounding board. It is no part of the Church's function to seek popularity and thereby get into situations in which the priest has to make an unpopular ruling on a moral issue. The delight of the Sukuma in unanimity and the sharing of decisions is so obvious that voting would be pointless.

The priest probably, then, has to choose the members of his own parish council, which, moral issues aside, would best be a balance of the middle-aged and the reasonably well-to-do and as far as possible good men by Sukuma standards. These councillors cannot be given executive power unless there is a willingness to accept particular responsibilities because the decisions will have to be enforced sooner or later and explained in public from the standpoint that they have already been decided, with the possibly inevitable result that the priest becomes a scapegoat. If the priest's expectation means some Western-type results and formalized deliberation the council will founder. It must surely be the job of these councillors to inform the priest of what he does not know and to give counsel. They must be men of sufficiently strong faith to tell the priest when he has been acting against the wishes of his parishioners.

Many decisions which have to be made will almost always be made outside the council, for the members, if they have been chosen well, will be able to manipulate and deliberate within the balances of their own community. Real problems must be given to them—fairly and squarely, even injecting problems which are unspoken. Every priest has an ever open-door policy but this does not succeed in getting as many people to speak as he would like, for few people like to approach a superior.

The councillors will be involved with such real problems as the bad, drunken, and thieving catechist, the father who refused to recognize his daughter's church marriage, school food problems that arise because the people do not wish to employ a salaried cook, the raising of local funds to pay catechists. There are always Sukuma nuances to these problems which are of immense importance, as in the latter problem; a certain priest was advised never to mention what the catechist's salary was to be since it would only make many parishioners jealous and they would refuse to contribute to make him wealthier than themselves, and he was also told it was not a good idea to advertise the amount of money required because the Sukuma did not respond to this sort of challenge.

They can advise on who is in need of getting loans and whether in fact a particular loan violates their own culture when relatives have refused, and whether it would not degrade the borrower; who is worthy to proceed to the first stage in baptism, for as a group they have an obligation to protect the Faith. The priest can then accept their advice and assistance and find it prudent to follow their findings, and it may be only rarely that he must make a contrary decision in the face of their advice. But need he in fact make this such a face-to-face issue as to denigrate the council and split the uniformity with which they are giving and receiving advice, and which may have taken months if not years to build up? It would be wise to get the decision made further back and have the bishop make a ruling. This is not as equivocal as it may appear; authority is more readily accepted from the unknown of higher status than from one who is holding a council meeting in which he is not exercising his ordained obligations.

Although it would be convenient to have council meetings immediately after a Mass which the members are attending, it is probably not the best time because too many people see the councillors go off to one side. This creates the exclusive element which does not go with the Sukuma temperament. Hangers about may want to attend, others may be jealous in this situation although previously they may have been willing enough to accept the announcement of the councillors' names for the year.

The less there is in writing the better; it will be the priest alone who will remember the rules for council meetings. They scarcely enliven proceedings even if they do not actively depress. The records are lost or ineffectively circulated or not discussed at all, and if the record of the last meeting is raised for confirmation it will often result in the current meeting's becoming a rehash of most of what was decided previously.

Even obtaining signatures to a decision means nothing in terms of Sukuma reality; reluctance to sign such records or decisions may be a warning that the matter has not in fact been decided, and signatures might indicate only that, despite some reluctance, they have agreed to give the parish priest their support. Probably an advice and decision book kept in the priest's or a generally trusted catechist's handwriting for reference only in further meetings would be the best that can be hoped for organizationally. It would probably be unwise even to get the members to initial Kisukuma minutes of the meeting; this ties them down and prevents them from exercising their essential compromises later.

Probably the most definite arrangement that can be made with safety is a "guide to the running of parish councils," which avoids any causative verbs; e.g., "will be done," "must be undertaken," etc.—except for initiating and concluding prayers. Even references in such a guide to the obvious fact that the Church's basic moral injunctions must not be broken by the members may be too strong, and stress should be on the virtues of charity and humility and so on.

The financial support for the parish church and its priests is an obvious subject for the parish councillors to organize. There is a fundamental difficulty in having the priest himself attempt to work up this support. He is not seen as one of them and his attempts must altogether be related to real or implied religious sanctions in the minds of the laity. If given this problem the parish councillors can approach it in several ways. If the parish priest has a regular schedule they can loosely organize a system of outstations so that Christians provide his meals on his visit; the number of Christians everywhere is large enough to make it unlikely that any family should have this obligation more than once a year.

Money is nevertheless a necessity and must be collected and the parish council, or its finance committee, can assess how much can be afforded by different areas. The regular giving of small amounts is seemingly more desirable than lump sums once a year, which are a strain on any family and appear dangerously parallel to a Church tax (*kodi ya kanisa*); it is not surprising that some call it that rather than a contribution to the Church (*zaka*). Church collections are often a failure and it is difficult to assess why it should be so when in their traditional magic-religious system payment is made before a service is rendered rather than afterwards at a time totally unrelated to any particular end.

Cash as a special commodity of limited use has already been discussed and there is no doubt that in relation to what it brings it has become much scarcer than it was when the Church was originally starting to collect support. Taxes may have been instituted in part by governments in order to get people to come for employment in economic projects directly related to development. Certainly up to a few years ago the main reason given by the people themselves for taking up road work annually in their locality or going for a period of migrant labor away from home was the need to get cash for taxes. Now there are innumerable demands on the limited amounts of cash available to the average household. Some are compulsory under law and the tax burden has certainly risen particularly since independence. Other demands are virtually compulsory, such as political contributions or membership dues of monopolist co-operatives.

Beyond this there are school fees and requirements, hospital dues, a much wider range of clothing and consumer goods, improvements in houses, and a plethora of temptations and demands which give Church contributions a very low priority for most families unless they are in particular need of a Christian service or assistance. It is this reluctance over money rather than charity as a whole which suggests that cash should be stressed as little as possible and that the priest should be as dependent for food as much as he can be on the charity of his parishioners.

It is quite reasonable to question the whole structure of Christian institutional life in Sukuma circumstances. Many priests are very reluctant to use a wide variety of Christian rituals in order to attract the laity because of their magical parallel. A great deal of hospital work can be criticized on parallel grounds; the number who attend and remain until a possible cure is effected is a

minute percentage of the total patients coming. The majority are
there for magical reasons which have nothing whatsoever to do
with a pragmatic understanding of Western medicines.

Since this work cannot have much observable effect on the to-
tality of disease, would not a policy of "compassionate neglect"
be a far more useful contribution to parish life? Would it not be
better to concentrate medical services on particular features of
sickness or health in which an effective result can be obtained,
such as maternity work or a clinic for those physically or men-
tally defective who will never receive adequate care in their own
communities?

Possibly much of this social work which weighs down the
Church administratively is a scaled-down version of social work
in Western countries; it has been set down in Usukuma without
being designed for a specific purpose or end. If the Church takes
on general medical work there is absolutely no end to the drain
on its finances. To budget for general medical purposes means in
effect that little will be accomplished, whereas a school for the
blind presents both challenge and fulfillment. An element of
resignation—almost of futility—toward some of the medical work
they were doing was noticed in conversations with Sisters, although
of course it was not expressed as such.

The search for leaders by the Church raises some interesting
problems. Even in the language it is difficult to find a word which
corresponds to a moral leader, and it appears that the word *batongi*
for parish councillors has no other use and is of obscure derivation.
In explanation of this role the Sukuma themselves say that he is
one who knows and receives the troubles of Christians and who
calls them to meetings of the Church. He is an assistant to the
catechist who collects church dues and leads the Christians in the
area in their worship. Or he is the man who looks into the problems of the Church and assists the priest; the person who expressed
it thus mentioned the fact that he had been given these responsibilities by the Christians of his Church.

It is apparent that councillors are not regarded as leaders but
as representatives. The two Maryknoll dioceses have a leadership
training center at Mipa and with this title it is difficult to argue
that it is a Catholic institution when other bodies with government

backing may wish to send their men there for training, whereas its function appears to be more of a catechist training school.

The term "elders" (*banamhala*) has the same difficulty. It is important to ask whether there are such things as leaders in a closely integrated society. There are people of status who keep matters ticking over, and in a broad sense they are acknowledged as leaders when there are no urgent problems at hand which require settlement. They want this status and in a stable situation those outside the group are content enough to let them remain in this position. They reach this position in Sukuma society by a combination of age, socially utilized wealth in the acquisition of connections, and intelligence. Any community contains this layer of elders with enough time in hand and activity enough to be used as arbitrators and filters for local decisions, but not too old to be able to carry out social functions of utility to the community.

Action is by consensus in most situations; the leader cannot act without this and indeed he has to manipulate a power structure which is so diversified that he can never get a consensus alone. His alliances have to be much more broadly based than the political or business structures of more developed societies. He can never deal in Church terms with some subsidiary problems, but he has to consider the effects of his pressures on his own subsequent life, his in-laws, the possibility of getting help with his cotton or food harvesting, the marriage of his son and daughter, the local co-operative and party branch. All these possible combinations restrain the prudent man from appearing too strongly to be a leader —if this were possible—and it is doubtful that a single individual could gain this all-embracing position.

Particular challenges will bring out particular leaders, but probably only for that limited purpose. Probably leaders are developed in the Sukuma situation in opposition to propositions rather than in support of them. The priest who inadvertently or in haste acts imprudently on the construction of a church would find a leader in opposition to him—a man who could coalesce the opposition. Any change which is not fed into the community first in a way which does not presuppose a particular situation will produce its leader of opposition. If a man is not a natural leader, then he will probably look on such training as a means of challenging existing leaders and the same man may well look on his move to another area after training as the reverse of what he wanted initially.

The search for leaders, then, may well be illusory—either the leader is self-evident within the parish or he does not exist. The difficulty may well be that the parish priest is concerned with the positive leader who acts constructively for the parish good, whereas leaders may exist negatively. They see in the character and leadership of the priest a challenge to their local position, or in Christian activity a new power structure which can be turned to their own ends. In general at least in Usukuma, Christian leadership involves such small and widely dispersed numbers that it may not attract anyone outstanding. Alternatively it may attract the type of man who sees a potential line of achievement in the local politics of the Catholic parish and who knows that he is not likely to succeed elsewhere.

Again leadership of the kind that the Church probably requires involves a greater time commitment than the average parishioner can afford to spare. He cannot spend time or indeed be expected to spend time on Church activity when this will penalize him economically and socially in the areas of his life not involved in Christian activity.

Leadership is not carried out for itself alone and probably in any parochial situation it is a struggle for power. The position can be maintained only if there is something offered and accepted and something received in exchange. The man who organizes the digging of the foundations for the new church might well appear to be a leader from the outsider's point of view, but he may equally well be taking a job which no one wants just because it has no power opportunities and has many negative aspects. Even if it could be accepted that leaders can be trained, it is then a matter of technique that has to have a universality of use which is highly unlikely to survive unless there is the character or integrity of a leader behind it.

For what, then, is a man to be trained? Even a prolonged absence may allow for a fundamental change in the power structure of the trainee's parish. Furthermore, the leaders of the community, whether this is considered a Christian community or not, have little to do with the priest, and the people may see them as Sukumas rather than as Christians. Special courses for leaders might well be taken as trying to incorporate these persons into the Church organization so that they would be controlled. Either they would agree and probably lose their leadership power or refuse and become resentful; at the best they might question why this is being done at all.

The parish itself seems to be a product of this increase in virtually lay organization on the one side, and on the other the Church's concern that no priest should have a personal following. The parish in Usukuma seems to be too amorphous, dealing with Christians of the lowest possible common denominator—the Christians fit into the organization provided or they do not get any service. No organization, much less a religious one, can expect to grow and lead if it is tied to these low standards of approach.

In some places surrounding Usukuma a special linguistic appeal was made to particular tribal groups of Christians so that there were linguistic parishes, with the result that priests crisscrossed each other in the course of their duties to minister to their particular type of Christian. There probably has to be some parish organization for the average Christian, but there should be a special approach to the special groups of importance. The co-operative movement immediately comes to mind, teachers, the factory workers, and so on.

Another aspect of the parish is the problem of boundaries. Parishes have to begin and end somewhere so that the bureaucratic aspects of Christianity can be reasonably organized; so that priests know where their formal responsibilities end and in order that the element of a personal following should be reduced as much as possible. To an expatriate priest, the border seems to be something well established and long lasting, possibly marked on a map, which the diocese knows and recognizes, but this has a very European flavor. The Sukuma do not look at borders in this way. They realize that expatriates of any shape and form pay much attention to borders and that these tend to be geographical abstractions on which their social and political problems have little bearing. Borders to them are undefined until they become an issue and it is doubtful whether they see anything illogical in this crisscrossing of priests—a special need requires a special service.

Moreover the Sukuma ignore borders unless they have some specific reason for using them or are forced by government to pay their taxes by locality. They think it nonsense that they should not use the nearest facility. If an out-station church is near to a parish border, they go there more often if the priest is there more often—they would consider it stupidity to do otherwise. Priests have also mentioned that if there is a difference in the speed of catechetical classes in adjacent parishes then the slower parish will lose catechumens. This occurred in deaneries which were stated to have identical catechetical policies.

It would seem unwise to pay attention to the issue if the Sukuma themselves are unconcerned and indeed what are the grounds for objecting? Maybe a priest is a little discontented, but the Church is gaining. Statistics are confused but can be posted and of course faith is gaining. The Sukuma would see a case for redefining the borders the moment there is a movement across a parish line, if one parish can for a time provide a better service, or it might be taken as the nucleus of a new parish. It might even be found an advantage to collect statistics on marriages, baptisms, and deaths on a deanery basis rather than by parishes. The priest sends in his statistical details to a deanery clerk who does all the work and maybe could answer monthly queries on a form sheet. In a parish of reasonable size most of these details are in the priest's head and the need to consult would be reduced in proportion to his length of tenure in a particular parish.

CHAPTER VIII

Liturgical Change

THE PURPOSE of adaptation is to assist Christians to understand and attain the Christian life and it seems that it might best be done by careful changes within the liturgy, a careful and prayerful inching forward, rather than starting with the more obvious and open spectacles. The Church looks at the liturgy from the inside and has tended to become judge in its own cause; the careful moral considerations and the specialization of ecclesiastical authority exclude the Sukuma's personal and local view of the Church.

Some clerical opinion discounts the recent liturgical changes and those which are still to come as of minor importance and considers that the role of the Church is not to adapt the liturgy to the people, as the outsider might interpret what has happened, but to adapt the people to the liturgy. It seems certain that a very high proportion of the laity see only the liturgical side of Christianity and that these minor changes from the Church's point of view are major changes in the eyes of the congregation. The two parties are looking at the matter from totally different standpoints.

It has already been suggested that ritual exactness should be relaxed, not so much because there are no historical precedents, but because these have no intrinsic relevance to the present-day Sukuma, and because the Church itself is stretching itself too far in suggesting seriously that these precedents have the exactness it maintains. It is suggested for example that it is not possible to substitute some local product for the Mass's bread and wine, something that would have great significance, because it would make the ceremony invalid. There surely has been a change in appearances, for there is little if any resemblance between the articles used at the Last Supper and those now used at Mass—factory-produced in another country for profit.

Some see the Westernization of the Church's ritual regardless of its original cultural origin as short-sighted and query, "Is it more Christian for a priest to drink the Sacred Wine from a golden chalice rather than from a silver one—or even from a well-polished gourd?" It was suggested that an ancillary consideration for the complication of ritual was that the Church restricts its use to the legitimated priesthood and that if it were simplified or adapted to Sukuma culture there would be less incentive to retain Catholic practice within the Church and schism might result.

Much dissatisfaction is alleged to be felt by the laity and it is said that this has supplied the impetus for the flurry of recent changes which have taken place. In the Sukuma field of Christian activity this may be less than a half-truth. Dissatisfaction there may well have been, but it is exceedingly doubtful whether this could have been attributed to religion alone. It has been part of a national feeling of dissatisfaction, little attributable to the Church alone.

The need for African clergy is surely not a new source of dissatisfaction, since Church policy in regard to this antedated by decades any similar policy in the colonial government. Dissatisfaction with priestly standards of living: this is not confined to the Church but extends to the whole area of expatriate activity, and it is doubtful that this has had many religious consequences, such as losing converts or the falling away of the baptized. The use of the vernacular in the ritual: change here and in the paraliturgical field has, if anything, been misunderstood and opposed by the establishment-Christians.

An older priest explained that but for careful preparatory explanations many Christians would be shocked by recent changes. At the same time the theological truth that ritual is a human institution is valueless as explanation; the Sukuma as much as any other people see ritual in conservative terms. Earlier changes such as the recitation of the Creed in Kisukuma, when it had been learned in Latin, was initially opposed and was accepted only after a period of trial suggested by the priest before they should make a final decision.

Possibly the Sukuma do accept some things too readily just because the priest or catechist is insistent on the correctness of a particular ritual or the truth of a religious statement. When they see no particular grounds for rejecting the idea or, in other words, when agreeing does not involve them socially, they agree with the person speaking, for they see no reason in unnecessarily making an enemy. From this of course comes the corollary that when circumstances change and social pressures build up against this agreement they will abandon it without hesitation just because the circumstances are different.

In other matters changes were introduced by the Church well in advance of the government's policy—such as the institution of parish councils, which the laity have been very slow to take up, although such an institution would give them powers over their priests and indirectly over the Church as well. Time and time again the query about a parish council has met with the response that there has not been one yet and that the priest has not had time to get around to it. Never the answer that the laity have been clamoring for such representation, which might have been expected to parallel the political developments of the nation.

The same appears to have been the case for almost every adaptation which was examined; there does not appear to have been a case in which a suggestion for liturgical or paraliturgical reform has come from the laity—at least none were mentioned. The laity have responded to or negated suggestions for adaptation presented by their pastor and have helped with ideas for varying a proposal so that it would be more acceptable. Perhaps it amounts to this: adaptations from priests alone presented tactlessly are refused, tactful suggestions are debated, varied, and absorbed, and Church directions are accepted almost without question after they have been explained.

In considering the process of adaptation, priests themselves have been surprised by these rather stolid reactions. Their theme at one time was that change was necessary but that hastiness at all costs must be avoided, with the African clergy counseling an even greater degree of slowness. The last years have seen an enormous amount of obligatory change ordered by the Church with little or no consultation with the Sukuma laity. Success or partial failure in their implementation seems to have depended on the patient and enlightening explanations of the priests. Change has happened, the Sukuma have obeyed, for that is what it virtually amounted to, and there have apparently been few side effects.

It has certainly been surprising to the priests involved, who have rather consistently been nervous of abrupt change, and somewhat of a relief. It may be said that as a result of the decisions coming out of the Council the Church is no longer dependent on the Sukuma for rejuvenation and revival and is now well ahead of anything that they had anticipated—once again in the lead.

In examining the changes against a Sukuma background it is reasonable to assume that they were either anticipated, possibly subconsciously, or that they have encroached on no Sukuma activities which would have opposed them. The circle of paid catechists had been dissolved, the proportion of Catholics in the younger age groups as in the population as a whole had begun to overwhelm the far older generation of early converts, the national language of Kiswahili had become a force supported by so many other agencies that its ecclesiastical use was inevitable. In these matters the Church was ready for a change and possibly only in considering Kiswahili would the laity have had any views, views at the parish level, which could not have been considered particularly valuable to a national or even diocesan decision.

As to the changes in ritual, the Sukuma have always been used to alien formulae which became part of their culture; ritually more than socially they are absorbed very quickly. Given the premise that a Christian ritual is acceptable, the form is not much trouble to them. It seems also that the changes which have occurred recently have gone further than most priests and bishops would have initiated on their own.

Every priest consulted felt the need for change in an age of change, but none seemed to be very confident as to what changes were needed. Again this seems a parallel to the differences in view between the expatriate officials of the colonial services and the policy decisions and objectives of their home governments, in that they have been overtaken by change which they perhaps feel they should have initiated themselves. There has also been an alteration in attitude, from the former view that change should take place slowly to the judgment that changes ordered by the Council should be filtered in slowly with adequate explanation.

The observer who is not an ordained priest sees great changes in ritual between 1964 and 1965 because his observations, and almost certainly those of the majority of the laity, are visual. The priest cannot be content with such a sociological analysis and he is quite right that there is no change in the religious meaning of the Mass, whether the altar is at the east end of the church with a celebrant with his back to the congregation, or in the center of the aisle with the priest facing inwards. In fact the priest is more than a little mystified that such changes should appear great to the outsider.

The greatest change has been the recitation of most of the Mass in Kiswahili, a direct move from Latin without an intermediate use of Kisukuma. While the Mass used to be said in Latin, the congregation recited or sang the main parts in Kisukuma. Even Sukuma priests have not opposed the introduction of Kiswahili, perhaps because a growing majority of any congregation have learned Kiswahili in school or become used to it through the everyday business of government and commerce. In view of the content of the Sukuma language it is indeed surprising that Kiswahili should have been adopted so easily and so readily—the predisposition to linguistic change must have been there already.

The Sukumas' opinions must be carefully sought and explanations given before any changes are made in what may have become for them legitimate Church routine. Consultation, experiment, reconsultation, and revision must be the method of progress toward significant adaptation. Every minor change may well be major in their eyes, such as whether the altar should be in the middle of the church or at the end. At no time should the priest experiment alone according to his own preferences. The colors in church may clash, with the priest in green, the altar boys in red, and the readers of the lesson in blue, apart from the decoration of the church itself, but this is their church and their choice. It is possible that the Mass itself with very few changes is the service of worship best suited to their traditional needs and that, with this necessary consultation, they will choose adaptations that are neither Sukuma or Western and will create a liturgical amalgam as the country itself changes its cultural values. Changes which seem important to the outsider may have little validity in the Sukuma context. Saying Mass facing the congregation may seem a big change, but in many out-station churches the priest has always said Mass surrounded by the people, so what he does at the altar has no strangeness for them.

If they have been consulted the congregation will consider that fundamental changes have taken place at their suggestion and with their consent, but there are unlikely to be many suggestions of changes touching the main mystery of the Mass, possibly because it is a mystery, and their own traditional activities contain such. Church statues, fonts, pews, shrines, and singing will all have their suggested adaptation, but all these are peripheral to the Mass, which is the core of Catholic observance and faith, and it is in this that adaptation may be most justified for the better edification and participation of the laity.

Some parts of the ritual, such as the kiss of peace at a solemn Mass, do not conform to their understanding at all and there is a temptation to change a symbol, clear in meaning to a person from one culture and meaning a totally different thing to a person from another background. Nothing, probably, is more potentially dangerous than the transfer of symbols and nothing is more naive than to imagine that a symbol moved from one context to another has still the same meaning. The fact that it is not understandable in Usukuma is not in fact any justification for change; it just becomes change for change's sake, which is seldom justified.

The Sukuma had nothing in their customs for greeting God, but genuflections came to be accepted as the correct way. In some parishes attempts were made to include the congregation more in the Mass by getting communicants to put their own hosts in the ciborium before it was taken up to the altar for consecration. Although this was potentially popular, it failed because some Christians were noticeably less clean than others. The kissing of the crucifix on Good Friday has given trouble, for the Sukuma do not kiss traditionally, and what is intended as a gesture of humility and love becomes an awkward bungling.

One parish thought that the traditional gesture of kneeling and clapping, used when meeting a chief in the past, would be a suitable substitute and more meaningful. Others have suggested that this traditional movement is not at all a suitable gesture in the circumstances, as it was intended in its original context to acknowledge political subordination. The Good Friday kissing of the crucifix was certainly never intended to be this and probably the gesture of touching with the hands the body of a deceased relative in farewell before burial would be more expressive.

For liturgical change to have any significance it must be a natural growth. How many of the congregation have in fact looked at the kiss of peace with the intention of understanding what it means? It is far more likely to be observed as a part of a regular ritual or not noticed at all. The Good Friday kissing of the crucifix is more important because it involves each member of the congregation in an individual act under the observation of others. It is not a conditioned reflex which could be applied to much ritual observance; if it gives him or her difficulty, which genuflection apparently has never done, then there is a clash of cultures, not of faith, which should be investigated and adaptation considered.

CHAPTER IX

Baptism

JUVENILE BAPTISM—the naming which gives an entrance into the Christian community—is a very simple and inconspicuous ritual, which compares badly with traditional rites as well as with the complicated and lengthy procedures which culminate in adult baptism. The naming of a Sukuma child when it takes on formal Sukuma social identity is an event of social importance depending upon the position of the parents and the birth order of the child; it validates their marriage and ensures the social survival of the patrilineage. Child baptism, which is usually devoid of supporting social events, is far too simple a ritual for it to assume great significance in their lives. Simple ritual itself has no particular virtues for them and this would seem to be borne out by the fact that, although any Sukuma could take on a Christian name without being socially challenged, the vast majority of would-be Christians feel that it is necessary to go through the prolonged process of instruction before taking on a Christian name which has ritual validity. Comprehension is not necessarily an essential part of belief, and parts of any ritual, such as the giving of the salt of understanding or wisdom in baptism, may be incomprehensible to the Sukuma without in any way invalidating their satisfactions from participating in such a rite.

Juvenile baptism gives no trouble to the Sukuma. It may appear as an insignificant rite over an insignificant person in terms of social status, while it establishes quite clearly with minimum expense that the child is incorporated into the Church. It is doubtful, however, whether the parents see that they have any continuing obligation to guide their children toward a Christian life, just as in traditional life name changing is a complete event in itself and requires no consequent obligatory activity. The priest may feel that it is necessary to get guarantees from the parents or even to institute periods for instructing them; he is not trying to force them at all, only wanting them to understand. But it is necessary to grasp that any guarantees the parents give will have little weight if any traditional situation should interpose.

When an adult comes forward for baptism it becomes far more a separation from a bad past than incorporation into a glorious future. The destruction of ritual objects, the social difficulties of reorganization into a Christian social life, even the cutting of hair before the baptismal ceremony, stress this separation from the past. It should be noted that apparently the priest takes the responsibility for the destruction of these ritual objects; the convert does not do it himself—he avoids the issue and thereby does not fully commit himself. For the priest to burn them behind the parish office or to have them as souvenirs in his house is a serious misuse of their traditional importance, and an opportunity has been lost for substituting one ritual for another on the same theme.

The great attention to head cloths given by the priests in some parishes as a memento or symbolic gift, a practice that was discontinued on the grounds of expense, stresses very clearly that physical separation from the past cannot be replaced solely by a spiritual incorporation into their future in the Church. The shaving of heads at baptism used to be general but has become unpopular; it makes the new Christians conspicuous in relation to customs, now generally abandoned, relating to the agricultural cycle, but the cutting of a small piece of hair would not be so difficult. Without some such replacement the social vitality and value of baptism are diminished.

Initiation rites are necessary parts of admittance to and promotion within any Sukuma society, and they are just as necessary for any small Christian group as in baptism and preparation for conversion into the Christian fellowship as a whole. If the Sukuma is to find satisfaction in these changes which he appreciates as being both spiritual and social, the transition from one role to another should be stressed with appropriate special ritual, including the period of neutrality when the person belongs to neither role.

The Catholic preparation for baptism seems to fit in very well with traditional ideas. The period of instruction is divided into stages marked by paraliturgical ceremonies, which are not an official part of Church doctrine and can be changed whenever necessary. In the initiation from the first stage the candidate receives a holy medal and his prospective godparent is required to be present. In the second stage he is introduced into the church, receives the salt of wisdom and is given a rosary, and so on up to the actual baptism. Such ceremonies reflect the rites of the catechumenate in the early Church, which now in the liturgical renewal are being given back their former importance.

The periods of spiritual preparation, retreats, and the times when the candidates have to be resident near the church for more intensive tuition may correspond in their ideas to the necessary neutral gaps between the old role and the new, while at the same time serving the Church's purpose of giving the catechumens an opportunity of seeing a Christian community in action. One parish reported that their catechumens stayed up all night singing before their baptism—an almost direct parallel to the manner in which initiates to the Bukwezi society are kept awake by various irritations and singing before the final ceremony.

An important issue to consider is the working out of means to make baptism more meaningful to the person to be baptized, his sponsor, and the Christian community. When large numbers are to be baptized the priests concerned can be forgiven for hurrying through the service; it is difficult enough to get a service moving at all when there are hundreds present and one person is sponsoring several different persons. Nevertheless the Christian community is present at Mass and baptism takes place at another time when only the interested persons are present. Spiritually they have been received into the Church but there has been no physical ritual connection. It might possibly be worthwhile to consider spacing out baptisms so that two or three were done at every Mass, in the middle of the service so that the community sees and the person experiences the congregation as witnesses. Also, the Easter Vigil is a good opportunity for this.

Another point of difficulty for the efficient effort of the Church to keep contact with its followers is the readiness with which the Sukuma change their names. Since they do this in their traditional life, the same readiness comes into Christianity and the difficulties of having different baptismal and confirmation names often make it impossible to trace individuals. One parish has apparently solved this difficulty, not so much by limiting the sponsors, but by giving all those confirmed at one time the same names, men and women alike, so that presumably they continue to use their baptismal names.

The rigidity and simplicity of the catechetical classes of the early missions has already been described, and it is inevitable that the periods involved will be shortened or lengthened according to the speed and ability of any particular class to master the tenets of the Church and become acceptable to the parish priest as potential Christians. It is also doubtful whether it is always advisable to divide classes according to the types of persons attending. The stronger should assist the weaker to learn and even for the former it would seem dangerous to telescope the stages by which the catechumen enters the Church or to abolish the religious retreats which hitherto have preceded these stages.

CHAPTER X

Christian Marriage

THE TRADITIONAL first marriage of a Sukuma is not attended by the social seniors of the marrying couple; it is largely an occasion for the young to enjoy themselves, and their elders are discreetly relegated to the more private satisfactions of beer-drinking and meat-eating elsewhere. Except for the marriage of important people, the numbers attending at the church are usually conspicuously small and this shows only too clearly that the Church's stress on the importance of the marriage ceremony and the obligations flowing from it do not coincide with Sukuma ideas, irrespective of the problem of monogamy.

In traditional marriage the bride-wealth included a bull for the bride's mother (*zagamba ya ngongo*), and a goat for her grandfather (*mbuli ya kilezu*), and elaborate procedures, such as the one involving the father-in-law, who is asked for permission to take the bride away after the period of the son-in-law's subordination in his house; all these stress the importance of the marriage rather than the wedding ceremony to the older generation, and these importances are twofold—a physical union and the passage of cows or whatever other bride-wealth has been agreed upon between the two families.

The Christian ceremony stresses for better and worse, richer and poorer, and provides appropriate symbolism to stress this. Consideration of the parallels between the wedding ring and the bride-wealth cow as sacramentally symbolic, and the blessing at an appropriate time and place of the bride-wealth payment, be it cow or cash, deserve attention. The fact that the Church has this symbolism should surely mean that an appropriate Sukuma symbolism should be incorporated into the service. To increase or make more complex the marriage ritual for the young couple themselves would not be a step toward making the ceremony a more important part of their lives because it would not be socially appropriate to them. Ritual to increase the discreet participation of their elders would be a correct step toward putting the marriage into its proper social setting, just as dancing and drumming might well militate against increasing the socially accepted participation, as these are the traditional activities of the younger generation.

In one parish there has been a successful attempt at having the elders present, in order to give away and receive the bride, and in another, the traditional stylized reluctance of the girl to be married has been incorporated into the service by having the girl standing at the back of the church and having to be encouraged to come forward. That the marriage service does require changes in order to make it more meaningful to the laity is always underscored by the number of converts who marry outside the Church or allow their children to do so.

An important function of ritual in traditional Sukuma society is to differentiate the roles of people living together. Sacrificial procedure shows clearly the differences between members of the patrilineage and the agnates. The old installation ceremony for a chief, who had no great security of tenure in precolonial times, was a means of showing him to be different from his economic equals, and the numerous ritual avoidances associated with both marriage and generation differences act as visual aids to behavior in complex social situations.

The marriage ceremony for the Sukuma is an external sign of social change, the older family is splitting up and extending and a new family is forming, just as the ceremony of ordination to the priesthood indicates a social change, regardless of spiritual values. They cannot be expected to abandon this important rite of passage for a religious ceremony which at the moment is essentially apart from the normal current of their lives as Sukuma.

The Church does indeed make some ritual differentiations by requiring the consent of parents to marriage and baptisms and the presence of sponsors or godparents, but these are simple ritual differences in comparison to the complexity of traditional rites. That Christians recognize this absence is shown by the great importance they attach to the role of godparents, giving it powers and obligations which go far beyond Church requirements. This role has become so important that marriage between children of the same godparents has become prohibited by custom.

The Church in Usukuma never takes godparents for an individual from the same family, and a godchild would not marry without at least consulting his godparent and possibly requiring his material help. Even the children of a godchild are classified as godchildren. They are classificatory kin and it is possible that the large groups of godchildren attached to catechists form exogamous clans and lineages parallel to or replacing loosely organized traditional groupings that are in decay. This need for differentiation is further demonstrated by the manner in which church congregations divide themselves, men on the right and women on the left.

The importance which they attach to godparenthood illustrates their interest in ritual positions, their desire for dependency, and their conviction that sponsorship in conversion cannot be anything but a personal relationship. Just as Sukuma initiation requires a sponsor for everyone, so does conversion, and they parallel the godparent and godchild as similar to the magician (*nfumo*), and his apprentice (*nhemba*). Similarly it is very rare for a Sukuma to forget the priest who baptized him and when the priest, who has baptized thousands, cannot remember he comments, "You have forgotten me and you are my father!"

An additional problem which further complicates Christian marriage is the change from the marriages of the older generation, in which the character of the prospective groom was of as much importance as the amount of the dowry. Today a frank commercialism has steadily encroached on any consideration of character, so that the man who offers most has the best chance of getting the girl. Traditionalism has become weaker without the Church's becoming stronger.

The various stages of a traditional marriage which may follow the church services require payments which are intended to be token and symbolic. Cases have occurred in which the bride's attendants have made their demands too high and the bridegroom and his friends have gone home before the marriage has been consummated. In one such case the father of the bride was angry with his sister for demanding too much and used the priest in an attempt to settle the dispute rather than having it go before the local elders. There is still a need for appropriate ritual, but it must not become a commercial element out of proportion to its symbolic worth.

CHAPTER XI

Paraliturgical Adaptation

PROBABLY THE MOST DIFFICULT problem of adaptation is to determine the border between changes that would assist the average Sukuma to be better Christians and changes that would, to all intents and purposes, produce secular spectacles in which the prayerful content would be considerably reduced.

The success of the Corpus Christi ceremonies at Bujora, near Mwanza, merit consideration particularly in comparison to that parish's experiments with the Way of the Cross and the Christmas Mass. In the former the priest was bound by the terms of the liturgy to a public procession, which had been usually confined to walking the boundaries of the church plot, but he changed this to a longer move onto open ground well beyond the church's boundary with the priest and the Sacrament carried in an open truck. In the absence of any traditional ability to keep the procession-way clear and orderly, this change may well have increased the dignity of the ceremony and have been a reasonable compromise between the enthusiasm of the people as occurred originally in Jerusalem and the need to protect the priest from being overwhelmed.

But in whose terms are we considering dignity and should not the entire ceremony be in their terms? Taking the Blessed Sacrament in a truck was to get there in terms of Western Church dignity, or to please the people. The most solemn traditional Sukuma ceremonies for the coronation of a chief seem to have had no order at all, with everyone pushing, shoving, and shouting. The surprise and delight of one newly arrived priest, after the solemn processions of his home parish, at seeing the chaos of the Sukuma Corpus Christi processions were evident: "It was terrific, just as it must have happened at Christ's entry into Jerusalem."

Although processions do not seem to have had any part in their traditional life, they are a part of modern Church practice which the Sukuma particularly appreciate. Here they are not essentially different from the processions of southern Europe, which have always been public demonstrations of the Church's existence. Perhaps the greatest success of this parish was their manipulation of subsequent events so that the occasion became a secular feast with a Christian flavor, involving many hundreds of non-Christian men and women who would not otherwise have been aware of this feast day and its importance in the Christian year.

The missionaries have always been very nervous of the many popular dance societies which exist all over the area, and even more wary of the dance directors or leaders (*ningi*), who seem to them to be inculcating magic and sensual immorality. On this occasion, however, the parish priest, recognizing their popularity and realizing the ever-changing topicality of their songs, invited them to attend and dance at the church and processional ground after the priests and Sacrament had returned from the procession. Far from lauding the non-Christian character of their activities, the dance leaders composed and sang songs in honor of the occasion, Christianity in general, and the parish priest in particular.

He had made a change that increased the topicality of the Church's image without having to make any adaptation of the liturgy. The ceremony appears to have become a popular event without the Church's having made any concessions to gain this popularity. In other parishes these festivities have attracted a wide variety of pagan groups, some of which should not have danced and sung at a Christian gathering. The laity have now been required to plan in advance, so that such situations do not arise. In some parishes this practice was introduced and almost as an automatic reaction to its popularity and seemingly nonreligious character abandoned again, reverting to a purely Christian ceremony.

While admitting the appearance of non-Christian elements in such ceremonies, it seems a great waste of opportunity to make the parish church the center of some of the major social occasions in the calendar. It is as if the Church wished to retire again and become the center of a small nuclear group in opposition to the life of the rest of the community. If Christianity is an all-embracing answer to the problems of life, then it has to provide some of the answers in public and in ways that are peripheral to the purely religious.

The Way of the Cross on Good Friday and the Christmas Mass involved different problems of adaptation at Bujora. In both cases the parish attempted a straightforward play illustrating the most important events in the Christian faith. There is a basic difference between a passion play, which has no direct part in the liturgy, and a prayerful Way of the Cross, which has such a part. It cannot be both at one and the same time and, further, there is a tendency to make the ceremonies too long to maintain the attention of the audience or congregation. The drift away from the spectacle and in and out of the church will show this, while at the same time paralleling people's attitudes to their own traditional ceremonies. In either case, the importance of the occasion as the visualization of the Christian drama means that there are difficulties if there are unbelievers around, who may talk and smoke; people who do not care should not be there.

It is no part of the Church's role to provide paraliturgical spectacles in order to attract the people at large, according to North American and English Christian attitudes, but this is a narrow appreciation and interpretation of the problem. In almost every other country paraliturgical ceremonies are a normal part of the community's public life—the Vatican itself could scarcely be described as restrained in this respect. Almost everywhere the Church does carry out such public spectacles. It may be no argument but it is significant that most communities appreciate such public excitements; if the Church does not provide for this and reap the concomitant fringe benefits, some other organization will certainly develop such institutionalized activities. The Sukuma have many other activities which have in the past and will in the future provide them with excuses for not attending church, so that it would be best to look at the positive rather than the negative aspects of such activities.

In theory the Sukuma should not look on the Church's activities as alternative entertainment, but there must be some subconscious consideration of this aspect. When an entire community is not at least nominally Christian, prayerful ceremonies should probably be confined to the church itself, because of the danger of profanation. On the other hand, if the ceremony is to take on the character of a passion play, it must be related to the life of the players as Christians and there should have been spiritual preparation for the acting of the roles. In the eyes of their communities the actors cannot be separated from their private lives, and attention should be paid to the symbolism of their positions. A newly delivered mother may well be an unsuitable choice to represent Our Lady, particularly if it is not known whether she is ritually clean according to traditional standards, which will still be at the back of most people's minds.

It does seem that these attempts at the adaptation of Christian ideas in a traditional framework have not been fully successful because they have been neither one thing nor the other. On the one hand they have not really assisted the power of the Church in its administration of the sacraments, while on the other hand they have not been fully lay occasions. The priest of this parish could have taken a back seat and left the administration of these matters to talented laymen; for him to have given the seal of legitimacy to the proceedings would have been sufficient. He must have spent an immense amount of time and effort, which was time lost from his priestly functions.

Church architecture has purposefully been given a very small place in these discussions. Whether the Church is round or rectangular may be irrelevant except to show the Church's preoccupations with property in whosoever's name it is held, but a church which has no walls and only a thief-proof sanctuary might well attract the Sukuma with its coolness and lack of regimentation, since it would be a compromise between the Western practice of Christianity and their traditional out-of-doors ceremonies. Certainly if this was the design it would avoid the unseemly incidents of fighting for seats after the Palm Sunday procession and even jumping in through the windows. If the unusual architecture of a circular aluminum-roofed church attracts the overseas visitor, then there is surely something there which the Sukuma would not like, as indeed the round church brings the comment, "Why build it round when every modern building is rectangular or square?"

It is surprising, considering the concern of the Church for the

future of the Faith and the necessity of change, particularly in
what have until recently been or still are missionary dioceses,
that little work has been done on what Sukuma Christians actually think about their Church. The statistics kept in every parish
would give a statistical background if compared to census information in order to evaluate progress and to guide future planning,
a comparatively simple exercise. Beyond this the sampling of
Christian opinion on the multitude of matters concerning the
Church's functions has never been attempted. Support for the
need to make Christian ceremonies coincide with the Sukuma
life cycle and its crises would come from even a crude analysis of
Mass attendance and Communions.

Some priests object to this sort of analysis on the grounds that
faith is an individual practice and cannot be measured in numbers, but it is just this amorphous numerical approach which char-
acterizes their catechetical practices. This is fair comment when
the parish census and its utility have even come to be discussed in
Catholic novels from America[15] as a prelude to parish development, and religious sociology as the study of religious vitality
rather than of religion[16] has long been seriously undertaken in
the predominantly Catholic areas of Europe.

Priest after priest can give opinions resulting from worries and
hard thought and suggest solutions related to their local or general experience, but no one was met who could give a statistically
based opinion on what the parish's Christians liked or did not
like, their reasons for conversion, and so on, and yet the Church
with its organization and immense efforts is virtually moving forward in a planless vacuum outside the purely religious sphere.

---

[15] *Cf.* James F. Powers, *Morte d'Urban.* New York: Doubleday, 1962, Ch.8ff.

[16] *E.g.,* F. Boulard, *An Introduction to Religious Sociology: Pioneer Work in France.* Trans. by M. J. Jackson. London: Darton, Longman and Todd, 1960. This book contains an extensive bibliography.

CHAPTER XII

Sukuma Music and Song

THE ADAPTATION of ritual to local needs is just one aspect of the continuing process of social change; there can be no specifically religious changes which do not have social effects, nor social changes which do not effect the Church and religious practice. Very little change can be induced with a particular purpose in mind, without causing additional subsidiary changes which were not expected in the original planning. Adaptation must be done by filtering changes into existing practices, through enlisting the opinions and advice of the laity as to what changes are prudent and acceptable to them—it can never be successful as directed change except by the purest chance, and above all there must be no sudden jumps brought about by the potential popularity of a particular move.

Assuming a need for symbolism in ritual, the Sukuma have made almost no use of its material expression in art form. There are a few stereotyped designs on their woven baskets and pots but not decorations on their houses. There are no clay models used in their initiations or in the magician's equipment, and they are not common in children's play.

While any ritual act can be described as symbolic, it seems that their language is used for the symbolism which might otherwise have found its way into art. It is an extremely complex language, not so much grammatically as in the meanings attached to words, in the creation of special words, and in the shortness of phrases expressing complex and important ritual processes. In general there is use of loaded words meaning far more than their translation would suggest. In this regard they are an imaginative people, taking pleasure in verbal complexities and appreciating subtleties that they themselves have created. So it seems that the ritual expression most likely to attract them religiously will be in the use of their language in its full complexity, not so much that they may take part in ritual with words and accompanying actions, but listening and appreciating.

The Sukuma love the singing of popular songs which have very contemporary wording. In translation there is little to appreciate, since the wording appears to be both short and repetitive while referring to things of which the priest with an excellent knowledge of their culture can have only very limited appreciation. Some priests say that these quick changes in what is fashionable in music will not do in the liturgy, but then again that is assuming that the European tradition of church melodies and words lasting for several decades and even centuries is suitable for the Sukuma. The Sukuma have a great love of singing, whether the words are topical or not, and the success of the non-Catholic churches with hymns in no way related to the traditional life is very striking evidence of this love.

The Church has done much to utilize this love by the preparation of Sukuma-style song books, but prior to this the Sukuma have usually preferred tunes from their own culture. Monotonous chanting accompanies most of their services, although they have adapted hymns to be used at Mass. The difficulty is that the Sukuma do not have paraliturgical singing in their traditional life. The tunes which they would most readily use are dance melodies for which words are composed on the spot. As in other cultures, fashionable words and tunes go together and they cannot be separated just by changing the venue to a church.

In the opinion of many priests and the earlier converted Christians, the danger lies not in the association of tunes with dancing, but rather in the relation of the dancing itself to pagan practices, such as the use of magic to ensure success, and the possibility of inappropriate words. Some also object to this music because the dancing is confined principally to the younger, unmarried component of the population and, although it has been said that the Sukuma have no immoral dances, they consider that the Church cannot accent such traditional values when the songs are commonly filled with sexual and "pagan" innuendo, and the dance leader, as the center of interest, mimes with obscene gestures to attract the crowd to his group. It seems possible that the Church is cutting itself off from a lively part of Sukuma life by taking this attitude. Dancing is important to the younger generation and they predominate.

Thus it is that the older practicing Christians have a great dislike of using dance melodies in church, and Christian themes transferred to Sukuma melodies have been described by them as no longer prayerful. The Gregorian chant of the Catholics and the Sankey and Moody hymn singing of the Protestants are readily acceptable to them just because they are different from the only melodies indigenous to them, which have always been used for non-Christian practices.

The new faith required new music, rather than adaptation, and numbers of Sukuma tunes have now been produced, composed in the Sukuma musical idiom but without any association with dance melodies. This does not represent a development of traditional practices, for it is alien to their ideas for the audience at a dance to sing the complete song—the leader sings the important parts and the remainder follow with a repetitive chorus. It is their choral values which have to be developed rather than struggling forward with labored attempts at different methods. Priests have commented on the dullness of the responses in a litany, but perhaps this fits in with their ideas of how it should be said or sung and they do not expect liveliness or full participation.

In the same way a narrative hymn or a litany sung by a leader with these same dull responses might be especially acceptable, instead of the repetition of common hymns. A community in Usukuma is orientated toward hearing in their own musical idiom, and a gospel story known to all but sung to unrehearsed wording by a Sukuma priest to a repetitive response might take the dirge out of the service.

It is necessary to consider the purpose of this singing and the stress that the Church has placed upon it. Possibly it was to fill the gap with a largely illiterate congregation who could be taught Christian doctrine much more easily through this medium. But do the Sukuma, in fact, wish or need to sing at Mass? There are certainly no parallels in traditional sacrifices, yet priests and others put in hours of valuable time teaching singing to congregations which appear to be not too unresponsive. The current theme of adaptation by making the congregation participate may well be against their cultural tradition. Singing together may be a specifically lay activity never previously associated with the religious, while silent participation may coincide better with their traditional values.

CHAPTER XIII

Christian Social Movements

THE SUKUMA PRESENT a great opportunity for Christian social movements, for they have a natural delight in the creation and running of small societies. While the principles must be Christian, the practice must be Sukuma or interest dies away under the overlay of Western experiences. The purpose of such societies is to provide for a particular event, to unite communities which are widely spread, to provide balances between one strong grouping and another, to form alliances against misfortune and provide for the sharing of success, to contain specialized knowledge, and increasingly to provide the individual with some sense of personal identity in terms of modern change, in the midst of which he has become increasingly lost in the mass. Looking at the co-operative movement in Usukuma socially as well as economically, it seems that they want relatively exclusive groups in which they can feel at home.

In any such society an institutional ritual must be developed which is known and used only by them. It is not suggested that secret societies should be formed, only that the in-group should be distinguished, in their own eyes and in the eyes of the outsiders, from the out-group; for example certain prayers that may be used only by the Legion of Mary in general and by a particular branch. This conclusion is borne out by the manner in which Christian work societies, formed with enthusiasm and joined by enough people to make them function adequately, tend to fade out quickly because there is no adequate magico-religious component in their structure.

Even if these background necessities are recognized and acted upon, the result might be the creation of specially privileged groups, which would be against the spirit of humility fundamental to the general conception of Christian social action; members expect to get social and economic benefits, not necessarily immediately but foreseeably, in return for the specifically Christian effort involved. It would be futile to expect the Sukuma to behave in a way which is not found in the functioning of similar societies in Europe and America.

Much religious work there is done in the free time of the participants or by those who are sufficiently well provided for to be able to fill up spare time with such worthy activities. The service club typical of the middle-grade business executive in America and Europe performs many charitable acts and deserves praise, but its members join for prestige reasons, business opportunities, and social amenities, creating, as well, special rituals to distinguish themselves from other comparable groups. Such a group, devoted entirely to charitable ends, would be nothing less than a monastic community and even then it would devise a distinctive religious procedure.

Few Sukuma have sufficient individual, social, and economic security; they cannot waste their spare time in such selfless social work, much less neglect the importance of status and the extending of their economic and social power through the medium of such agencies, which is significantly seen in such activities carried out in spare time elsewhere. They see a Christian society in terms of their own uncertain daily lives, and its religious justification may well be subordinated to their private need for insurance—factors which to the average Sukuma are both collective and individual. Charity in the abstract would seem to be impossible under normal Sukuma conditions and indeed it is doubtful whether it can exist anywhere without ancillary social or psychological benefits for those who practice it.

Another important point to recognize and develop is that of the social gradations which they use and appreciate. They do not expect and do not practice any functional social equality in their own lives, either in the past or in the political present, where it may be only a talking point or the justification for a flamboyant gesture. Accordingly Christian societies must not only have a large number of office-bearers but also a membership that is graded.

This necessity for having large numbers of office-bearers in proportion to the membership, if a heterogeneous society is to flourish, has been observed in street gangs in Kampala, Uganda,[17] so it may well be a specific East African requirement for success. The relative success of Third Order Dominicans in the Sumve area seems to be allied to this, for members are allowed to wear the habit of the Order on special feast days. The parallel lack of success in some places of the Legion of Mary, administered on organizational principles based on Western experiences, with small groups and few office-bearers, stresses the importance of these Sukuma attitudes.

For almost every social activity they prefer to form a society, whether it is for worship, hunting, cultivating, or dancing. Such societies are localized in their branches but often have connections all over the country. The membership is always graded according to superior esoteric knowledge, popularity, expenditure on entertainment, and personal ability in manipulating the divergent personalities of the members.

Sukuma societies, based as they are on personal interactions and not on written constitutions and the formality which comes with writing, cannot be sustained where there is not this personal interest. The structure of today in one group of personal relationships is gone tomorrow, new alliances have been formed, new situations have arisen. Since these societies have no formal structures, adjustments are made and the consequences give rise to new adjustments, and so on. No Sukuma organization that has any formal foundations will succeed; it must be loose in form and widespread in its objectives. Possibly the rule is not to start with a program which may not fit it; the successful Sukuma society starts like a blank sheet of paper on which the people themselves write their program.

The decay of many of the corporate and satisfying aspects of traditional life has resulted in a great increase in the popularity of dancing groups or societies in some areas, and in the corporate activities of co-operative and political cells. Increasing education and the influence of economic changes must surely undercut the

---

[17] B. Dahya, "*The Nakasero XI—A Street Football Team.*" East African Institute of Social Research. Conference papers, January 1962, No. 129.

influence of various activities in traditional form, but not the need for such activities. In this trying environment, with the wide spacial separation of family groups, no modern developments have provided forms of entertainment better designed than the traditional ones. The social success of the Corpus Christi ceremonies at Bujora has shown that these dance groups can be tied to a Christian purpose without losing their attraction. The younger men and women require corporate social activity, and by stressing the moral and ignoring the social requirements of their lives, the Christian churches are missing a special opportunity.

Even if this problem is considered purely as a question of whether or not there should be any return to traditionalism, the Christian's attitude to the educated Sukuma's rejection of traditional dancing at the moment and his acceptance of Western dancing has to be considered. Interest in Western dancing is not so much an active choice, but rather arises because a need of traditional dancing is no longer felt. When political celebrations cause traditional dancing to take place in the towns, it is carried out and attended by rural Sukuma and not the urban dwellers; its function, as with traditional dances in England, is to assert Africanness in an increasingly Westernized elite-led culture.

All this social activity in the form of societies must be seen against the dullness of people's everyday lives and the distance from one household to another. People are looking for distractions, for they have few activities to break the monotony, just like the farming communities in the Midwest of America, which take a parallel pleasure in such community activities, with meetings and competitions to provide opportunities for social contacts necessary for business and marriage.

Although the Sukuma have this aptitude for societies, they are not geared to the making of decisions by individuals or by small exclusive groups. Leadership and decision-making is very much a group affair, a balancing of divergent opinions and the taking of the middle way. Spreading power, particularly financial power, is far more important than confining it to small nuclear committees composed of activists partially acting in their own interests. A successful society, in terms of Western drive and decision-making, does not exist for them, and in accepting these values as goals it is probable that the Sukuma point is being missed. Success lies in the fact of joining and thereby acknowledging the society's potentiality as possibly useful, and not in the fact that the individual is not being left out. Particular people and particular purposes at the time are more important than any possibility of such a society's continuing for years.

Success in Sukuma terms also has some elements of competition, possibly not in achieving a declared aim, but at least in edging ahead of another group with the same target. The clear-cut success leaves everyone flat, whereas competition in which one or another group is alternated in the lead supplies the interest which they appreciate. The Bugika dance society may have led this week, but the lead was not cut and dried; no one declared a result, so that the Bagaru can recover their position on another occasion. These dance societies rise and fall in popularity just like any other society, but they appear to be stronger in the north than in the south.

Although their own societies are all created for special purposes, so that Christian ones devoted to charitable ends present no great problem, each of the societies provides economic advantages for its members. Members help each other in their cultivation, sickness, ceremonies, and marriages. They would resent any attempt to confine a Christian society to charitable or spiritual action. This presents difficulties because spiritual assistance from priests and its inevitable extension into the economic field will not always be successful. In the apportioning of blame for failure the greatest part falls on the outsider, the well-intentioned advisor, who is not part of their own society. The pitfalls are clear if the successful Third Order of Dominicans group should wish to start a cooperative shop for their own use and profit.

Some of these difficulties have apparently been solved in the Christian Credit Union in Bukumbi, near Mwanza, which has worked well for ten years under the titles of *ilika ya kwitogwa* or *ludugu lwa kwitogwa*, "the loving brotherhood." Although now the money is in the bank, for some time the money and bookkeeping were dispersed among the members as an insurance against theft and peculation. By this means no one was isolated in a position of potential moral danger. While the society provided credit for its members, they also contributed for a requiem high Mass for any member who had died, and each general meeting was preceded by a Mass for the dead members. Thus they had ceremonies personal to them as a society which were at the same time closely connected with ancestor remembrance.

A fresh examination is needed, with the parallels that can be drawn from the failures and successes of individual cotton co-operatives. The appeal of the co-operative is built on tradition and it has political support, regardless of whether or not it prevents the progressive Sukuma from getting ahead. If an altar society is required and it cannot give status to its members commensurate with the effort required, then let it be tied to a savings group, with each member contributing each month and one taking all the money. This allows them to get things for which they would not have the strength of mind to save alone, and to get discounts. The Legion of Mary might do much for troubled Christians, provided that membership is balanced to co-operative buying which would allow each woman to spend her cotton money wisely, cheaply, and secretly.

CHAPTER XIV

The Individual, the Family, and Adaptation

THE IMPORTANCE of family and lineage to the Sukuma outside of the small and relatively unimportant townships in the area should be stressed in Christian religious and social practices. Even the permanent town-dweller who has largely individualized his life as much as he can, still sees himself as a member of a larger family group than he can accumulate in the town. Some have commented on the difference in social or religious atmosphere at Masses said by priests on tour from that of the regular parish Masses, because the congregation can sit as close as possible in kinship units, which may not indeed relate to the Christian family system.

It can be readily understood that sitting around the priest in what appears to be disorder, whether at Mass or during instruction, is very much nearer to the Sukuma's idea of what is comfortable and proper than being forced to sit in lines by the arrangement of church pews. Many priests speak of wanting the Christian family to sit together in church and stress their almost total failure to achieve this—failure preordained because the Sukuma do not think socially in these kinship terms. No one knows in what order they do in fact sit in church or whether there is any order at all, but in a church devoid of pews the congregation will group in some way or another and maintain these groupings over periods, and it seems likely that kinship will be the primary link in the absence of anything or anyone more important.

Against this is the fact that even in the most traditional household everyone is given something to sit on, if not a stool, a log, and also with improvements in clothing, it would not be practicable to use the floor, which cannot be kept clean, and the younger Christians have spent relatively large sums on clothing which they cannot afford to dirty. Even if pews are accepted, it is possible to query the necessity for a stereotyped arrangement; at a Sukuma meeting an open space fills up with people bringing their own chairs, which are arranged in a semicircle.

Kinship is not noticeably present in the liturgy and where it is present it is not presented as an essential. The catechism never comes to the small virtues and it is these which represent everyday reality to most Sukuma. In the training for baptism they are taught many things which are not immediately important to the ordinary man. Much of the catechism stresses matters which are personal to the individual for his salvation, whereas there is a serious need for service to the community such as there was in traditional life.

People look for Sukuma values in Christian principles; for example, they see the commandment to honor father and mother as a Sukuma-Christianized directive to obey, and recognize that the marriage vows are disobedient to these same values. That this individualism in their religious practice is new to them is stressed by the difficulty they experience in praying alone; for them it is never an isolated act and they seem to find it easiest to pray in a group in the form of a dialogue with responses.

Possibly also as a result of this stress on individual redemption, the Christian's conception of sin as individual apparently gives him some difficulty in understanding that this does not prevent the effects of sin from extending to his family. The individuality of the Christian's responsibility for his own salvation is made so clear in instruction that it may exclude traditional responsibilities. When he does understand that he has committed a sin affecting his family, there is pressure on him to hold a propitiatory sacrifice where it can be got rid of publicly in a traditional manner with as many people present as care to come.

The problem for Christian churches to consider is not whether adaptation is necessary or not—because there can be no question that some changes are necessary—but whether these changes are to alter church practice to coincide with some parts of a fading traditionalism or to look to the future and coincide with the broad

features of the Sukuma personality. That they had a certain practice in the past can only be indicative of their way of thinking and
it cannot be justification for trying to incorporate it into modern
ritual, however attractive and appropriate it may appear to be.

The necessity for ritual, which had a multiplicity of functions
in traditional life, must be accepted, and there is no case for suggesting that this fundamental need for ritual has disappeared. An
appreciation of a sacramental religion is obvious in the Sukuma,
corresponding as it does to their rites of passage; some even remark that the African Inland Church cannot possibly be a proper
religion because it has only two sacraments. The greater danger
has been in the wholesale abandonment of traditional practices
with the assumption that external discipline can replace the need
for interior grace and control. By becoming Christians they must
not have such a void in their lives, and this emptiness can best be
filled by a religious practice which is Christian in function but
Sukuma in form.

INDEX